Supporting Older People Using Attachment-Informed and Strengths-Based Approaches

by the same author

Changing Offending Behaviour
A Handbook of Practical Exercises and Photocopiable
Resources for Promoting Positive Change
Clark Baim and Lydia Guthrie
ISBN 978 1 84905 511 6
eISBN 978 0 85700 928 9

of related interest

Counselling and Psychotherapy with Older People in Care
A Support Guide
Felicity Chapman
ISBN 978 1 78592 396 8
eISBN 978 1 78450 751 0

Person-Centred Thinking with Older People
6 Essential Practices
Helen Sanderson, Helen Bown and Gill Bailey
ISBN 978 1 84905 612 0
eISBN 978 1 78450 082 5

Confused, Angry, Anxious?
Why Working with Older People in Care Really Can
be Difficult, and What to Do About It
Bo Hejlskov Elven, Charlotte Agger and Iben Ljungmann
ISBN 978 1 78592 215 2
eISBN 978 1 78450 494 6

Supporting Older People Using Attachment-Informed and Strengths-Based Approaches

IMOGEN BLOOD and LYDIA GUTHRIE

Jessica Kingsley *Publishers*
London and Philadelphia

Figures 2.1 and 9.2 are reproduced with kind permission of
Baim and Morrison (2011), Pavilion Publishing and Media.

First published in 2018
by Jessica Kingsley Publishers
73 Collier Street
London N1 9BE, UK
and
400 Market Street, Suite 400
Philadelphia, PA 19106, USA

www.jkp.com

Library of Congress Cataloging in Publication Data
Names: Blood, Imogen, author. | Guthrie, Lydia, editor.
Title: Supporting older people using attachment-informed and strengths-based
    approaches / Imogen Blood and Lydia Guthrie.
Description: Philadelphia : Jessica Kingsley Publishers, [2018]
Identifiers: LCCN 2018009188 | ISBN 9781785921230
Subjects: LCSH: Social work with older people. | Social case work.
Classification: LCC HV1451 .B63 2018 | DDC 362.6/7532--
dc23 LC record available at https://lccn.loc.gov/2018009188

British Library Cataloguing in Publication Data
A CIP catalogue record for this book is available from the British Library

ISBN 978 1 78592 123 0
eISBN 978 1 78450 387 1

Printed and bound in the United States

Contents

Acknowledgements

The authors would like to thank the group of expert readers who commented on drafts and generously shared their knowledge, views and experiences. These are: Clark Baim (Change Point), Helen Bown and her colleagues at the Barnwood Trust, Rob Fountain (Age UK Gloucestershire), Jo Hunter (of 64 Million Artists), Beth Noray (Independent Dementia Trainer), Ian Popperwell (Commissioner and associate at Imogen Blood & Associates), Jane Price (Nurse and Health Manager), Pam Snowball (Bolton Council) and Heather Tyrell (Rhondda Cynon Taff Council) .

We would also thank those who have supported the publication process – Meenakshi Parmar and Shelly Dulson at Imogen Blood & Associates for their support around referencing and diagrams; and Stephen Jones, Emma Holak, Samantha Patrick and colleagues at Jessica Kingsley Publishers for their encouragement and guidance.

We would also like to acknowledge Gladstone's Library in North Wales, which has provided us with an inspiring and comfortable retreat in which to meet, eat, think and write, away from our extremely busy lives!

Imogen would like to thank Jenny Pannell, Ian Copeman and Rachael Litherland, who have worked alongside her to hear and synthesise the voices of older people which have informed this book. She would also like to thank Joe, Solomon, Wallace and Daphne for their personal support during the writing of this book.

Lydia would like to thank Dr Steve Farnfield, Dr Alison Roper-Hall and Dr Arlene Vetere for sharing so generously of their wisdom and compassion, and helping her to develop her understanding of attachment theory and family systems. She would also like to thank Clark Baim, her Co-Director at Change Point, for his consistent encouragement and attunement. She would also like to thank Mark, Beth and Sam for their patience and support.

Lastly, we would both like to thank all those who have participated in our training courses, focus groups and research interviews over the years, without whom we would have very little to say!

Preface

Attachment-based practice and strengths-based practice: the ethos of this book

In his introduction to *Developing a Wellbeing and Strengths-Based Approach to Social Work Practice*, Alex Fox argues that formal support services need to fit around and enable informal support relationships in families and communities. This:

> will require a new (or rediscovered) set of social work skills and attitudes: a social care workforce with the humility to use its power and access to resources not to take charge, but to enable people and families to take charge. (Think Local Act Personal 2016, p.3)

Our intention in writing this book is to support those who work directly with older people and their families – whether as social care, health or housing professionals, or in the community and voluntary sector – to practise in a way which embodies the values of humility and respect for the individuality and the strengths of those we work alongside.

We know that most practitioners would aspire to work in this way; however, it can sometimes be difficult to see how best to apply these values in practice, especially when so many of our processes and performance systems remain managerial and outcome focused. Our intention is to consider what it means and looks like to work with older people in the context of their families and other networks and to reflect upon the skills and attitudes needed to actually do 'strengths-based practice' in an attachment-informed way.

If those working with older people in social care, health, housing and the voluntary sector are to work in a truly empowering and strengths-based way, then it is essential to understand how people (including themselves) behave in relationships when they feel under threat. This is where attachment theory can play an important part. People tend to come into contact with professional services when they are in a time of need or difficulty, due to illness, bereavement or crisis. These are all experiences which can contribute to a perceived sense of threat or danger, and can therefore activate our attachment systems, in order to protect ourselves and maximise the likelihood of staying safe and meeting our basic emotional needs. Likewise, the attachment system of the worker can be activated by an encounter with a person who is experiencing sadness, anger or an unmet need for comfort and belonging.

There is an emerging evidence base regarding the relevance of attachment theory right across the lifespan, but this tends to be available only to those who can access academic journal articles. It is our aim to offer an accessible introduction to attachment theory – in particular, Dr Patricia Crittenden's Dynamic Maturational Model of Attachment and Adaptation (Crittenden 2008) – and to prompt practitioners to consider its relevance to their work, both in relation to themselves and the people they work with.

Attachment theory puts the concept of the relationship at the heart of practice. In common with ideas of 'relationship-based practice' and 'relational care', it recognises the complex and dynamic nature of human behaviour in relationships (Wilson *et al.* 2011). The relationships we build with the individuals and families we work with can represent both the means of offering professional support and can form an important element of the support itself.

Our aim has been to curate and translate, to bring together learning from existing research – including our own qualitative research conducted with around a thousand older people over the past decade – in order to propose the skill set for this new way of working with older people. We have assembled a 'toolkit' for practitioners at the end of the book, consisting of simple models we have used and developed through our own training and consultancy. This includes both tools for working with individuals and families and tools to support professional supervision, since reflecting on ourselves as individuals represents a vital element of this practice model.

Do we need a book about 'older people'?

At many stages along this process, we have paused and considered whether it makes sense to write a book specifically about 'older people':

after all, this huge social group is surely as diverse as it is similar. Most of the models we present here have been – or could be – used with other age groups. We fully recognise, and celebrate, the individuality and diversity of older people. Like any other age group within society, older people will differ from each other in terms of race/ethnicity, social class, gender, sexuality, religion, disability, and so on. Often these differences and inequalities will be much greater than the commonalities shared as a result of being 'older'.

However, we believe that, despite this, it still remains useful to write about older people as a group. Health, social care and housing services are often organised and delivered according to age. In a modern industrial society in peace time, older people are far more likely to be experiencing ill health, or the loss of loved ones, than other groups within society. Older people also share experiences of age discrimination and are, as a group, often marginalised, stereotyped, patronised and 'protected'. It is on these shared experiences which we will focus.

We are writing this at a time of increasing inequality, combined with a huge retraction of the welfare state, both of which will impact significantly on our ageing population. By focusing on relationships, we are not negating the impact of poverty and social exclusion. Political transformation is needed; yet our message here is that change can also begin from the bottom up – that those working on the ground have a pivotal role to play in empowering those they support. It is important that we can clearly articulate the kind of practice that we believe older people and our communities deserve, so that we can then tailor the systems and policies which will nurture it.

The organisation of this book

It is our aim that this book supports both an enhanced understanding of the theoretical underpinnings of attachment theory and strengths-based approaches, as well as offering practical tools and examples to support practice.

Chapter 1 describes the policy context, and introduces seven principles of strengths-based practice, exploring how each might be relevant to older people.

Chapter 2 begins with an introduction to attachment theory, including examples of how we learn our attachment strategies in the earliest months of life but, crucially, have the capacity to learn new strategies, right across our lifespan, in response to changes in our environment. Attachment theory is a theory about adaptation and survival.

Chapter 3 offers an introduction to systemic ideas about working with older people in the context of their social networks and families. We consider issues raised by the need to adapt to the roles of 'cared-for person' and 'carer', and we offer ideas about working with family networks to resolve conflicts.

Chapter 4 considers the question, 'What makes a good life in care?' and draws upon our own qualitative research over the past decade with older people living in supported environments, including care homes and extra care housing, though much of the material in this chapter will also be of relevance where older people are receiving care in their own homes.

Chapter 5 focuses on maintaining social connections and networks, which is a key part of practising in a strengths-based way. We will offer case studies and good practice examples to illustrate how barriers can be overcome.

Chapter 6 examines how an overly cautious approach to risk can be a threat to strengths-based practice. We will consider how agreements can be reached when individuals, families and workers have different views about risk, and will offer case studies of good practice.

Chapter 7 focuses on supporting people who are approaching the end of life, and those who are experiencing or anticipating bereavement. Death represents the final separation from loved ones, and coping with the prospect of death is a profound challenge to the attachment system.

Chapter 8 emphasises the importance of workers being sustained and supported by high quality, reflective supervision. Working with older people and their networks can offer huge potential for learning, growth and reward but can also be emotionally challenging. Reflective supervision represents a key element of supporting staff to remain emotionally balanced and healthy, particularly if it operates within a strengths-based organisation.

In *Chapter 9*, we present 11 tools for practice.

We hope that you will find this book thought provoking, engaging and of practical use in your valuable work.

1

An Introduction to Strengths-Based Practice with Older People

Jakob's story

Jakob is 78 years old and lives in a housing association flat. Originally from the Ukraine, he has no living relatives, did not know anyone in the area, and English is his third language. Although he was not eligible for support from adult social care, he was ringing the duty team several times a week in great distress. When social workers made follow-up visits, he did not want to take up anything they suggested, was reluctant to leave his flat and seemed lonely, anxious and unhappy.

Julie – a tenancy support worker – met Jakob and used gentle reassurance and a structured 'Circles of Support' approach (see Chapter 9, Tool 8) to help him think about possible solutions to his problems. He said that he would like to meet other men his age who share his passion for chess. Julie found out about and accompanied him to a local social club for older men. He now attends the club regularly, travelling there on his own on public transport. He plays chess with a man who shares his language and love of the game and has started to teach chess to others at the club. As a result of his increased confidence, Jakob now goes to his local pub on his own for a quiet drink and chats to the bar staff and other customers, and he has joined a local 'good neighbours' volunteer scheme. He no longer calls the duty social work team (though he keeps in touch with Julie) and his feelings of anxiety and loneliness have reduced. (Adapted from Bowers *et al.* 2011, pp.29–30)

In this story, Julie demonstrates a 'strengths-based approach' in the support she gives to Jakob by:

- taking time to build a relationship with him. She doesn't rush in and make assumptions about 'this sort of person', she doesn't impose her views of what would help him, or make a hasty referral to services that happen to be available

- helping Jakob to work out what matters to him, based on his interests, rather than his 'needs'. Chess turns out to be the key, rather than a referral to a befriending service to meet his needs around social isolation

- building Jakob's capacity to get to the club on his own. Recognising how daunting it might be for him, Julie goes along with him the first time he visits the club, to help him find the place and meet the rest of the group. Soon he is happy to go independently, using public transport, which should build his confidence to try out other journeys. If Julie had simply handed him the address or – at the other extreme – booked regular transport to take him there, would this have happened?

- supporting Jakob to build a 'real world' network of support for himself gradually and naturally (rather than setting up a care package from 'service land'). This includes the local pub, people living in his neighbourhood and other men at the chess club. It is interesting that Jakob quickly chooses to make a contribution, by teaching chess to others and volunteering for his local 'Good Neighbours' scheme. This seems to be a key part of his recovery.

Strengths-based approaches are sometimes contrasted with 'deficit-based' care management. This model – which was introduced by the 1990 National Health Service and Community Care Act – is based on the idea of a professional 'expert' conducting an 'assessment' in order to seek out, understand and fix problems, needs and issues, and piece together a package of services to meet them. In the deficit-based culture which has dominated, certainly statutory services over the past decade or two since the Act, those trying to get assistance from social services have usually found that they need to engage in 'problem talk' to demonstrate their eligibility for services. In other words, they need to describe their problems in a way that demonstrates they have high enough needs to be eligible for services.

By contrast, the following definitions of strengths-based practice have been proposed:

> Strengths-based practice is a collaborative process between the person supported by services and those supporting them, allowing them to work together to determine an outcome that draws on the person's strengths and assets. (Social Care Institute for Excellence 2015)

In our example, Julie worked *with* Jakob to help *him* achieve what *he* wanted in his life.

> Strengths-based approaches concentrate on the inherent strengths of individuals, families, groups and organisations, deploying personal strengths to aid recovery and empowerment. (Pattoni 2012, p.4)

The ultimate aim was to empower Jakob to build his capacity, confidence and social networks so he could live a fulfilling life, without needing formal 'services'.

> A strengths-based approach to care, support and inclusion says let's look first at what people can do with their skills and their resources and what can the people around them do in their relationships and their communities. People need to be seen as more than just their care needs – they need to be experts and in charge of their own lives. (Alex Fox of Shared Lives, quoted in Social Care Institute for Excellence 2015)

The solution Julie and Jakob developed drew on his skills and resources – his language skills, his love of chess, his desire to help others and his ability to get around independently. It also built on the resources in the communities to which he belonged: the bonds with others who shared his language and gender, as well as his local neighbourhood, with its pub and 'Good Neighbour' scheme.

Policy and legal context for a strengths-based approach

The Care Act 2014 and the Social Services and Well-Being Act (Wales) 2014 contain several key principles which support the shift to strengths-based practice.

First, these pieces of legislation require a focus on promoting a person's holistic 'wellbeing'. This means that local authorities and those commissioned by them should go beyond assessing a person's need or eligibility for a care – or other service; they should be looking more broadly at a person's life, including their strengths and interests. The Care Act 2014 identifies the following aspects of a person's wellbeing, as set out in Figure 1.1 and expanded in the list that follows:

Figure 1.1: Wellbeing within the Care Act 2014

- Health: physical, mental and emotional

- Accommodation

- Economic status and social circumstances

- Personal relationships

- Occupation: work, learning and leisure

- Control over day-to-day life

- Protection: from abuse and neglect

- Dignity and respect

Second, both pieces of legislation set out the principle that the person themselves is best placed to judge their own wellbeing (unless it can be proven that – in relation to a particular decision or scenario – they do not have the mental capacity to make that judgement – a point to which we will return in Chapter 6). This means that we need to work collaboratively and treat people as the 'experts in their own lives'.

Finally, the Care Act 2014 guidance refers quite explicitly to strengths-based approaches, by requiring local authorities to 'Consider the person's own strengths and capabilities, and what support might be available from their wider support network or within the community to help' (Department of Health and Social Care 2018, para.6.63).

Similarly, the Social Services and Well-Being Act (Wales) 2014 Code of Practice:

> requires the assessment process to start with the person themselves and understand their strengths and capabilities and what matters to them, and how their family, friends and local community play a part in their life to help them reach their personal outcomes. (Welsh Government 2015, p.5)

Principles of strengths-based practice

In this section, we identify and discuss seven core principles of strengths-based practice and consider how and why these principles can be particularly relevant for older people.

Principle 1: Collaboration and self-determination

As we have heard, strengths-based practice involves a genuine willingness to share power, to pool expertise and to come up with solutions together. The role of the professional helper is not one of an 'expert' working out what the person needs; it is about recognising that each person is an expert in their own life – in living with *their* health condition, in *their* home, and in knowing what matters to *them*.

Professionals typically have *general* expertise – they may know their way around the 'system', from benefits entitlements to housing options; they may know various different techniques for supporting someone to transfer from a wheelchair; they may have supported lots of different people with dementia. Collaboration is about *working together*, combining general and personal expertise to create a solution, to make a decision, or simply to agree how the person wants to be supported out of the wheelchair in a way *that works for them*.

Why is this particularly relevant to older people?

Older people are all too often disempowered within health and social care services: others know best, decisions about them are made without them and, as a result, what matters to them is not always taken into account.

Principle 2: Relationships are what matters most

Time and time again, when older people are asked what matters most to them, the quality of their relationships with other people is usually top of the list: relationships with family, friends, new acquaintances, neighbours they occasionally greet, care professionals, hairdressers, and so on (Bowers *et al.* 2009; Blood 2013; Blood, Copeman and Pannell 2016b).

Relationships are absolutely central to our wellbeing and can be a key resource from which we draw strength. Yet adult social care (in contrast to children's services) has tended to focus only on the individual 'client' and thereby risked overlooking the people who matter most to them. Partners, children, friends and neighbours have been quickly and simplistically categorised as 'carers', when they are often the key to building resilience.

When we work for an agency or service, our interactions and interventions can become very process-led. We may have a series of tasks we need to get through in a timed visit; we may need to complete an assessment, make a referral or sign someone up to a new tenancy. Our performance is typically judged by these outputs – how many, how quickly and – perhaps – how effectively we do these. Assessments and referrals end up being seen as outcomes.

However, when you ask older people about their experiences of services, it is clear that these absolutely hinge on the relationships they have (or do not have) with workers. Often, ironically, the parts of the service people value most are the parts where workers connect as human beings, rather than simply as professionals.

> [The care workers] really care – they are more like friends really... one night, I was in a terrible state...I just had a horrendous night and they didn't leave my side for the whole night – they were there at my bed, they lay down next to me, they held my hand... You can't put a price on that. (Older person living in a care home, Blood and Litherland 2015, p.30)

I like to chat and enjoy some banter with the carers, but you can't do that if they change from one day to the next and don't care about you as a person. (Older person living in an extra care housing scheme, Blood, Pannell and Copeman, 2012, p.5)

From older people's perspectives, the relationships are not a nice-to-have-if-there's-time or a means to an end (after all, it is a lot quicker to get the processes done if people are cooperating with you). For them the relationship *is* the service.

Relationship-building has to be the foundation of strength-based practice: without it, we cannot collaborate with people, connect with them as individuals and try to understand behaviour which may appear unusual, or may present a challenge. This is why attachment theory – a way of understanding how and why people behave the way they do in relationships, which we introduce in Chapter 2 – can enhance and complement strengths-based practice.

To build these sorts of relationships, we need to be present and allow ourselves to connect with people. Working at this level is not always easy: the people we support may move on or die; they may push us away or become overly dependent on us (all themes to which we return in the following chapter). Supporting people in crisis, pain or at end of life is, as Yvonne Sawbridge argues, 'emotional labour' – workers need to manage their own emotions enough to give others the sense of being cared for (Sawbridge and Hewison 2011). If this is to be safely sustained, workers also need to be cared for and supported. You need to be managed in a strengths-based way if you are to work in a strengths-based way with others. We will explore this in more detail in Chapter 8.

Why is this particularly relevant to older people?

Older people can be at particular risk of loneliness and isolation, and recent studies and campaigns have highlighted their impact on both mental and physical health. Supporting people to maintain and rebuild their connections is often central to promoting their wellbeing and we talk more about this in Chapter 5. For some older people, relationships with professional helpers may be the only regular social contact they have.

Getting to know each other and building trust can help to counteract the impact which an unequal helping relationship can have on the older person's sense of self. This can be particularly acute for older people who have not needed help in the past and whose identity has rested on being independent or being the provider and carer for others.

Principle 3: Everyone has strengths and everyone has something to contribute

When we go into a situation as a 'helper', our natural tendency is to focus on all the things a person cannot do: the problems and losses in their life, the things they need help with. However kindly and sensitively help is given, this can reinforce the person's sense of frustration and shame at being someone who 'needs help'. The fear of being a 'burden' and the desire to feel you are making a contribution to 'counterbalance' this is strong for many older people; in fact, it is strong for many people, regardless of age.[1]

Strengths-based practice seeks to turn this on its head. It tries to find out and build on what the person does *not* need help to do, what keeps them strong, what they are good at, and how they can be supported to make a contribution.

Question for reflection: recognising own strengths

Venkat Pulla asks the key question, 'How can we find strengths in our clients if we cannot find strengths within ourselves?' (Pulla 2013, p.64).

Reflect on your own strengths:

- Which skills and personal qualities are you most proud of?

- What keeps you going and makes life worth living?

- What would your friends and family say they value most about you?

- What would your colleagues and clients say your strengths are?

- What learning can you draw from trying to identify your own strengths to help you support others to find theirs?

---

1   Breheney and Stephens (2009), in a study of older people, found that people were generally reluctant to seek or accept offers of help from others if they did not feel they would be able to reciprocate, since this would undermine their sense of self-worth that was very much bound to self-reliance and independence.

A strengths-based approach aims to build people's longer-term resilience – the abilities and support net which can help them adapt to adversity, challenge and loss.

Joan's story

Joan is 80, she lives alone and experiences difficulty breathing due to chronic obstructive pulmonary disease (COPD). Her housing association have fitted a stairlift so she can get up and down the stairs in her three-bedroom house. When we met with Joan she told us how she feels 'pretty useless' because her breathing means she has to keep sitting down to rest. She remembers how she used to be able to clean the whole house in a day, where now she finds it increasingly difficult to keep up with the housework.

Joan lost her beloved husband of 50 years very suddenly to cancer nine years ago. She still misses him and told us it had taken her a long time after his death to feel that she can go out again, 'I am trying now to build up my networks again – but I still feel very lonely – really, I lead a lonely life.' She explains that she struggles to get on the bus, partly due to the breathing, and partly due to anxiety. Joan describes herself as a naturally sociable person, and her daughter has been taking her to various clubs, but when she returns home, she quickly begins to feel lonely and depressed again.

She saw an advert for The Silver Line and found out that it was possible to volunteer to be a 'telephone friend' without needing to leave your house. Joan has started volunteering and is supporting two other women who have recently lost their husbands by phone. She is really enjoying this, because she is able to help them whilst enjoying the company herself, 'Plus, I find I am able to think and talk about the loss of my husband in a way that I hadn't been able to before.'

Why is this particularly relevant to older people?

Ageing eventually brings challenges in some areas of our lives or our health – our hearing or memory may worsen or we may find it difficult to walk as far as we used to. This requires us to adapt how we view and present ourselves and the roles we play. Old age is typically portrayed as a time of loss, decline, deficit and dependency: older people need to counter this by adapting their identities, and finding new – or adjusting former – ways of making a contribution. For Joan, being able to support others as a 'telephone friend' is clearly a two-way street; it perhaps goes some way towards balancing the sense that she is 'useless' in other areas of her life.

Certainly, in relation to mobility (and emerging research evidence suggests this is also the case with our brains[2]), it is true that, if you 'don't use it, you lose it'. Even the most compassionate care and support can become disabling if everything is done for you, so enabling a person to contribute may be the best way of supporting them.

Principle 4: Stay curious about the individual

There is as much diversity amongst older people as there is amongst younger people: no two people are alike. As Professor Tom Kitwood once famously said, 'When you've met one person with dementia, you've met one person with dementia.' However, when you work with older people (or any group of people) all the time, there can be a tendency to look for common features that allow you to place a person in a category with others. A team shorthand can develop, 'We've seen this type before,' 'We know how this story goes.'

Strengths-based practice invites us to stay curious about each individual – to look for what makes a person different, not what confirms that they are the same as someone else (or everyone else) we have worked with.

Unusual, puzzling or 'challenging' (as it is often labelled) behaviour is all too easily dismissed by others as a sign that an older person is 'losing their mind'. The response of services tends to be to assess risks and manage behaviours rather than seek to understand them.

Strengths-based practitioners assume that all behaviour – even in a person with advanced dementia or psychosis – has a function. There is meaning here, and it is our job to hear it and find it, especially if the person is not able to communicate it in a more conventional way, because of cognitive, physical or emotional barriers (Stokes 2008). In Chapter 2, we will cover this in more detail and introduce a tool to support this detective work.

---

2   Speed of processing training (a form of computer-based brain training) has been found to almost halve the risk of developing dementia when done by older adults regularly over a ten-year period. You can get details at www.brainhq.com

Mary's story

Mary has recently moved into a care home on account of her worsening dementia, which is putting her at increased risk of falling. A care worker comes to explain that she is going to help Mary to take a shower. She seems fine with this, but halfway through the shower, when the care worker passes her the soap, Mary shouts at her and pushes her away violently.

The care home manager decides that two care workers should shower Mary in future, due to the risk of violence. Understandably, the care workers are anxious about giving Mary a shower, but the team decide they will take a firm, no-nonsense approach. Mary's resistance increases: her outbursts become more frequent and more aggressive. Soon staff are refusing to provide personal care to Mary and her placement at the home is starting to look unsustainable.

Following a training session in strengths-based practice, the care home manager decides to try and find out more about Mary's history and what might be causing these outbursts. She decides to speak to Mary's younger sister who visits her occasionally. She explains Mary's behaviour and asks the sister whether she knows of anything in Mary's past which might explain it. The sister explains that Mary was sent to a convent school and that, although they never spoke explicitly about it, she had noticed changes in Mary after this. She became more distant and private and would became very anxious when they went to public swimming pools or the beach. It had come out in the press many years later that a number of girls had been sexually and physically abused by nuns at that school. The sister was not sure if this had happened to Mary or not, but, if it had, it could certainly explain her behaviour.

The manager brought the staff together and relayed this conversation to them. They started to imagine how stressful it might be to be disorientated in an unfamiliar environment reliving traumatic experiences from many decades ago. They realised that staff (especially two at once) wearing uniforms, taking a no-nonsense approach, accompanied by harsh lighting and bathrooms that looked quite institutional could easily be taking Mary back to these events. Her lashing out in defence suddenly started to feel like a rational response to what must feel like a very threatening situation.

The team came up with a number of simple ideas as to how they could make taking a shower feel less threatening for Mary. They noticed her humming along to a Frank Sinatra song and this inspired them to set up a CD player playing Frank Sinatra in the bathroom. They bought some scented candles to soften the lighting and counter the smell of bleach, and took the view that they needed to make Mary feel like she was in a spa rather than an institution. One staff member went to support Mary to take a shower. She wore ordinary clothes rather than a uniform, and spoke very gently to Mary, trying to keep the atmosphere as relaxed as possible; she was very careful to make sure that Mary always felt her privacy was protected.

Mary responded really well to the new approach and was supported – by one member of staff – to take a shower without further outbursts.

Why is this particularly relevant to older people?

Once someone becomes 'an older person', and especially where they develop a health condition or disability, all the other parts of their identity tend to get lost behind the diagnosis and the stereotypes. We forget that older people have a sexual identity, that they have had lives – careers, passions, loves and losses – that they have been young. It is only when we get curious about the person behind the condition, the person 'underneath', that we can start to connect with and empower them.

Older people are often portrayed as 'other': their behaviour and what they have to say is all-too-often dismissed as a 'symptom' of ageing, or proof that 'the dementia has taken them over'.

Our own fears of ageing can mean that it is easier to view older people as a different species than to see them as an older version of a younger person, since this can remind us that 'we' will become 'them' at some point. This is reinforced by media and government portrayal of older people as a problem to be fixed.

Principle 5: Hope

Strengths-based practitioners maintain a general outlook of hope. They believe in human capacity to change, that it is never too late to rebuild broken relationships or learn new skills and that people can change behaviours which have been labelled 'entrenched' or 'self-destructive' if they choose to.

This is not the same as being relentlessly upbeat or glibly optimistic: workers need to be able to stay with someone in times of depression or despair and hear their pain, without brushing it off and telling them to pull themselves together. Sustaining hope as someone approaches the end of their life is not about telling their relatives you are sure they will pull through. Sustaining hope where someone has received a diagnosis or had an accident is not about reminding them there are people in a worse state.

Why is this particularly relevant to older people?

If we are to support people to be happy in later life, we need to challenge the dominant narrative about ageing: 'It's too late for all that!', 'They've been like that for years, they aren't about to change now!'

Roberts (2012) argues that our 'self-concept' becomes particularly important as we get older and are faced with negative and ageist assumptions and expectations. Aspirations and dreams should be invited and nurtured, even when a person is in the last weeks or days of life or is coming to terms with a diagnosis or disability. In the words of Agnes Houston, who is a member of the Scottish Dementia Working Group, 'a diagnosis of dementia is not the end, but the beginning of a new life' (Weaks *et al.* 2012, p.8).

Principle 6: Permission to take risks

Strengths-based practice swims upstream in a risk-averse culture within health and social care services. It recognises that the risk of falling over while you dance or of getting lost on the way to your friend's house often outweighs the risk of doing nothing. In fact, it recognises that, by dancing regularly, you run less risk of falling over and injuring yourself (Aesop 2017) and that, by preventing loneliness, you promote your physical as well as your emotional and social health (Holt-Lunstad, Smith and Layton 2010). Furthermore, there's little point preserving a life that's not worth living.

This is not to say that risks should not be carefully balanced. However, in a strengths-based approach, we consider the resources someone has and work with them and their supporters to find ways for them to do the things that matter to them while *reducing* (but not necessarily eliminating) risk. It might involve dancing next to a sofa, inside a circle of cushions or whilst sitting on a chair, or calling your friend before you set out and using a mobile phone with GPS tracking enabled.

Likewise, in our practice with older people, we need permission to try new things, safe in the knowledge that things not working should not be deemed a failure. We can easily imagine that the care home staff supporting Mary might have come up with a few initial ideas to help her feel relaxed while taking a shower which did not work. Perhaps the first Frank Sinatra track they played reminded Mary of her late husband and upset her, or perhaps the hypothesis about the abuse was wrong – maybe Mary never liked showers full-stop. If we are to take a detective-like approach to understanding the function of behaviour and if we are to support people to find ways of doing what matters to them, there are bound to be dead ends and false starts. The key is to draw learning from these, not to cast blame on individuals and go back to the way we have always done things.

Why is this particularly relevant to older people?

Older people are often treated and spoken to like children. As James Charlton (1998) points out, the argument that disabled people (and this seems to apply equally to older people, many of whom are disabled) are vulnerable and need 'protecting' has often been used to marginalise and control. Instead, strengths-based practice challenges the idea that older people should be wrapped in cotton wool and encourages them to live their remaining years to the full.

Norma Jean's road trip

When 90-year old American, Norma Jean Bauerschmidt was diagnosed with uterine cancer, doctors started talking to her about her options in relation to surgery, radiation and chemotherapy. When asked how she wanted to proceed, she said she'd like to 'hit the road'. She set off on a 13,000-mile road trip across 32 states in a campervan with her son, daughter-in-law and their dog. Over 400,000 people followed their journey on the Facebook page 'Driving Miss Norma'.[3] In the year-long trip, she had lots of 'firsts': from riding in a hot air balloon and on a horse, to getting a pedicure and having her first taste of key lime pie, oysters and fried green tomatoes. She entered a hospice on the last leg of the tour and died a month later. Her daughter-in-law explained, 'Over these past 12 months, all of us have learned so much about living, caring, loving and embracing the present moment.' (Sims 2016)

---

3   www.facebook.com/DrivingMissNorma

Principle 7: Build resilience

Strengths-based practice seeks to find an alternative to offering a quick fix ('sticking plaster') or a long-term ('dependency') response, by instead supporting people in ways which build their own capacity to cope now and in the future.

Thinking back to Jakob, who we met at the start of the chapter, a quick-fix solution might have been to refer him for time-limited befriending. However, even if he had connected with the befriender, it is quite likely that the calls to the duty team would have started again at – or soon after – the end of intervention. Another alternative might (resources permitting) have been to provide transport for him to attend a day centre, or he might even eventually, if the endless call-outs to the duty team had persisted and nothing else seemed to work, be moved to residential care. If these service offers had been accepted by Jakob and proved to be 'successful' (i.e. at engaging with him and achieving a range of other outcomes for him), Jakob would effectively have been locked into a long-term relationship with services: he would become a 'service user' or a 'resident'. Instead, Julie supported him to continue to be Jakob: she developed his capacity to cope without services, and to build his own 'natural' networks.

The concepts of 'independence' and 'dependency' have become politically loaded in the wake of cuts to local authority funding. 'We aim to promote independence' has begun to sound like a polite way of saying, 'You are not eligible for any services from us.' However, strengths-based practice recognises that services can overprotect and de-skill people, and that most people would rather live 'normal' lives in which they get support (and give it back to) their natural networks. Surely most of us would rather have a friend than a befriender? As professional helpers who want to do more good than harm, our job is to strengthen and supplement natural networks, not to replace them. We will talk more about how to do this in Chapter 5.

Being 'resilient' means you can not only endure losses and challenges but that you can bounce back from them. Social research has traditionally focused on identifying and testing 'risk factors' – in other words, how we can predict who is most likely to experience poor outcomes. There is, however, an increasing trend to try and understand 'protective factors' – how it is that some people manage to achieve good outcomes despite experiencing loss, trauma or poor health.

In the National Survey for Wales (National Statistics 2014), 70 per cent of adults who said they were in 'very good' health (compared to 31% in 'very bad' health) said they had been 'calm, peaceful and happy' most or all of the time over the previous four weeks. This is a large gap, yet it is also striking that nearly a third of those with the poorest health still report feeling calm, peaceful and happy most or all of the time. We can imagine why the other two-thirds might tell us they feel anxious and unhappy, but why is it that this third do not? There may be some 'survey effect' here, with people wanting to present positively or feeling that the last four weeks were a lot better than the previous four weeks, but these findings do suggest that a significant minority have learned to adapt to the pain, uncertainty and barriers they may face.

Why is this particularly relevant to older people?

Older age creates new challenges: it brings losses and changed circumstances to which we need to adapt, but it also requires us to find new ways of coping with these changes. We may have lost a partner or friend who was our emotional rock, we may no longer be able to turn to work or physical activity as a way of switching off from emotional challenges.

Psychologists have suggested some of the key features that promote resilience at any age (Konnikova 2016). Under each, we include an example from our research with older people:

- the degree to which we feel we have control over the outcomes in our lives, including our own happiness (as opposed to feeling this is dictated by external events or fate)

  > After I lost my dear wife I thought 'well, I've got to do something', so I joined a Welsh male voice choir and never looked back since. (Blood *et al.* 2016b, p.31)

- the meaning we make of the events and circumstances we encounter in life: do we define them as traumatic or unfair, do we generalise ('nothing good ever happens to me'), blame ourselves for them or assume that 'everything will be terrible, whatever I do', or do we treat challenges in our lives as opportunities for learning and self-development?

  > I'm completely content with life. All of it has prepared me for what is coming ahead. (Blood *et al.* 2016b, p.17)

- our confidence in our ability to manage: that we have the skills or ability, the support, the help, or the resources necessary to take care of things.

> I think the fact that I was in the RAF for years helps that. You have to learn to be responsible for yourself. You can't rely on handouts. (Blood *et al.* 2016b, p.17)

A key message here is that resilience is a process rather than a personality trait, which means that it can be learned — at any age. MacLeod *et al.* (2016) argues that we need to take a holistic view of older people's lives if we are to promote their resilience. Mindfulness and psychological approaches such as motivational interviewing (see Chapter 9, Tool 7) can help people to develop positive emotions and develop the motivation to take control of their circumstances. However, it is also crucial to look at their physical activity and health, and external resources like their relationships and the place they live.

We developed the simple wheel in Figure 1.2 from the findings of our research with 140 older people in Wales (Blood *et al.* 2016b). The segments show the different resources which these older people told us help them to respond and adapt to the challenges of ageing. We have described the wheel elsewhere as the 'Anatomy of Resilience' — the different parts of a person's life which together make up their capacity to cope (Blood and Copeman 2017).

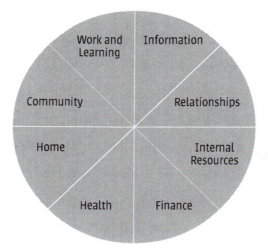

Figure 1.2: The Anatomy of Resilience wheel

A note about 'internal resources'

By 'internal resources', we mean:

- psychological resilience, coping strategies, sense of humour, etc.

- beliefs, which may include faith or general outlook on life.

A note about work and learning

Although older people have typically 'retired', we included this segment in the wheel because issues related to work and learning often came up in our conversations with people about what mattered most to them. For example:

- Many retired people had taken on unpaid work – as volunteers, as councillors or board members, or as carers for grandchildren, partners or older relatives.

- Some continued to practise their trade (one man in his 70s was still decorating for friends and family), or to mix with people they used to work with.

- A commitment to learn new things, 'keep busy' and make a contribution were critical to the identity of most of the older people we spoke to, even when they faced health challenges.

- For many people, it was important to talk about their earlier work and other roles: these are central to who they are.

- How retirement is managed and experienced can have a significant impact on finances, relationships and self-esteem in later life.

Conclusion

In this chapter, we have introduced seven principles of strengths-based practice and considered why they are particularly relevant to older people. In the remainder of the book, we will be introducing you to theories and tools which will help you to apply these principles to the people you support and/or the staff you manage.

We hope you will already be thinking about older people you have encountered in your professional and personal lives who could benefit from these approaches, and you will probably also have identified examples in which you are already working in this way. In Chapter 9, we include core tools for strengths-based practice: Tool 1, for mapping out the resources which people have and Tool 2, which explores the art of asking questions which draw out strengths and meaning.

But what about the minority of people who we are struggling to support effectively, yet probably take up the lion's share of our time and emotional energy? These may include:

- individuals or families who react to us in ways that we struggle to understand: responding with seemingly disproportionate levels of anger or other emotions, perhaps constantly pulling us into new dramas, only to push us away. Or the people who are adamant that they are fine and refuse to let us in, even when it is clear that they are on the brink of crisis

- those who are not able to communicate clearly with words and whose behaviours are perplexing, disturbing or even dangerous, and for whom a move to a more secure institutional setting can feel like an inevitability.

In the next chapter, we introduce attachment theory, which we believe can provide the foundation for a collaboration and strengths-finding approach with these people.

2

Introduction to Attachment Theory

Attachment theory offers us a way of understanding how humans behave within relationships in order to get our emotional needs met and protect ourselves when we feel threatened. Our attachment system helps us to increase our chances of surviving and staying safe by developing patterns of behaviour and responses known as our 'attachment strategies'. Attachment theory was first developed by John Bowlby, a psychiatrist and psychoanalyst, who became interested in the experiences of children who were separated from their families during the Second World War as evacuees (Bowlby 1982).

Early writing and research on attachment focused on how babies and young children developed their attachment strategies. In more recent times, research has demonstrated the significant impact of these strategies right across the life course. Indeed, John Bowlby wrote that attachment strategies play a vital role 'from the cradle to the grave' (Bowlby 1982, p.208).

This chapter will outline an introduction to attachment theory, describe three different types of attachment strategy, consider how our attachment strategies change across the lifespan, and explain how an understanding of attachment theory can be applied to the experiences of older people and their families.

The Dynamic-Maturational Model of attachment and adaptation (DMM)

Dr Patricia Crittenden developed the Dynamic-Maturational Model (DMM) of attachment and adaptation, a model of the development of attachment strategies (Crittenden 2008). The DMM emphasises attachment patterns as self-protective strategies which we continue to adapt across the lifespan in response to perceived dangers and threats. The DMM considers attachment strategies not as labels, or as a fixed part of a person's personality, but instead focuses upon their function: to protect the self in moments of threat. They represent an individual's best attempt, given their capacities and resources, to achieve safety, comfort, proximity and predictability in moments of danger. Attachment strategies serve a crucial function to promote survival, and so attachment behaviour can be most helpfully understood as serving a function or purpose for the individual, even if they aren't aware of that function.

Patricia Crittenden (2008) writes that when:

- faced with perceived *danger*, we seek *safety*

- faced with perceived *distress*, we seek *comfort*

- faced with perceived *isolation*, we seek *proximity* to our attachment figure

- faced with perceived *chaos* – including internal chaos – we seek *predictability* (or what is familiar to us).

This is a very important point – when trying to make sense of a person's attachment behaviours, at whatever age, we need to pay attention, not just to the behaviour but to the function of the behaviour. In other words, in what way can that behaviour be understood as that person's best possible attempt to get their basic needs for safety, comfort, proximity and predictability met? These ideas are represented in Figure 2.1.

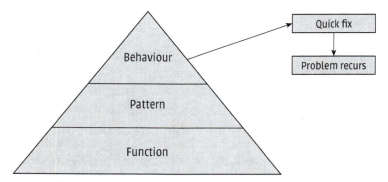

Figure 2.1: The behaviour–pattern–function triangle
Reproduced with kind permission of Baim and Morrison
(Attachment-based Practice with Adults). Pavilion Publishing and Media.

When we are puzzled by a person's pattern of behaviour, especially a pattern which is repeated, we often try a 'quick fix' solution, which is sometimes based upon our agency's policies. For example, if a person living in a residential care home becomes distressed in the shower (like Mary, who we met in Chapter 1), the manager may have the idea that it would be best to use two staff members to shower the person safely, in line with agency policies.

However, this does not address the root of the problem – the underlying reason why the person is becoming distressed – and so very often the problem recurs. In fact, if the reason for the distress is that the person does not like being seen naked in the shower but can't say so, then allocating two staff members to supervise the shower is likely to make it feel more threatening for them.

It is by paying attention to the pattern that we can begin to get an idea of the function or the meaning of the behaviour for the person. In other words, what needs is the person trying to meet when they behave in this way? Once we understand that, we will be more able to work together to find and try out possible solutions. We can begin to build an idea about the pattern of the behaviour by asking questions such as:

- When did it start?

- When is it more likely to happen/less likely to happen?

- Are there times when it is better/worse?

Case study: making sense of puzzling behaviour using attachment theory

Rose is a 63-year-old woman who lives on her own in a flat which she rents from a housing association. She has lived there for 12 years. Her husband, Derek, died when she was 54, and she has lived alone since then. She has two adult children, Marie and David, who both have their own children and live some distance away. They both call her at least once a week, and visit a few times a year. She usually spends Christmas with one of her children.

For a few years now, Rose has been buying large quantities of cleaning products, such as bleach, washing-up liquid, washing powder, toilet cleaner, toilet rolls and cloths. She keeps them in the living room of her flat. There isn't much space for anything else in her living room, and she can't sit in there any more. She is now storing boxes in her kitchen and bedroom as well, as the living room is full. It's hard for her to keep the flat clean because of all the boxes. Her children are concerned that she is spending a lot of her money on these products, and they don't really understand why.

The housing officer from the housing association has visited Rose a couple of times, and is worried about the potential health and safety risk from the cleaning products. The housing officer contacts David, who shares the concern, and agrees to try to encourage Rose to clear them out of the flat. Rose is scared that she might lose her tenancy, so she agrees with the housing officer's idea that the cleaning products be removed. The housing association arrange for the cleaning products to be removed, and for Rose's flat to be cleaned. Rose tells her children and the housing association worker that she's sorry for the trouble that she's caused, and that she understands why the items have to go.

However, eight weeks later, during a visit to his mother, David sees that Rose has replaced the cleaning products, and that the living room is full again. At this point, he realises that he needs to find out more about the reasons why Rose might be buying cleaning products. The housing association makes a referral to a tenancy support worker, Beverley, who meets with Rose at her flat. Initially, Rose is very apologetic for 'causing so much trouble', and says that she 'doesn't understand why she kept being so silly'. Beverley asks Rose to talk about when she started buying cleaning products, and Rose explains that it first began about nine years ago, and had gradually increased. Beverley asks her what she did with all the cleaning products, and Rose explains that she was known by all the residents in the housing development as the person to go to if you ran out of cleaning products. Because there wasn't a local shop within easy walking distance, families found it easier to call on Rose if they ran out of washing-up liquid or toilet rolls. They used to pay her for the items, so that she wasn't out of pocket. Beverley begins to realise that there is an explanation for Rose's behaviour which is more to do with relationships and social connections than cleaning products.

Reflecting upon Rose through an attachment lens

Rose's buying of cleaning products was seen by her children and the Housing Association as the problematic behaviour – the tip of the triangle. They decided upon a 'quick fix' – the removal of the items. Rose said that she agreed to this and understood the problem.

However, this approach was only effective for a few weeks, so it is clear that there is something else going on. By talking to Rose about what it means to her to have a stock of cleaning products, Beverley begins to understand that there is a relational aspect to her behaviour.

Rose explains to Beverley that some days the only contact she has with other people is when someone comes to her door to buy cleaning products from her. She has felt increasingly lonely since the death of her husband, and she is conscious that both her children are busy, and she doesn't want them to feel as though they have to visit her more often. Being able to offer help to people in this way gives her a sense of belonging, and a sense that she is fulfilling an important role for the people around her. Rose's stockpiling of these items represents her best attempt to meet her need for social contact (proximity) and gives her a sense of identity and belonging (comfort and safety). It's an unusual way of meeting completely normal needs, which all human beings have.

Beverley realises that helping Rose to keep her tenancy will involve much more than just arranging for the cleaning products to be removed again. She arranges to meet Rose again at home, and during the conversation, she tries hard to reassure Rose that she isn't judging her, and isn't angry. This is because she realises that this is a moment of real challenge and threat for Rose, and she wants her to be able to stay calm. She talks to Rose about the idea that stocking up on cleaning products might be meeting her needs for social contact, and a sense of being useful to other people. Rose says that this idea makes sense to her, although she'd never put it into those words.

Making an attachment-informed plan

Beverley and Rose talk about how Rose could meet those needs in a way which wouldn't put her tenancy at risk, and which would give her the opportunity to use her skills and her desire to contribute to the community. Rose has the idea that she could find out more about what happens at the local community centre. She finds out that there is a community cafe which runs there twice a week, and that they are looking for volunteers. She decides to join the team of volunteers and finds that this activity helps her to feel that she has an important role in her community, and is making a contribution. Through the community cafe, she also starts to volunteer for the local food bank. When Rose is ready, she and Beverley work together to clear her flat. Later, Rose reflects that she feels relieved that her flat is empty of cleaning products, and that she feels much more satisfied with her life now she is volunteering with the community cafe and the food bank.

Now that we have seen how understanding the function of behaviour, or the meaning of the behaviour to the person, based on normal needs for safety, comfort, predictability and proximity, can be a helpful, strengths-based approach, we will move on and learn more about the development of attachment strategies from birth onwards.

How babies develop attachment strategies

At birth, babies are entirely dependent upon a 'stronger and wiser' human to protect and care for them, and to keep them alive by providing food, warmth, comfort and protection. Attachment theory calls this parent or carer an 'attachment figure'.

Babies are born with the ability to signal when they need care or protection – for example, if they are hot, cold, hungry, scared, in pain, or otherwise unsettled. This might be triggered by something happening inside of them (like hunger) or something outside of them (like a loud noise). When distressed, the baby will behave in ways which attract the attention of the attachment figure, by crying, reaching out, gazing and clinging on. If the caregiver responds sensitively and promptly to the infant's signalling, by getting close and doing something to meet the baby's need (such as using a gentle voice to calm the baby down, or by offering food, warmth or a clean nappy) then the infant will be soothed, and they will stop crying. In this way, 'attachment behaviours' help the baby to gain vital, life-sustaining protection and comfort from the caregiver. Through many repetitions of this cycle of signalling and response on a daily basis, over time the infant learns to view the caregiver as a 'safe haven' – a trusted source of comfort and protection in times of difficulty.

Babies are also born with the instinct to adapt their behaviour in response to the particular person who is caring for them. Through thousands of repetitions of simple everyday exchanges between the caregiver and the baby, the baby will learn from the caregiver's responses how to behave in order to get the best out of their attachment figure. It is this process of learning which gives rise to the development of attachment strategies. For example, what volume and duration of cry is most likely to gain the caregiver's attention, and to result in them coming towards the baby and offering care?

In this way, the baby's attachment behaviour represents their best attempt to obtain the vital protection and comfort from the caregiver they depend upon for their survival, in moments of perceived threat.

The ways in which the attachment figure interprets and responds to the baby's attachment behaviours will affect how the baby learns to recognise the signals from inside his/her body and how to interact with their caregiver. Although we call these attachment patterns 'strategies', this is not meant to imply that the baby is conscious of these processes or is making deliberate choices; these processes develop before the baby is capable of weighing up options and choosing between them. Attachment strategies in early childhood, and to some extent across the lifespan, operate at an unconscious level, beneath the reaches of conscious awareness. These patterns form the environment in which the early brain develops, and become deeply embedded in the neural pathways of the brain and the central nervous system. These early patterns have a profound impact on the way we function within relationships in order to feel safe.

Of course, many babies have the experience of being cared for by more than one adult, although most babies have a primary caregiver who looks after them for the majority of the time. Researcher Elisabeth Fivaz-Depeursinge has developed an assessment called the Lausanne Trilogue Play paradigm, which shows that babies as young as six months old are capable of responding differently to two different caregivers – they can recognise that two adults may respond differently to them, and develop different attachment strategies to fit in with them (Fivaz-Depeursinge, Frascarolo and Corboz-Warnery 2010). So, attachment is about far more than just a two-person relationship.

Saying that the development of our attachment strategies begins in the earliest months of life is not the same as saying that they are set in stone in early infancy. As we develop across the lifespan, we develop more complex attachment strategies; we have a larger repertoire of behaviours for signalling our needs to our attachment figures and for seeking comfort from them. The nature of our attachment figures changes with age; we may form new attachments with partners, and we may become caregivers, if we have children of our own, or we may take on a caring role in relation to our own parents, or partners, or other family members.

Strange Situation procedure

Mary Ainsworth developed the Strange Situation procedure in order to assess the attachment patterns between an infant (12–15 months) and their caregiver. The experiment involves closely watching how the infant behaves during two brief separations from and reunions with the caregiver (Ainsworth 1979). Mary Ainsworth found that the responses of the infants broadly fell into one of three patterns, which she called Types A, B and C. These terms are still used today, and we call Type B a secure attachment pattern, and Types A and C insecure attachment patterns. The names given to these types of strategy tend to imply that a 'secure' strategy would somehow be preferable to an 'insecure' one. However, as we will see below, a secure strategy is only advantageous if the caregiver, and the social context in which they are living, provide safety and comfort for the baby. Insecure strategies, Types A and C, may be an infant's attempt to 'get the best' from a carer who is not able to offer safety and comfort in a predictable way. Studies show that about 60 per cent of the population in modern, industrialised democracies would be assessed as having a Type B strategy. Types A and C account for the remaining 40 per cent, so they are not at all unusual, and not necessarily a cause for concern.

We will now look at how the infant develops a Type A, B or C strategy in response to their caregiver's behaviour.

A note on terminology

Readers may be familiar with terminology such as 'dismissing/avoidant' (A), 'secure/autonomous' (B) or 'coercive/ambivalent' (C) to describe attachment strategies. In this book we will use the terms A, B and C to describe the different patterns. Type A refers to dismissing/avoidant, Type C refers to 'coercive/ambivalent' and Type B refers to 'secure/autonomous'. We also won't be talking about disorganised attachment as a separate strategy. There are two reasons for this. First, recent research has suggested that it is more helpful to think of strategies being dysregulated rather than disorganised (Duschinsky and Solomon 2017; Granqvist *et al.* 2017). Second, disorganised attachment is more commonly associated with infants and children, and is a term which is less usually applied to adults, and therefore less relevant to this book.

The development of attachment strategies

Predictability and attunement

There are two aspects of the behaviour of the caregiver which have the most significant influence on the development of the baby's attachment strategy: the *predictability* of their responses, and the degree of *attunement* of their behaviour towards the baby.

Predictability refers to how consistent the caregiver is in the way they behave towards the baby; how likely are they to respond to the baby's attachment signals in similar ways at different times and on different days? This is important, because if the caregiver is predictable in his or her responses, the baby can learn cause-and-effect links (e.g. 'If I am hungry and I cry, then I will be fed and I will feel better'). If there isn't a consistent pattern, then the baby will struggle to learn these links.

Attunement refers to how accurately the caregiver is able to work out the underlying reason for the baby's attachment behaviour, and their ability to respond in a way which will calm and soothe the baby (e.g. the baby cries because he or she needs a clean nappy, and the caregiver is able to work out the reason for the cry and to respond in a helpful way, by changing the baby's nappy rather than feeding the baby because she or he thinks the baby is hungry). This doesn't mean that caregivers have to get it right first time – it is the process of observing the baby and trying to work out how they are feeling and what they need to help to soothe them which counts.

The B strategy

The Type B strategy is known as a secure attachment strategy. In the Strange Situation procedure, infants using Type B strategies show some degree of anxiety or sadness at missing the parent when they are separated, and greet the parent when they return to the room by approaching them and raising their arms to be picked up. Once the caregiver picks them up, they are quickly soothed and they soon want to return to play.

The B strategy is associated with predictable and attuned care on the part of the caregiver. If, when the baby cries out, the caregiver behaves in a way which is both predictable and attuned, the baby can be confident that their caregiver will comfort and protect them should they be distressed or in danger. The baby comes to rely on the caregiver as a 'secure base', a source of comfort and safety. This can give the infant using a Type B strategy the confidence to explore the environment around them, because they know that the caregiver will protect her if she becomes sad, angry or scared.

The baby who is developing a Type B strategy is learning that signals, or information, from inside her body – physical sensations of temperature, hunger, tiredness, and emotions of fear or need for comfort – have an important purpose. If the baby recognises her feelings, and expresses them through attachment behaviour such as a cry, then the caregiver will move closer, and help the baby to feel better in a predictable and attuned way. The baby is also learning that information from outside her body, such as patterns of cause and effect, are also useful. For example, babies are capable of learning from the earliest weeks of life links such as 'If I cry, someone comes and makes me feel better,' in much the same way that dogs are capable of learning 'If I return the ball to my owner on command, I receive a treat.' A baby developing a Type B strategy is learning that these two sources of information – inside the body (feelings or affect) and outside the body (thoughts or cognition) – are equally valuable, and both need to be paid attention to.

The A strategy

The Type A strategy is known as an insecure attachment strategy. In the Strange Situation procedure, infants using Type A strategies will not show very much sadness or fear when the caregiver leaves the room, but will carry on playing. If you look very carefully, the way they play might change – it might become more superficial – if the infant was playing with a toy piano, they might just play the same note rather than experimenting with making up a tune. This suggests that the infant is feeling sad or afraid on the inside, but is not acting on it. When the caregiver returns, infants using A strategies don't rush up to greet the caregiver straight away. There is often a short delay of a few seconds. Then, when the infants do approach the caregiver, they often lower their eyes, and don't make eye contact straight away. After they have been greeted by the caregiver, they quickly return to playing.

The Type A strategy is associated with predictably non-attuned behaviour from the caregiver. In other words, when the baby cries out, the caregiver consistently behaves in a way which does not solve the baby's problem. For example, when the baby cries, the caregiver either ignores the baby, shouts, or in cases of maltreatment, harms the baby in some way. The important point is that this happens in a consistent way. In these circumstances, the baby learns, 'If I cry, either nothing happens, or something happens which makes me feel worse.'

A baby who is developing a Type A strategy is learning that information from inside her body (her feelings and physical sensations) are not safe sources of information to pay attention to, because if she shows her feelings, by crying or by signalling that she needs comfort, she is either ignored or made to feel worse. Instead, it is more useful for this baby to pay attention to what is going on in the world outside her body – sequences such as 'If I cry, my mum frowns at me', 'If I smile, my mum smiles at me.' This baby learns that cognitions – thoughts about patterns and sequences – are more useful than her inner feelings in order to get her basic needs met. Therefore, this infant learns to pay less attention to what she is feeling, and more attention to the world around her.

The C strategy

The Type C strategy is also known as an insecure strategy. In the Strange Situation procedure, an infant using a Type C strategy will show great distress on separation from the parent by crying and protesting. He will quickly seek out contact with the attachment figure when they re-enter the room, but he will not calm down quickly. He is likely to resist soothing – he may arch his back if the parent tries to comfort him, or cry more loudly, or even show signs of anger. When the parent tries to leave the room for the second time, he may try to stop him from going, by clinging to his leg, or try to follow him out of the room. The infant can appear to be quite distressed and angry.

The Type C strategy develops in response to unpredictable and inconsistently attuned care from the attachment figure. When the baby cries, the parent sometimes responds quickly and in a sensitive way. But at other times, the parent responds after a delay, sometimes sensitively, and sometimes less sensitively, and sometimes not at all. There are lots of reasons why this could be the case; there may be a lot of children in the house, or there could be an adult who needs caring for. Or there could be issues of domestic abuse, mental illness or substance misuse in the family.

This type of unpredictable response from the parent is very difficult for the baby to make sense of, because the baby is unable to learn what the link is between crying and a response from the parent. Sometimes, if the baby cries the parent responds in a way which makes the baby feel better, but at other times, this doesn't happen. Crucially, the baby can't understand the reason for these different responses at different times. What is likely to happen is that the baby learns that when he keeps crying for an extended period of time, this is more likely to generate a response from the parent. Therefore, the baby's cries and other emotional signals are likely to become exaggerated; cries become sobs, a need for comfort becomes clinginess, anger becomes a tantrum, and the baby is likely to resist being soothed. The reason for this is not to do with the baby's personality, but because such exaggerated signals are more likely to win a response from the parent.

The development of attachment strategies beyond infancy

Now that we understand how the baby's experiences of caregiving lead to the development of Type A, B and C strategies, we can consider how our attachment strategies develop across the lifespan. Of course, the attachment strategies we develop are highly influenced by the relationships we develop with our parents, siblings, and later on, partners and (perhaps) our own children. They are also influenced by how much danger we face in our lives – at the mild end, this could be danger due to family circumstances such as divorce, or frequent changes of caregiver, or at the more severe end, this could be danger due to abuse, neglect or maltreatment. In general, the more danger or threat we face, the more likely we are to develop a more rigid attachment strategy, with less flexibility, and we may find it harder to adapt to changing circumstances or changing relationships.

The development of Type B strategies across the lifespan

A person using a Type B strategy is able to pay attention to both thoughts and feelings in order to make sense of the world around them. This enables them to reflect on their own emotional needs, and to balance them with the needs of other people. They are able to both ask for help when they need it, and to care for others. They are able to balance their thoughts and feelings with those of others because they trust that, should they express a need for comfort, their attachment figures will be able to meet that need in a predictable and attuned way. A person using Type B strategies has a greater capacity to cope with life's challenges across their lifespan, because they have access to the full range of strategies and are able to recognise their needs, ask for help appropriately and accept help when offered. Of course, a person using Type B strategies is just as vulnerable as anyone else to difficult life events, such as a bereavement, the end of a relationship, or an accident, but they are more likely to be able to recover, given time.

The development of Type A strategies across the lifespan

As discussed above, a person may develop a Type A strategy if they experience their caregiver as unattuned in a predictable way. They become more tuned in to their thoughts about the world around them, such as patterns and sequences of behaviour. On the other hand, the child learns that displaying real emotions, such as anger, sadness, fear or a need for comfort, is likely to result in rejection from the caregiver, which will lead to the child feeling worse. Therefore, what drives the Type A strategy is the fear of intimacy and being truly 'known' by another person.

At the milder end of the spectrum, later in life, a person with a Type A strategy may develop caregiving strategies – getting some of his or her own needs met by offering care to others. The Type A strategy can also be associated with high achievement in academic or professional life, but the individual may struggle to recognise their own emotions. A person who has coped with more threat may become increasingly cut off from their own feelings, and become socially isolated, because human relationships have proved so difficult for them. Or, they may surround themselves with a large number of people but keep them all at arm's length, and keep the relationships superficial to protect the self from intimacy. Or, they may behave in a controlling way within relationships, in order to keep people at the distance which feels comfortable to them – not too close, but not too far.

The more danger or threat a person with an A strategy has had to cope with, the more likely it is that they may experience sudden emotional outbursts, which are not characteristic of them. The analogy of a pressure cooker is useful here; just because the person is not very aware of their feelings doesn't mean that they aren't having them. Most of the time, the person may be able to keep a lid on their emotions, but under certain circumstances the pressure may build until the lid blows. The person may act in a way which is violent (anger), or have a panic attack (fear) or sob in a way which feels beyond their control (sadness) or may seek comfort through inappropriate physical contact with others. Sometimes, these unexpressed feelings can also lead to physical symptoms, such as unexplained skin complaints, or stomach problems. It's as though the body is displaying the symptoms to show the person that they are not paying enough attention to their feelings. These outbursts of unexpressed feelings are called 'intrusions of negative affect' (Crittenden 2008). The word 'negative' does not refer to the emotion itself, but to the reaction of the caregiver to the expression of that emotion by the child. The intrusion, or outburst, represents a bursting out of the emotion which the caregiver could not tolerate being expressed.

The development of Type C strategies across the lifespan

The Type C strategy develops when the child experiences unpredictably attuned care from their attachment figure – when they express a need, the carer sometimes responds in a sensitive and attuned way, and at other times either does not respond in good time or responds in an insensitive way. The carer's unpredictability is very confusing for the child because the child can't predict how the carer will respond, so the child comes to rely upon their experiences of their feelings in order to make sense of the world. The carer is more likely to come to take care of the child if they cry loudly and for a long time, and so the child learns to express their emotions in an exaggerated way.

As the child grows older, he or she may learn to behave in ways which are more likely to gain the attention of the unpredictable attachment figure. This can lead to increasingly risky behaviour, as the child will keep needing to raise the stakes in order to gain the attention of the caregiver. Additionally, as the child gets older, he or she is likely to learn that it is important to hold onto the caregiver's attention once it has been gained. Therefore, the child learns to keep changing the way they are expressing their emotions. For example, a child might throw their shoe at a wall in an expression of anger. When the caregiver gets close to them, probably to tell them off, the child may begin to cry and say that 'No one ever asks me how I feel about things!' This could elicit some comfort from the caregiver and go some way to meeting the child's needs. For the caregiver, it can feel that they are engaged in an ongoing sequence of unsolvable problems, with the child alternating between anger and vulnerability. Through their development, they learned that there is little to be gained in trying to see the point of view of other people; as their main caregiver behaved unpredictably, understanding their motivation gave only limited benefit. Rather, what was protective was to tune into their own feelings, demonstrate them in an exaggerated way, and then, once the caregiver's attention had been gained, change the emotion which was being expressed.

In later life, this can mean that a person with a Type C strategy may find it difficult to develop and maintain close relationships. They may appear at times to be overwhelmed by feelings of sadness, anger, helplessness or fear. When they have faced more threat, they may at times act in a way which is aggressive to others, and alternate that with helplessness or vulnerability. It must be remembered that this strategy is unconscious, and it represents the person's best attempt to get their emotional needs met.

How can attachment theory be useful when working with older people?

Attachment theory is most commonly associated with the early stages of life but has just as much relevance when thinking about older people and their family networks. The very process of ageing, which for most people can be associated at some point with physical and emotional vulnerability, can increase a person's need for comfort and safety. Equally, family members or partners may themselves find their attachment strategies become activated by their concerns and anxieties about the welfare of their older family member, and their natural fear of age and mortality. Attachment theory can encourage us to regard a person's self-protective strategies as strengths, which have been protective for them at some point in their life. Becoming curious about their life experiences and important relationships can help us to gain an enhanced understanding of their current behaviour. This can encourage workers to steer away from labelling people on the basis of their behaviour, and to have the courage and creativity to see beyond wholly service-led solutions to supporting people to feel safer.

Challenges to the attachment system in later life

As we grow older, for most people, the chances of us needing support from other people increase. The support we need may take the form of help with meeting our basic physical needs, or our social and emotional needs. For an adult who may, during their earlier adult life, have been in an independent, caregiving role (such as raising children, for example), the transition to being in a position of needing support from others can be a difficult one. In earlier adult life, they may have simultaneously given and received care – so their relationships were symmetrical. In older age, this balance can be harder to find, and they may find themselves more dependent on others than previously.

The need to negotiate new roles can lead to tension and a sense of vulnerability. For some people, this vulnerability may be increased by social problems such as poverty, discrimination or insecure housing, or by illness. The unique challenges of later life can lead to a person developing different attachment strategies in order to maximise the chance of having their needs met in a new context, characterised by new relationships.

Common experiences of older age may include coping with the loss of a partner, siblings or friends. As a result, many people find themselves reflecting upon their life story, and looking for meaning or significance. There may be changes in social and family networks – many studies suggest that family ties take on greater significance as a person gets older. For some people, it may also include the need to cope with new and unfamiliar environments if they decide to move out of their home. People who need to rely on paid helpers face the challenges of forming trusting relationships, potentially at a time when they may feel vulnerable. All of these experiences are likely to evoke stress, threat and perceived danger in individuals, and therefore activate their attachment responses.

There is a small but growing research literature about how people meet their attachment needs in later life. It seems that we are capable of developing new attachment strategies to cope with changing contexts, such as a needing to adapt to receiving physical care from another person, or a move into a residential setting. Our attachment strategies are robust, but not rigid, and, as Bowlby said, we remain capable of learning new strategies from the cradle to the grave. This capacity helps us to adapt to changing environments, needs and relationships in older age, and as such is a key strength.

There is some research which suggests that people who use Type B strategies may be better equipped to adapt to the changes brought on by older age because they have more flexible strategies, and are more likely to be able to recognise their changing needs and ask for help if they need it (Bradley and Cafferty 2001). They may, of course, at the same time continue to offer comfort and support to others around them until the end of their lives.

People using Type A strategies may typically find it difficult to tune into their emotional worlds and recognise that they need support through relationships in order to feel safe, comfortable and connected. This may mean that they are unable to ask for support in a timely way, and may even become angry or irritated if they are asked by well-meaning others if they need help.

People using Type C strategies may prioritise their attachment needs over their care needs, and may therefore ask for help and support from others in order to feel safe and comfortable. They may alternate between asking for help, and then rejecting it, in a way which can leave people around them feeling confused or frustrated about how best to help them. For people using either Type A or type C strategies, understanding how their attachment strategies represent their best possible attempts to meet their needs for safety, comfort, proximity and predictability can help people around them to understand the meaning of behaviour which can otherwise be difficult to understand.

Clive – an example of a person using a Type A attachment strategy

Clive and Josie are both in their late 70s, and have been married for 40 years. They live together in a house which they own. Josie had a stroke three years ago, and her speech and her physical mobility are still affected. They have a daughter, Dawn, who lives in the same town and sees them weekly. Until recently, Josie has only needed Clive to help her with washing her hair. He has also done most of the household tasks. Recently, Josie has started to have problems with wetting the bed in the middle of the night. She is embarrassed about this, and Clive has been very supportive. He has tried to keep on top of the extra washing and has bought a plastic sheet for the bed. Dawn has noticed that her dad is looking more tired, and each week she asks him if he is OK. She's noticed that when she asks him this, he smiles at her, and says, 'I'm fine, lovey, and so's your mum' and then quickly asks her about her work situation (he knows that she has been having difficulties with a new boss). Dawn suspects that her dad might not be telling her the full story. One day, she sits him down and, very gently, asks him to tell her what the matter is. He snaps at her, saying, 'Stop being so nosey. We're doing fine. I don't need any help.'

The next time she visits, she says that she will help her mum to wash and dry her hair. When they are alone in the bedroom, Josie shows Dawn that the wardrobe is full of bags of wet bed sheets. Dawn tells her dad that she knows about the laundry problem and wants to help them both. He becomes very angry and shouts at her. He tells her that she is interfering in their business and should go home and sort out her own problems. She is upset at his hurtful words and leaves the house. She really wants to support her mum and dad, but isn't sure how.

Clive's story

Clive grew up as an only child; his mum and dad had two stillborn babies before he was born. When he was a baby, his mother became very anxious whenever he cried, because of the traumatic losses she had suffered. His father was emotionally distant, and not very involved with him as a boy. He learned that the best way to get his emotional needs met was only to display positive emotions, such as happiness and contentment, and to hide away feelings of sadness or anger. On the rare occasions that he showed sadness or anger, his mother was unable to cope, and turned away from him – she was unattuned to his needs in a predictable way. As he grew up, he became very good at reassuring his mother that he was OK – psychologically, he took care of her by putting her emotional needs first. By cutting off from his own genuine emotions, and presenting only positive emotions, he was able to get some of his needs met by being physically close to his mum. As an adult, Clive finds it very hard to recognise what he is feeling. He and Josie have a very supportive and loving relationship, but Josie has often commented to Dawn that Clive struggles to talk about his feelings.

At this point in time, Clive is struggling to care for Josie in the way that he always has done until now. He finds this new challenge very difficult to manage, because of his belief that his role is to care for her by putting her needs first. He feels very ashamed that he doesn't know how to cope with her night-time incontinence, and has a strong urge to hide the problem away. When Dawn finds out and confronts him (albeit very gently), the emotions of anxiety and shame are too much for him, and he is overwhelmed by anger. He then feels very bad for shouting at her.

Why might Clive behave this way?

Clive learned, throughout his childhood, that displaying positive emotions to his mother and appearing outwardly 'fine' was the best strategy available to him to get his needs met as far as possible. This Type A strategy has worked fairly well for him throughout his life. He is now unable to cope with looking after Josie without some more support. Part of him realises this, but he feels very afraid, both about Josie's deteriorating health, and about what might happen in the future. This fear and uncertainty is activating his attachment strategy. Snapping at Dawn represents a bursting out of the fear and sadness which he has buried. He struggles to ask for help, because he learned that when he showed his attachment needs to his mother, she was unable to respond in a way which made him feel better. He learned that it was safer to ignore these needs and not to ask for help. So being in a position now of needing to ask for help seems very threatening to him.

How can Dawn support her parents?

It might be helpful if Dawn can stay very calm and talk with Clive in ways which help him to feel safe. Clive is unlikely to be comfortable naming his feelings straight away, so it might help him if Dawn is factual and helps him to consider all the options. Supporting Clive and Josie to put together a simple chart, looking at the pros and cons of all the different options, might help. Helping Clive and Josie to recall their strengths as a couple, and times when they have coped with difficulties, might also help.

Marieta – an example of a person using a Type C attachment strategy

Marieta is 78 and lives in a supported living flat, on her own. Her husband died three years ago. She has one son, who lives two hundred miles away. He has a very demanding job and isn't able to visit her very often.

Marieta has recently begun to press the alarm button to call the scheme manager, Bernadette, saying that she has fallen and needs assistance. When Bernadette arrives, she is often frustrated to find that Marieta has called her to help with a problem that, in her opinion, she could cope with for herself, such as having misplaced her glasses or her telephone. When Bernadette reminds Marieta only to call for her if she has a genuine problem, Marieta often becomes angry and tells Bernadette that she thinks she is lazy. She accuses her of being much nicer to other people who live in the flats. On other occasions, Marieta is very kind to Bernadette, apologises for having been angry with her, and tells her that she doesn't know how she'd manage without her.

Bernadette now finds that, when she sees that Marieta has rung her alarm button, she starts to feel anxious, as she doesn't know whether Marieta will be angry, or distressed, or apologetic. Bernadette is noticing that she is now reluctant to attend when Marieta rings her alarm and tries to avoid her.

Marieta's story

Marieta was the youngest of seven siblings. Her father died after a long illness, when she was three, and her mother had to work very hard to bring in enough money for the family. Marieta was cared for mainly by her older siblings. Each of her siblings had slightly different ways of caring for her – some were strict, others were very flexible – and this meant that Marieta could not predict what the response would be if she expressed feelings of sadness, anger, fear or a need for comfort. Marieta learned as a young child that, when she needed to be cared for, she was more likely to receive a response which would make her feel better if she displayed her emotions in an exaggerated way. As she got older, she learned that the best way to keep her siblings close, and therefore able to comfort her and help her to feel safe, was to change the nature of the problem which she presented to them, so that they did not leave her.

Why might Marieta behave this way?

Following the death of her husband three years ago, Marieta has felt increasingly isolated and lonely. She would like her son to visit her more, but he is very busy at work, and has just got married. His wife is pregnant, and while Marieta is very much looking forward to being a grandmother, she is also concerned that this will mean that he will have even less time to spend with her. Having grown up in such a large family, Marieta is finding it difficult to spend so much time alone. Her attachment strategy is activated by her isolation, and her fears about becoming a grandmother, and her son being less able to visit her.

Bernadette is the person who Marieta feels closest to, and this is why Marieta is behaving in this push–pull way with her. Bernadette is responding to Marieta's unpredictable behaviour by withdrawing, which Bernadette senses. Bernadette's withdrawal makes Marieta feel more anxious and rejected, which causes her to escalate her behaviour in an unconscious attempt to pull Bernadette closer to her.

How can Bernadette support Marieta?

If Bernadette continues to try to avoid Marieta, or to keep her distance from her, the situation is only likely to escalate. First of all, Bernadette can help Marieta by being as predictable as possible – agreeing times when she will speak with her and sticking to them. It may help Bernadette to be very clear about what she is experiencing from Marieta and agree some ground rules. Paying attention to Marieta, by visiting her for a conversation when there isn't a problem, is likely to help Marieta to feel 'borne in mind' by Bernadette. In the long run, it might be helpful of Bernadette to try to support Marieta to consider how she wants her life to be. This might involve some strengths-based conversations, considering Marieta's resources and skills. It may also involve supporting Marieta to have a conversation with her son and his family about how they see the future.

Further reading

Baim, C. and Morrison, T. (2011) *Attachment Based Practice with Adults*. Brighton: Pavilion.

Crittenden, P.M. (2008) *Raising Parents: Attachment, Parenting and Child Safety*. Cullompton, Devon: Willan Publishing.

Howe, D. (2011) *Attachment across the Lifespan*. Basingstoke: Palgrave Macmillan.

3

Working with the Whole Family

Many older people derive great strength and resources from their family connections, and like people of all ages, define themselves at least partly in terms of their relationships with their family network – as a parent, a sibling, a partner or a grandparent. It is often changes in family circumstances – such as a change in the level of contact, or the illness or loss of a loved one – that can prompt a crisis for an older person. Therefore, it seems important to consider an older person in the context of their family relationships, including partners, siblings, children and extended family. However, many services are delivered with only the individual older person in mind, and people employed to deliver services may have little or no contact with family members.

A social worker on a training event run by one of the authors commented that, having recently moved from a team where he worked with children and families to a team where he worked with older people, he was struck that whereas services tend to think of a child as firmly rooted in the context of their wider family and social network, it is more common to consider older people as separate individuals in isolation from their families and friends. Clearly, adults have different rights and needs from children, but networks of relationships and family connections are just as important for them.

When family members of older adults are considered by the providers of services, their perceived role as 'carer' can overshadow any other relationship they may have with their loved one. Many people in this position speak about the shock of being labelled a 'carer' first and a 'daughter' or 'husband' second. In the words of a woman interviewed for our study in Wales, 'I don't see myself as a carer, I just see myself as my father's daughter. He looked after me when I was a child, so is it not my time for payback?' (Blood *et al.* 2016b, p.26).

Looking after a loved one who can no longer fully take care of themselves because they are getting older has been part of the natural cycle of family life across the whole span of human history. Many people who are supported by their partners or children in their older age will have themselves cared for those family members in the past – either during their childhood or during periods of illness. The giving and receiving of care within a family or partnership is a mutual process, the direction of which shifts over time. However, it is well recognised that taking on a caring role can be a source of stress and strain. Carers are much more likely to experience mental and physical health problems than the general population, and caring can impact on every aspect of life. The stresses of caregiving are often divided into primary and secondary stressors (Pearlin, Mullan and Semple 1990). Primary stressors include acts of caregiving, such as helping with washing, dressing and personal care, and offering emotional support. The secondary stressors include the impacts on the other aspects of daily life, including finances, employment and social relationships.

There are many different reasons why family members offer care to each other. Many family members – as in the quote above – decide to look after a loved one because of a sense of love, or a recognition that they have received care from that person, and so caring for them seems like a natural extension of the love which they have shared, as parent and child or as partners. Others offer care because of spiritual, religious or cultural beliefs or expectations. There is evidence that the response of family caregivers to their caregiving role is related to their motivations to provide care. Brodaty and Donkin (2009) found that caregivers who are motivated by a sense of duty, guilt or societal expectations are more likely to resent their role. Those who identify positive reasons for caregiving are less likely to express a sense of burden, and are more likely to access social support if they need it.

Carers who themselves belong to marginalised groups (for example, due to their race, sexuality, income or social position) may face discrimination, and may find it harder to seek support from mainstream services. Moriarty, Manthorpe and Cornes (2015) also remind us that many who offer care to loved ones but do not define themselves as 'carers' may not ask for support because they may not see themselves as needing, or deserving, it.

Caregiving and family relationships

A family that is caring for a family member due to an illness of older age is more likely than other families to experience conflict. The illness or care needs of the older person are likely to evoke strong emotions and to remind other family members of their own vulnerabilities. As one participant in the Better Life programme stated, 'People like to think that old is different. They don't like to be reminded of their own mortality' (Blood 2013, p.17).

Caring for an older family member can evoke the attachment strategies of all those involved, as they are reminded of their own mortality and as they cope with the day-to-day needs of their loved one. It can also evoke other long-standing tensions and rivalries which may exist within the family. Conflict can be based upon disagreements about the distribution of financial resources, inheritances and perceived favouritism. There may be long-standing family secrets, concerning domestic abuse, sexual abuse, affairs and children born outside marriage, which may remain unspoken, but nonetheless add hidden dimensions and complexities to conflicts which appear to be about the care of an older person.

A study in 1991 found that 40 per cent of adult caregivers were experiencing conflict with another family member which they believed was caused by the impact of their caregiving responsibilities (Strawbridge and Wallhagen 1991). The main cause of the conflict was due to disagreements about how much support each sibling was offering to the parent. Other sources of conflict were disagreements about how serious the parent's health problems were, disagreements about how different siblings were interacting with the parent, and differences of views regarding major decisions such as whether a parent should enter a residential care home and how it should be funded.

These findings were supported by Peisah, Brodaty and Quadrio (2006), who examined 50 cases of family conflict which were considered by the Guardianship Tribunal in New South Wales, Australia, all of which involved a person with dementia. These conflicts were so entrenched that they had to be referred to a tribunal, so they are not representative of the majority of family conflicts; nonetheless, much can be learned from them. Most of the conflicts were between siblings, and the majority involved differences of opinion about money, or about the provision of care, or about where the person with dementia should live. Another frequent source of conflict was disagreement over the diagnosis, with a commonly observed pattern being the person diagnosed with dementia in alliance with another family member challenging the diagnosis and accusing other family members of being bossy and controlling.

The majority of the conflicts between siblings involved one sibling taking the role of main carer and being accused by other siblings of providing inadequate care, taking the parent's money and failing to communicate with the other family members. The researchers conclude that 'having a dependent parent provided an opportunity for siblings to play out a competition to be the best, most caring child' (Peisah *et al.* 2006, p.489).

Of course, this tension can go both ways. In research for the Barnwood Trust we interviewed a woman who gave up her employment to live with and support her mother, who would otherwise have needed to move into residential care due to her dementia (Blood, Copeman and Pannell 2016a). The woman told the researchers that she was expected to pay rent by her brother, as he believed that she should not be living rent free in her mother's house, despite having given up her employment.

Attachment patterns within families

Families are emotional systems – within families, individuals are linked by complex webs of relationships, roles and expectations of each other. When an older family member begins to require support, it is likely that new patterns of interaction will need to be negotiated. Roles may have to be revised, and power may shift, either horizontally between the generations or vertically among sibling groups. Familiar patterns and roles may be threatened, requiring family members to act in new and unfamiliar ways in relation to each other. The family script – the family's shared expectations of how family roles are performed – may need to be rewritten (Byng-Hall 1995). These changes will also be informed by the social, cultural and religious context within which the family lives, and their beliefs about ageing, illness and gender roles.

Families which are able to be flexible and to communicate their thoughts and feelings are most likely to be able to adapt to meet the challenges. These are likely to be families whose relationships are based upon Type B secure attachments, whose members are able to show care for each other in predictable and attuned ways, and to move flexibly between using their thoughts and their feelings in decision making.

Attachment relationships within families are usually complex; among sibling groups, it is very common for different siblings to use different attachment strategies in relation to their parents and each other. Dallos and Vetere (2009) discuss attachment strategies in terms of communicational patterns, rules that regulate which subjects can be spoken about, with whom, and in what way.

For example, with Type B secure patterns, family members will be encouraged to express both positive and negative feelings, and their emotions will be heard and validated by other family members, who will then be able to reflect upon what has been said and negotiate a solution.

In families that use Type A attachment strategies, certain topics or themes may be off limits, and it may be difficult for emotions to be acknowledged. Conversation may focus on practical issues, such as plans, rotas and schedules.

In families that use Type C strategies, emotions may be communicated very freely, and may escalate as each person competes to be heard. This may lead to a conversation which is dominated by emotional expression, where thought and reflection are difficult.

Minuchin's overall categories of family patterns are a broad fit with patterns of attachment: 'adaptable' families equate with the secure Type B pattern, 'disengaged' families with Type A patterns and 'enmeshed' families with Type C patterns (Minuchin 1974). As people whose roles involve supporting families to cope with these challenges, we can use our knowledge of attachment theory to help the family to remain safe enough to be able to reflect on their emotions and their thoughts. For more ideas about how to do this, please see the final section of this chapter and Chapter 9, Tool 4.

Interactional patterns within families

Within a family, behaviour is never a one-way street; each person influences, and is influenced by, each other. Family interactions form loops and spirals rather than straight lines. John Burnham, a family therapist, has written about the patterns of interaction within a family that is facing a dilemma about how to think about their child's behaviour – does he have Asperger's syndrome or not (Burnham 2016)?

The family were of the view that this was the key question, and that answering that question correctly would help them to function better as a family. We have adapted this example and related it to a family affected by their mother's (possible) dementia.

Marcella's story

Marcella is 76 and has two children, Tracey and Simon. She lives with her daughter, Tracey, and her two grandchildren, and she sees Simon weekly. Tracey and Simon have both noticed that Marcella sometimes can't remember the names of her children and grandchildren, or the words for common items. Tracey has suggested to her mother that she goes to see the GP for an assessment, but Marcella becomes angry at this suggestion, and accuses Tracey of interfering and treating her like a child. After they argue, Tracey becomes slightly less tolerant of her mother, and more critical, pointing out occasions when Marcella forgets a word or appears momentarily confused.

Tracey is speaking with her close friend, Susan, about her mother. She realises that her relationship with her mother is strained at times and wants things to be better between them. Tracey says to Susan that it would really help her to know whether her mother has dementia or not, because it would help her to cope better. Susan asks her what difference it would make, and Tracey says that, if her mother has dementia, she would find it easier to be patient with her when she can't remember things. Susan asks Tracey what difference it makes when she is more patient with her mother, and she replies that her mother seems calmer and is able to remember more when she is patient with her. Tracey then sees her mother as having 'improved' and comes to the conclusion that her mother doesn't have dementia. She then becomes less patient, and more critical of her mother, whose memory then seems to 'worsen'. Talking with Susan about the patterns of communication between her and her mother, Tracey recognises that the thing which makes a difference to her mother's behaviour and capacity to cope is how she responds to her if she becomes confused. Tracey realises that what matters to her is the kind of relationship she has with her mother, as opposed to whether her mother's confusion is caused by dementia or not, and she decides to focus on this. One way of thinking about this pattern of family interactions is to use a 'strange loop' model (Cronen, Johnson and Lannaman 1982).

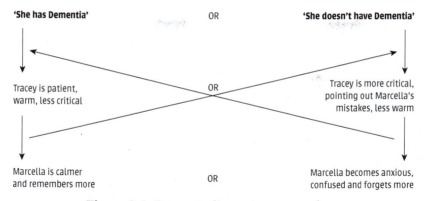

'She has Dementia'   OR   'She doesn't have Dementia'

Tracey is patient,   OR   Tracey is more critical,
warm, less critical   pointing out Marcella's
                                                   mistakes, less warm

Marcella is calmer   OR   Marcella becomes anxious,
and remembers more   confused and forgets more

Figure 3.1: Dementia diagnosis: a strange loop

Figure 3.1 highlights how Marcella and Tracey behave in ways which affect each other. It doesn't matter where the pattern starts – whether Marcella's forgetfulness or Tracey's criticism comes first – the pattern is the same. The model helps to reduce blame by focusing on the whole pattern rather than one person. Noticing the pattern helped Tracey to see that what really matters is not the issue of the diagnosis of dementia, but the question of what kind of relationship she would like to have with her mother. The model is also strengths based – it can help Tracey to recognise that she already has the skills and the ability to calm and soothe Marcella, and to help her to remember more. Changing the question from 'Has my mother got dementia?' to 'What kind of relationship do I want with my mother?' opens up more possibilities for Tracey and reminds her that she is already able to be loving and patient with her mother. Of course, this is not to discount the importance of a diagnosis, which can offer certainty, and possibilities for treatment and support. But focusing upon relationships as well as diagnosis can help Tracey to consider how she wants her relationship with her mother to be in the here and now of each interaction between them.

In this example, we have applied this model to a family relationship. However, we could also use the approach to consider relationships between people who are paid to offer care and the older people they care for, in order to focus on patterns of interaction and the ways in which we influence each other.

Attachment and caregiving

Much of the research in this area has focused upon the impact of caring for a person with dementia. In 2014, the Alzheimer's Society estimated that over 60 per cent people with dementia are cared for by family members at home, most commonly by a partner or adult daughter (Prince *et al.* 2014). Whilst providing care for a loved one can offer an opportunity for people to develop new and potentially rewarding aspects of their relationship, it can also lead to strain and difficulty for both parties. Looking after a family member with dementia can impact upon the physical health, mental health and finances of the person who takes on the caring role. Forty-eight per cent of carers have themselves been diagnosed with a long-term illness or disability (NHS Digital 2017).

The emotional effects can be more difficult to quantify. People with dementia and their carers often report a sense of loss – loss of identity, and loss of the relationship they had experienced prior to the diagnosis of dementia. Caregivers can experience 'ambiguous loss' – the sense that their loved one is both present and absent at the same time due to the cognitive and physical impacts of the illness (Boss 1999). People with dementia can experience a multi-layered sense of loss; we should not underestimate the strain involved in becoming, at least to some degree, 'a person who needs care', combined with the disorientation and frustration that accompany memory loss.

The onset of dementia is likely to activate the attachment strategies of the person with dementia and of their loved ones, because of the threats to self-identity and the impact upon the sense of connectedness to others. People with dementia often speak of the disorientating impact of being unable to fully remember the narrative of their life, and the fear of being unable to recognise their loved ones. The fear of the impact of the illness can have almost as great an impact as the illness itself. The onset of dementia can also induce a sense of fear in the people around the person with the diagnosis – 'Will my mum still be my mum?' 'What about when my husband no longer recognises me?'

These threats can activate the attachment strategies of those involved and prompt them to either rely on thoughts (Type A) or on emotions (Type C) in order to protect the self, and increase the chance that basic emotional needs will be met. We will now consider the different attachment patterns that may operate between adult children and their parents, and in couple relationships.

Attachment in caring relationships between people with dementia and their adult children

This section focuses upon the nature of relationships between people with dementia and their adult children because this is an area where there has been a considerable amount of research. However, attachment patterns are universal, and there is every reason to consider that attachment patterns between people without dementia and their adult children may operate in similar ways, if their attachment systems are activated due to the threat of illness.

There is a body of evidence which suggests that the nature of the caregiving relationship between a parent with dementia and their adult child will be impacted by the nature of the attachment relationship they experienced before the onset of the illness. Of course, this is not to say that their attachment strategies are the only important factors; issues such as their financial security, other support networks, their housing situation and their social context will also play a role in the way they are able to adapt to cope with the impact of the dementia.

In order to learn more about how attachment strategies can affect relationships between people with dementia and their children, Howard Steele and his colleagues studied 17 mothers and their daughters (Steele, Phibbs and Woods 2004). The mothers all had dementia, and the daughters were all in the role of caregiver for their mothers. They interviewed the daughters using the Adult Attachment Interview (a semi-structured interview which gives a very accurate picture of the attachment relationships between the speaker and their attachment figures). The mother and daughter were then reunited after a one-hour separation, and the researchers paid close attention to the way in which the mothers greeted the daughters. They rated how pleased the mother appeared to be on reunion with her daughter, by paying attention to the mother's facial expressions and body language, and the overall emotional connection between the pair shown through eye contact and responsiveness to each other.

The findings of the study were that daughters whose Adult Attachment Interviews demonstrated that they used Type B secure strategies in relation to their mothers had mothers who were more likely to be rated as greeting their daughters with pleasure and joy upon reunion. Daughters who expressed unresolved grief and loss during the Adult Attachment Interview, or who were assessed as using insecure Type A or Type C strategies in relation to their mothers, were greeted much less positively by their mothers on reunion. The researchers concluded that the severity of the mother's dementia was not a significant factor – this result held true regardless of the nature of the mother's dementia.

Another study found that attachment style was the only significant predictor of caregiving difficulties and psychological strain in children who were caring for their parents (Hazan and Shaver 1990). Adult children who used Type B strategies with their parents reported feeling less strain as a result of offering care and felt less 'burdened' by their role as carers. Using secure, Type B strategies seems to both insulate the caregiver from the psychological impact of caregiving and to result in the person with dementia being able to show joy in the presence of their child. Of course, there is a relationship between these two things – it may be that the joy shown by the parent helps the adult child to find meaning in their role as caregiver and helps them to feel more positive about it. This outcome is far more likely if the parent and the adult child share a relationship history where it was safe for the child to express attachment needs, in the expectation that the parent would meet those needs in an attuned and predictable way.

A study by Chen and colleagues has suggested that an adult child who is using Type B, secure attachment strategies in relation to their parent with dementia is more able to care for their parent in a sensitive way (Chen *et al.* 2013). For example, if the parent becomes confused or frustrated, a son or daughter who is using Type B strategies will be more able to reflect upon their parent's behaviour and understand the way in which the illness may be affecting their parent. They are more likely to be able to rationalise the behaviour, and therefore to continue to offer comfort, support and encouragement, rather than responding emotionally or rejecting their parent. In turn, the parent with dementia will be influenced by the calm presence of their son or daughter, and is less likely to become more distressed, thus preventing escalations.

Chen's study also suggests that sons or daughters who do not use Type B strategies tend to be more likely to respond with hostility or criticism when their parents act in a way which causes them stress. The researchers call this 'expressed emotion'. High levels of expressed emotion are linked to high levels of distress in caregivers, and in the people being cared for, as both parties are influenced by, and influence, each other.

Expressed emotion in a person using Type A strategies

Angela cares for her mother, Marina, who has a diagnosis of dementia. Marina finds having a shower to be very distressing, and she often resists Angela's attempts to help her to wash. Angela finds it difficult to recognise her emotions, and when her friend asks her how she's coping with her mother's illness, she replies that she's fine. One day, Marina refuses to get into the shower, and then wets herself. Angela is overcome by a wave of anger and frustration, and shouts at her mother. Afterwards, she feels very ashamed, and they both cry.

Because of her use of Type A strategies, Angela tended to bottle up her strong emotions. She was not able to recognise that her anger was building up, and she was not consciously lying or concealing that information when she told her friend that she was fine – she was just out of touch with her body and her signs of anger. When her mother wet herself, Angela felt an explosion of anger – which we can think of as an 'intrusion of negative affect' bursting through her A strategy (see Chapter 2) – and lashed out verbally against her mother. She and her mother were both very shocked, and Angela was deeply ashamed.

Expressed emotion in a person using Type C strategies

Connor's mother, Eleanor, is in a residential care home, and has been diagnosed with dementia. The staff observe that at the start of a visit, he tends to be very attentive to his mother and tries hard to talk with her about her grandchildren, and about her experiences in the care home. However, there is a regular pattern emerging; when Eleanor is unable to remember details of her week, or to remember facts about her grandchildren, Connor becomes angry and critical. He can be overheard to say, in a critical tone, 'Come on Mum, you're not really trying. We talked about this last week. I wrote it down for you...' Eleanor then becomes distressed and unsettled, and sometimes cries. At that point, the staff intervene and suggest that Eleanor needs a break.

Connor sometimes becomes angry with the care staff, criticising aspects of his mother's care, and reminding them how much the care home is being paid to take care of her. When the manager speaks to him about his complaints, he cries and says that he feels that no one understands how difficult it is for him to visit his mother. The staff have an uneasy relationship with him and try to keep their distance.

He notices this, and in turn he feels less welcome and more likely to react emotionally.

Connor is using Type C strategies in his relationship with his mother. He finds it very difficult to accept that she is sometimes able to respond to him and meet his attachment needs for connection, and less able at other times. This activates his Type C attachment strategy, and he exaggerates his display of anger towards her when he feels frustrated. Unconsciously, his expressions of anger are inviting his mother to focus on him and meet his attachment needs for closeness and connection. She is not always able to do this, which leads to him feeling rejected. When the staff intervene, he tends to exaggerate his vulnerability, and to describe himself as misunderstood and doing the best job that he can, and then to criticise the job they are doing. He is preoccupied by his overwhelming emotions, and by the emotional impact of his mother's dementia upon him. This means that he is less able to learn about how best to communicate with his mother and to share a sense of connectedness.

Later in the chapter, we will consider how best to work with families and carers in an attachment-informed way.

Attachment between couples in caring relationships

Again, we will focus upon the experience of couples where there is a diagnosis of dementia, as this is an area where there is a considerable amount of research. As before, there is every reason to suppose that much of the learning about how to support couples in attachment-informed and strengths-based informed ways will be generalisable to couples who are experiencing other challenges linked to getting older.

The diagnosis of dementia presents a big threat to the relationship between partners or spouses. Partners of people with dementia speak of experiencing losses in different aspects of their life and relationship, such as companionship, emotional and sexual intimacy, mental stimulation and having someone to share worries with. Whilst the challenges of adapting to a life with dementia are very real, the impact of a diagnosis of dementia will be different for every couple.

Chris Roberts – 'I have dementia but it doesn't have me yet'

Chris Roberts was diagnosed with dementia at the age of 50, and he and his wife, Jayne Goodrick, speak publicly about the impact of the diagnosis on their family; for example, in June 2016 they were the subject of a BBC *Panorama* programme, for which they recorded video diaries. Their philosophy is that they stay positive, and work as a team, alongside their five children, to overcome every hurdle which dementia puts in their way. For example, when Chris stopped being able to boil the kettle because he couldn't take the lid off, they bought a kettle with a button-operated lid. They gave a joint speech at the 27th Alzheimer's Europe Conference in Berlin in October 2017, during which they talked about their coping strategies, and urged professionals to remember the importance of reaffirming families' strengths, and the value of hope. Chris ended the speech by saying, 'I am still me. I am living with dementia, not dying from it, and so is my family. I have dementia, but it doesn't have me yet.'[1]

Perren and colleagues carried out a study looking at the attachment patterns of couples where one of the couple had been diagnosed with dementia (Perren *et al.* 2007). They found that the attachment strategies of the caregiver influence both the levels of distressed behaviour from the person with dementia, and the wellbeing of the caregiver. A key finding was that caregivers using Type A strategies were associated with expressions of agitation and aggression from their partner. This highlights the importance of the reciprocal and interactional nature of caregiving – each person influences and is influenced by the other person. It seems that the less the caregiver is comfortable with emotional closeness, the more distressed their partner becomes, perhaps because their attempts to elicit comfort and safety from their partner do not work, and so they become frustrated. This is challenging for both people in the relationship. The same study demonstrated that caregivers using Type A strategies were less likely to report that they were coping well with their caregiving role.

Wadham and colleagues carried out a review of research into the impact upon couples of one partner developing dementia (Wadham

---

1 A recording of the speech is available at www.youtube.com/watch?v=_EK6LtGC3jM

et al. 2016). They identified four areas of impact which the couples identified as important:

1. *Togetherness*: couples felt that the dementia impacted them both as individuals and also as a couple. Many of the couples talked about trying hard to keep hold of a sense of 'being together' and they often did this by seeing the dementia as an external force which they needed to unite against by working together. Couples spoke of needing to make adjustments in order to carry on doing things together, but recognised that, over the course of their whole relationship, there had been times when they had depended on each other, and that patterns of dependency had been mutual and shifting over time.

2. *Upsetting and redefining the balance*: the person with dementia was less likely to be able to carry on with all of their usual daily tasks, some of which were taken on by their partner. Some couples planned this transition, and others were more reactive and responded to issues as they arose. Some partners enjoyed learning how to take on new tasks, such as gardening, managing the household finances or cookery, and others resented it. These changes provoked mixed emotions for both partners and altered how they defined themselves and their relationships.

3. *Shielding one's partner from the effects of dementia*: people with dementia wanted to protect their partner and to minimise the extra burden on them. In turn, partners often wanted to shield the person with dementia from a complete awareness of the impact of the dementia by helping them to stay as independent as possible and by gently steering them in ways which were not obvious to them, and allowed them to retain a sense of independence.

4. *Resilience*: couples tried to focus on what they could still enjoy together. Many of the individuals expressed sadness in recognition of what they felt they had lost. Some couples spoke of their relationship having become strained, due to anger and frustration, and other couples spoke of coming to terms with life being different due to the illness, but still being able to enjoy aspects of being together as a couple.

The review found that couples responded differently to dementia; for some, it led them to focus on the essential aspects of being a couple, whereas for others, their relationships became more limited and strained. The review reminds us that, although services often focus upon monitoring the physical and cognitive health of the person with dementia, there would be great benefit in bearing the couple in mind, as their ability to retain a sense of togetherness as a couple will have a significant impact on their wellbeing.

The 'Getting Along' programme

Damian Murphy has developed a four-session programme called 'Getting Along', which offers support to couples affected by dementia. The sessions cover reflecting upon the couple's relationship in the past, the present and the future; considering how the diagnosis of dementia has affected their sense of identity; and reflecting upon issues which the couple are finding difficult to manage.[2]

A strengths-based approach – nurturing what remains

Justine McGovern, in her review exploring the lived experience of people with dementia and their partners, writes that dementia is best thought of as a family issue, rather than an individual one (McGovern 2015). She builds upon Rolland's theories of family and illness (Rolland 1994) and suggests that the illness becomes part of the family system, almost like another family member, and therefore we should hold the whole family in mind when we are considering how best to support the person with dementia. She suggests that focusing on monitoring the levels of physical and cognitive capacity tends to highlight areas of loss and decline, and things which the person with dementia can no longer do. McGovern argues that couples affected by dementia tend to cope better when they adopt a strengths-based approach and focus on their shared connection – what she refers to as 'we-ness'. She encourages couples, and people who support couples, to look for what remains rather than what is lost – what emotional connections can the couple still enjoy? This may involve a

---

2   A five-minute film about the programme is available at www.youtube.com/watch?v=gEe9NbCq2Pg

shift from cognitive matters, such as shared conversations and plans, to more emotional matters, such as staying in the present and enjoying moments of emotional attunement. This is not to discount the sense of loss or sadness which a couple may feel, but instead to offer ideas about how couples can best respond to the challenges posed by a diagnosis of dementia.

McGovern gives the example of Art and Carrie, who decided to focus upon sharing fun experiences together. Carrie, who has dementia, enjoys eating popcorn in the cinema and feeling the emotions which are evoked in the moment by a film, but they are both aware that she may not recall the film, and can't describe the plot afterwards. Art focuses on sharing Carrie's connection to the emotional content of the film, and the contented moments they share together eating popcorn in the cinema.

McGovern recommends that people who are supporting couples affected by dementia should learn how to support couples to nurture 'we-ness' through non-cognitive approaches, such as staying in the present moment, and using non-verbal skills to increase closeness and intimacy (e.g. touching, brushing hair, putting on hand cream or body lotion, holding hands, replacing words with touches). The hope is that this strengths-based, relational approach will help couples to retain a positive connection with each other, which will help them to retain hope and promote wellbeing. Some of the practical ideas we include in Chapter 4 on everyday creativity may be useful here for couples and families.

A wonderful example of celebrating 'we-ness' was reported in the *Washington Post* (Klein 2018). Michael Joyce, who has dementia, proposed to his wife, Linda Joyce, to whom he has been married for 38 years. Rather than reminding him that they are already married, Linda Joyce accepted his proposal and arranged a ceremony by a lake with friends and family. A friend conducted the ceremony, and their favourite music was played. Linda Joyce chose to interpret Michael Joyce's proposal as an expression of his deep love for her, and the ceremony marked a celebration of the emotional connection which they share.

What are the factors linked with positive caregiving experiences?

In their study, Yu and colleagues identify four important themes which are spoken of by carers who report positive caregiving experiences (Yu, Cheng and Wang 2018):

1. *A sense of personal accomplishment and gratification*: this arises from developing skills that help to promote the wellbeing of the person with dementia, such as ways of helping them to feel calm, or to gain pleasure from an activity. The gratification is felt by the carer when they see that the way they are relating to the person with dementia is improving their wellbeing, which in turn improves their own wellbeing, as they both influence and are influenced by each other.

2. *Feelings of mutuality in a relationship*: this arises out of being present in the moment with the person with dementia and taking pleasure in shared connection. It is also supported by reflecting upon the life story of the couple and remembering times when the support and caregiving has been mutual and reciprocal.

3. *An increase of family cohesion and functionality*: some caregivers value the impact of the dementia on the whole family system, as family members support each other to cope, which adds another dimension to their relationships.

4. *A sense of personal growth and purpose in life*: some caregivers say that the experiences of caring for a person with dementia cause them to re-evaluate their priorities, to focus more on relationships, and that they have benefited as people from developing their patience and compassion through caregiving.

What are the factors which help partners to focus on the positive aspects of caregiving?

Not all people who care for a family member with dementia are able to identify positive aspects of caregiving so readily. Yu and colleagues' study also identifies three factors which partners who *are* able to focus on the positive aspects of caregiving share in common:

1. *Self-affirmation*: feeling able to cope with the challenges of caregiving, and confident and prepared to cope with future challenges. This is also linked to social affirmation – receiving recognition and emotional support from other people.

2. *Self-regulation*: caregivers who felt positive about their role were able to use cognitive strategies to cope with their strong emotions. These included reflecting on the mutual nature of giving and receiving care across the whole history of their relationship and finding meaning for their current caregiving role. Acceptance of the diagnosis and focusing on what remained rather than on what had been lost were also found to be helpful.

3. *The context of the relationship*: people who felt very connected to their partners before the onset of dementia were better able to adjust to their new reality, and to continue to enjoy aspects of their relationship. The researchers also found that people who had a positive religious faith found that this helped them to come to terms with their caring role.

These three themes correlate well with our themes of attachment and strengths-based practice. Self-affirmation is clearly linked with strengths-based approaches – the belief that 'I have coped in the past and will be able to cope in the future' – and the use of support from social networks. Self-regulation reminds us of the importance of noticing and soothing our immediate emotional response to a challenge and using cognitions as a coping strategy. This is akin to the parenting style of a sensitive, attuned carer, who is able to use the mind's reflective function to appreciate the meaning of the baby's communication and to react calmly, using both thoughts and feelings. The final point, the context of the relationship, affirms that people who have a secure Type B attachment strategy in relation to each other are more likely to be able to cope with the challenges posed by an illness such as dementia, due to their capacity to reflect and to learn coping strategies.

Practical ideas for supporting families using attachment and strengths-based approaches

Families who are struggling to cope with adapting to the challenges of caring for an older family member can be referred to see a specialist family therapist. However, this is not available to the majority of families, and most people who work with families are not specialist therapists. This list offers some ideas and approaches which are designed to fit within the scope of most workers who may support families.

- *What is the threat?* Is it possible to help the family to consider what they are most concerned about? This may differ between family members, and helping them to put it into words may help to reduce anxiety and make it less likely that their attachment systems will be activated. The example of Joyce and her two sons in Chapter 6 gives an example of how to support siblings and their parent to talk about their fears.

- *Can you help to build a sense of safety?* Once the family have been able to express their fears and concerns, are you able to offer information or reassurance? If family members feel that their fears have been acknowledged, they are more likely to be able to reflect on their thoughts and feelings, and to communicate in a balanced way. This kind of communication is based upon the two notions of predictability and attunement, which we discussed in Chapter 2. It is very important to try to be predictable and consistent, (doing what you say you are going to do), and attuned or emotionally sensitive. This may also involve helping family members to discuss their fears about the future and to make plans in good time.

- *Use a strengths-based approach.* Yu and colleagues' research reminds us of the importance of empowering family members. Help them to recognise that they already have the skills which they need in order to care for their loved one. Discuss with them examples of times when things have gone well and help them to recognise what they did which helped to achieve a positive outcome. It can be tempting to put yourself in an expert role. This can be useful at times, especially if the family are asking for your professional advice.

However, the family needs to become the expert on caring for their loved one, and motivating them to use their strengths can help with this.

- *Try to remain neutral.* This isn't the same as not having any opinions, being passive or not sharing your expertise. It can be very helpful to share tips which have helped other individuals or families, particularly if you have been asked for your advice. Furthermore, if you believed that a person was being treated abusively or was at risk, it would be your duty to find out more and to take action, as necessary. Neutrality here means not taking sides; it can be very easy to identify with one family member at the expense of another. You may see a son who visits his mother three times a week in a more positive light than her daughter, who visits three times a year. However, we can never fully know a family's history or the motivations of individuals. If we take sides or position ourselves closely to one family member and further away from another, then we become less useful to the family, because we can become stuck and reinforce a sense that the situation cannot change. It is our role to help the family to retain hope and to consider that there might be room for things to be different. Alison Roper-Hall, a psychologist and family therapist who specialises in working with older people, refers to this position as retaining our 'manoeuvrability for change' (Roper-Hall 2008, p.495).

- *Help the family to find meaning.* It has been shown that family members who have a positive attitude to caregiving cope better with the challenges which it poses – this links to the 'meaning making' we highlighted as a key element of 'resilience' in Chapter 1. This can mean thinking about the caregiving as one chapter of a relationship which has spanned many different chapters and remembering times when the person being cared for has fulfilled other roles, perhaps involving caring for them. Using a family tree or telling the life story of the older family member can help to support this.

- *Help the family to focus on what remains.* As discussed earlier in the chapter Justine McGovern uses the term 'we-ness' to describe the emotional connection which partners can celebrate when one partner has developed dementia. Even when a person's cognitive powers are impaired due to age or illness, their capacity to experience and express emotions remains, in most cases. Are you able to help family members to identify non-cognitive ways in which they can express their love for their relative?

- *Offer practical support.* A family's capacity to care for an older family member will be affected by their social context. Can you help them to check that they are receiving all of the benefits they are entitled to? Many millions of pounds go unclaimed in benefit payments each year. Can you help them to link up with other families in similar situations, or to seek support from a charity or local carers' organisation?

- *Reflect upon your own reactions.* If you find yourself having a strong emotional reaction, which pulls you towards one family member or away from another, it may help to reflect on the root of those feelings. It may be that a theme, a story, or a person is unconsciously reminding you of something from your own life. This is a normal human process, but it may help you to find a time when you can think quietly and reflect on your emotions.

- *Learn everything you can about the family's social context.* If you are working with a family that differs from you in terms of race, culture, religion, class, and so on, it may help you to learn more about how they see the world.

- *If you get it wrong, try to make a repair.* If you sense that you have ruptured your rapport with a family, you can try to apologise and make a repair. You might get a sense of this if a family changes how they relate to you, by showing anger or becoming more reserved. We all know that to get things wrong is human – we expect that. What we don't expect is a really good repair, often involving an explanation and an apology, and a plan for making sure it doesn't happen again. There is further discussion – of attuned repair – in Chapter 5.

4

A Good Life in Care

Around 300,000 older people live in care homes in England and Wales (ONS 2014). We have dedicated a chapter to this part of the health and social care sector because of its size, the nature of the model and the consensus that change is needed. However, some of the material in this section will be relevant to those supporting older people with high support needs in other settings – in their own homes or in extra care housing.

In this chapter, we argue that good care cannot be delivered without consideration of people's emotional, social and psychological needs. We explain how strengths-based practice can be embedded throughout the daily life and care practices of a care home to enable residents to make a contribution and remain as independent as possible, and how each member of staff has a role to play in this. We argue that 'activities' should not just be about organised trips and occasional events but also about the practice of connecting with residents throughout the day. We give lots of examples of how this can be done. We offer practical techniques for understanding residents' life histories, for meeting their attachment needs through a multi-sensory approach, and for applying this knowledge of them within the delivery of personal care.

Anybody working in a care home can introduce some of these practical ideas into their work and relationships; however, we recognise that excellent management is needed to embed and sustain these approaches across the whole home. In his *Care Home Inquiry* for the Joseph Rowntree Foundation, John Kennedy (2014) highlighted a number of significant structural challenges in relation to how care homes are provided in the UK. This mostly private market is over-regulated yet under-funded, and many of the care staff working in it receive little more than the minimum wage, despite caring for an increasing number of residents with multiple physical conditions and/or dementia. Kennedy found that the average cost of a week's residential care is significantly cheaper than the average cost of a week's stay in a bed and breakfast.

This book focuses on practice, not policy: our aim here is to give practical, theoretically informed examples of how change can start – and is starting – from the ground up, through the actions of staff, managers, volunteers, and older people and their families. It would, however, be remiss and naïve not to recognise how challenging it is to embed this change within the current system, and the importance of lobbying for change at a policy level too.

However, despite these constraints, there are care home managers and staff who are doing a good job. We will explore the following, strengths-based questions in this chapter:

- What does a 'good life in care' mean to older people living in care homes?

- What does it mean to apply a strengths-based and attachment-informed approach in care homes?

- What is it specifically that care home staff are doing and can do to promote this 'good life' in care?

- How are they managing to do this, given the system and context of limited resources within which they are operating?

What does a 'good life in care' mean to older people living in care homes?

In 2014/15, we undertook research in Gloucestershire care homes to hear the voices of older residents (Blood and Litherland 2015). We went into 12 different homes across the county and interviewed 88 residents, many of whom had significant cognitive and/or communication impairments. We were asked to consider what made a 'good life in care' from their perspectives, in order to inform the county council's Quality Assessment Framework for care homes. The research was funded by the Police and Crime Commissioner, so our focus was on what made (or would make) residents feel safe (or unsafe) in care homes, and how connected they felt to wider communities and networks.

Many of the people we spoke to – even those who told us they were lucky to be in a good care home – missed 'home' deeply. A significant minority used the language and imagery of prisons: they talked of 'escape' and felt 'held against their will' or 'trapped'; they talked of the staff in terms of 'them' and 'us'.

What seems to make the difference between somewhere feeling like a prison and somewhere feeling like home? Our interviews suggest there are a number of possible factors – décor helps, but feeling that you have chosen to be here (or at least involved in the decision); that you still have control; and that staff 'get you' and are there to support you to do the things you want to do (not just shoe-horn you into an over-arching regime) seem to matter more.

Quotes from older people living in care homes

All the staff are friendly. The red tape stops it being homely – they're going to do this, going to do that. Staff could have a bit more time to talk, and do things – there's so much pressure.

When you're in your own home you can do whatever you want whenever you want. I would ask permission to do certain things here.

(Blood and Litherland 2015, p.54)

Sarah Rochira, the Older People's Commissioner for Wales, conducted a review into the quality of life and care of older people living in care homes. She was struck by the fact that:

Care homes are often characterised by institutional regimes, where a task-based approach to delivering care concentrates on schedules, processes and checklists, rather than on the needs of the individual.

(Older People's Commissioner for Wales 2014, p.7)

In our research in Gloucestershire, many of the people we met had low expectations – of their lives now as older people and sometimes also of life in a care home:

I've had a lovely life up to now, so I can't grumble really.

Happy is a big word. I wouldn't exactly say I am happy really but I think you look at things differently.

(Blood and Litherland 2015, p.54)

Despite huge diversity in the attitudes, preferences, personalities and lifestyles of those we met and interviewed, six clear priorities emerged, and these seem to confirm the key messages of other qualitative research conducted with people living in care homes (e.g. Bowers *et al.* 2009; Williamson 2010; Blood 2013; Bigger Boat 2014). These were:

- *feeling safe*: this can mean different things to different people (which we consider in more detail below)

- *maintaining and developing relationships*: visits and contacts with family and friends, relationships with staff (and crucially the emotional support they provide) and other residents in the home

- *feeling in control and feeling useful*: having choices in relation to day-to-day life, having a say in what goes on in the home, and being involved through small jobs or roles

- *activities that offer meaningful occupation*: a choice of quieter, individual activities that might be flexible and spontaneous, as well as noisier, group or planned sessions

- *being supported to go out of the home and make connections with the local community*: bigger minibus trips are appreciated, but regular fresh air, visits to local shops, the park, or hairdresser's and opportunities to mix with younger people and those with shared interests were highly valued.

What makes people feel safe in care homes?

There is a lot of fear and anxiety surrounding care homes. In studies where we have interviewed older people living in their own homes, the prospect of 'being put in a care home' can create palpable fear. Widely reported incidents of abuse and neglect in the sector mean that relatives and commissioners are understandably anxious about the welfare of their loved ones and the quality of the services they choose and fund. In our conversations with residents in Gloucestershire, we were struck by how 'feeling safe' could mean very different things to different people, for example:

- *Good staff*: as one person explained, 'The carers are very very good, they make you feel safe.' This was partly about the staff being professional – knowing what they are doing and respecting confidentiality – and partly about having good relationships with them, through which they had grown to know and trust them. Others did not feel safe because they felt dependent on people they did not trust, and felt that being safe is conditional on 'getting on well with them and doing what is expected of you'.

- *Good management*: feeling confident that you could go to the manager if you had any problems in the home, that they would take you seriously and respond effectively. One person attributed the calibre of all the staff in the home to the 'really special' manager: 'it comes from the top, doesn't it?' We talk more about what good management looks like and what needs to be in place for it to thrive and be sustained at the end of this chapter, and in Chapter 8.

- *Physical security*: this was mentioned by many – especially by those who had experienced crime (or fear of crime) or who had experienced falls. Yet being able to get out was at least as important as others not being able to get in: some residents described feeling 'caged' or held against their will: 'If I could get out I would.'

- *A sense of control*: for some people, feeling safe was about being able to do things when you want to – like go to bed or stay in bed. Many people talked in terms of whether or not they were 'allowed' to do things and some felt that their suggestions or complaints would not be acted on: 'I'm too old to have a say – they probably wouldn't listen anyway.'

- *Calm environments*: these helped to make people feel safe; others explained that they felt unsafe in communal areas, often due to noise levels, the behaviour of other residents or a feeling that others were talking about you or being unfriendly.

- *For people with dementia*: we heard and observed how important it was to feel 'anchored' in surroundings which could often feel unfamiliar and confusing. One person explained that it would make her feel safer to have someone to talk to 'who knows me from old'. A relative felt that it helped her sister to feel safe that she was in a small, homely and familiar place where staff had the time and energy to continually reassure her about where she was, how she got here and who the people around her were.

Links with the community and the 'outside world'

There were some examples of links between care homes and the wider community, for example:

- One home had a regular 'knit and natter' session in the communal lounge, which was attended by older women living locally as well as those living in the home.

- Some homes had developed links with local schools and colleges and we met young people who were coming in to volunteer and spend time with residents, learning about their histories.

- Some homes and residents maintained close links with local churches and places of worship – ministers and priests sometimes visited residents and/or conducted religious services in the home; we even met a resident who still regularly played the organ at her local church.

However, there were huge variations in the amount of contact with the outside world which the care home residents had: some were taken out almost daily by either family members or staff, some were able to go independently for walks around the gardens or surrounding area; however, others could not remember the last time they had left the premises:

[Sadly, near end of interview, looking round a small room with no outlook] This is all there is for me.

I'm just shut in here – day after day.

Unfortunately, I can't get out for walks anymore – I can just about manage to walk around here on my frame but no...I can't get out of here. I'm here until I die.

(Blood and Litherland 2015, pp.33–35)

Some reflections on human rights in care homes

A full consideration of the case law and guidance in relation to the Deprivation of Liberty Safeguards (DoLS) is beyond the scope of this book (Social Care Institute for Excellence 2017).[1] However, as we think about a 'good life in care', and especially as we think about residents' opportunities to get out and about and connect with others, it seems important to raise awareness of some of the ways in which care home residents' human rights to liberty and freedom, and to privacy, can be infringed by the very way in which the organisation operates.

In both of the following vignettes, the residents clearly have mental capacity; there will be many grey areas where residents have dementia but have mental capacity at least some of the time (see the summary of the Mental Capacity Act in Chapter 6 for more detail) but no formal application has been made to the Court of Protection to deprive them of their liberty.

Human rights in care homes: two vignettes

Maggie has significant sight loss and lives in a care home. A few months ago, she fell over a box which the care staff had accidentally left in the corridor outside her room and injured herself. Now the staff have told her that she should not leave her room unless she is being accompanied by one of them; she should press the buzzer if and when she wishes to do this. Maggie is very aware of how busy the staff are and she does not feel she can ask them to come and lead her out through the corridor unless she has an urgent or specific need to do so. Staff very rarely come and offer this to her, so she sits in her room alone for most of the time, feeling trapped.

John thinks highly of the staff who run the care home where he lives – he feels they give him 'special treatment', so he is keen not to 'rock the boat'. John likes to pop out on his own to go to the library and fetch some books or visit the shop opposite to buy some sweets – he feels safe doing this on his own. However, it is the home's policy to keep the front door locked at all times and not to let any resident out unless they are accompanied by a member of staff or someone 'responsible' who is known to them. John explains that this is intended to keep the

---

1   For an overview of the use of DoLS in care and nursing homes, see SCIE's web-based resource at www.scie.org.uk/mca/dols/practice/care-home

> residents who have dementia safe – the home doesn't like to have 'one rule for some residents and one for others'. However, the home is very short-staffed and yesterday John had to wait until 5pm to go out to the shop because no one was free to take him.

In their article, 'Questionable practices, despite good intentions', Backhouse and her colleagues (2017) looked in detail at how staff in four care homes responded to the risks arising from dementia-related behaviours, such as aggression, sexual inhibition and calling out. They found that staff commonly used multiple strategies such as surveillance, resident placement, restrictions and forced care to keep residents safe. Although staff had the best intentions, Backhouse reflects that they are often left to deal with moral dilemmas about freedom and safety. Although these measures are often justified 'in the moment', they can all too easily become 'routine and preventative', leading to a culture in which human rights are infringed.

There are no easy answers to the challenges arising from inadequate numbers of staff (who are often low paid and poorly trained) trying to care for a number of people with advanced dementia in a communal setting. However, we hope that some of the values, theories and practical ideas from this chapter will prompt and support alternative ways of doing things. With more understanding and consideration of the emotional needs of people with dementia and with effective support from management, we believe that it is possible to understand the function of behaviours which present a challenge and find alternative ways of preventing many of these problems in the first place.

How can we apply the seven principles of strengths-based practice in care home settings?

1. Collaboration and self-determination

The combination of living within an institutional setting and depending on others to care for you creates an inherent power imbalance for care home residents. There will always be a degree of tension between the needs and wishes of the individual and the routines, rules and processes which have been set up to make sure the home runs smoothly within the resources it has and the external demands placed on it. In this setting, self-determination will almost always need to be balanced, and compromises will need to be reached. A person who needs assistance to walk safely may want to walk around the gardens or surrounding area as much as possible, but staff availability is likely to mean that this can only be done at certain times.

Working in a strengths-based way does not remove this fundamental tension, but it can mean that staff have honest, open and two-way discussions with residents to reach these compromises. It might mean sitting down with a resident regularly to find out what their priorities are, what they would like to do and working together to think about how this could best be achieved. Can a family member, a volunteer, or even another resident support them to walk around the gardens? Can they be taken to sit alone in the gardens and given a buzzer to press when they are ready to be escorted back in? A finding in our research is that most residents are acutely aware of the pressures facing staff and are very conscious of not adding to these demands. Given this, it is not safe to assume that residents will ask staff when they want to do something, as we saw in our example of Maggie, who has ended up effectively trapped in her room.

2. Relationships are what matter most

Good care homes make sure staff have time, permission and support to get to know residents and their families; they recognise that going and sitting with an isolated resident to watch a football match together or holding the hand of someone who is in pain is sometimes more important than doing paperwork or making beds.

Strengths-based practice also looks to develop and support people's 'natural networks'. This might involve bringing together two or more residents with a shared interest and considering ways in which they might be linked up with others in the local area who share that interest. It might involve supporting a resident to stay in touch with relatives living at a distance using Skype or Facebook, or providing emotional support to someone who wants to repair or improve a relationship (a point we cover in more detail in Chapter 5).

3. Everyone has strengths and something to contribute

Assumptions are all too easily made that, by the time a person moves into residential care, they have little left to offer and a decline into total dependence on others is inevitable. As Scourfield (2007) argues: 'It is often assumed that when someone enters residential care, their disability or illness is so all-consuming that they have no interest in anything other than their personal care and their day-to-day comfort' (Scourfield 2007, p.1136).

Yet the best homes take time to find out about a person's history – their skills, knowledge and passions – and find ways to use these to promote engagement, stimulation and opportunities for them to contribute. In Chapter 9, Tool 6, we consider how life story work can best be used in care home settings, including with those who have more advanced dementia. Later in this chapter, we also present a number of shorter practical ideas for getting to know and connecting with residents.

Some care homes adopt a 'household model'. This usually works best in smaller homes or those which have been divided into 'households' of around eight to ten residents. In these 'households', older people are encouraged and supported to take part in meal preparation as much as possible – buttering bread, shelling peas, laying the table – or in watering plants or feeding fish.

Atul Gawande (2014) tells the story of Bill Thomas, the incoming director of Chase Memorial Nursing Home in New York state, where half of the residents were physically disabled and four-fifths had a form of dementia. Depressed by what he termed the 'Three Plagues' of nursing home existence – boredom, loneliness and helplessness – Bill somehow persuaded his board and won an innovation grant to try something different.

He brought in two dogs, four cats and a hundred birds to live in the home, along with hundreds of indoor plants, a flock of laying hens, rabbits, a vegetable and flower garden and an on-site childcare and after-school programme for staff. Pandemonium and crisis followed – the staff team were divided: were they running an institution or providing a home?

But then the residents began to come alive – 'People who we had believed weren't able to speak started speaking' (Gawande 2014, p.124). People who had been completely withdrawn and bed-bound came to the office offering to take the dogs for a walk. All of the parakeets were adopted and named by residents. Over the next two years, prescription medication halved and deaths fell by 15 per cent. In reflecting on the impact of the animals on the lives of residents, Gawande concludes: 'In place of boredom, they offer spontaneity. In place of loneliness, they offer companionship. In place of helplessness, they offer a chance to take care of another being' (Gawande 2014, p.125).

This may be too radical a step for many care homes, but it does remind us of the importance and impact of continuing to have a role or responsibility, of having someone or something to look after, however high our own care needs may be.

4. Stay curious about the individual

Our example of Mary (in Chapter 1) who became extremely distressed when staff attempted to shower her reminds us how important it is to try to understand – or at least empathise with – the puzzling or 'difficult' behaviours older people will sometimes display in care settings. By staying curious about the individual and the function of their behaviour, rather than dismissing it as a 'symptom' of dementia which needs to be controlled, simple ways can often be found to make people feel safe and comforted, without resorting to force, segregation or medication. This approach can make life calmer, safer and more enjoyable for staff and other residents too.

5. Hope

At their worst, care homes are described as 'places where people are waiting to die'. However, in care homes which are filled with hope (and we can imagine Chase Memorial with its hundred parakeets might fall into that category!), there is a strong belief in the importance of living life to the full, right to its very end. Those who are too unwell to leave their rooms are not given up on or forgotten about; staff use touch, music and evocative scents (see the example of the 'snoezelen' below) to connect with those who find it hard to communicate verbally.

6. Permission to take risks

As we have seen, this can be a particularly challenging topic for care homes; relatives (and sometimes older people themselves) choose care homes because they believe them to be the 'safest option'. Lopez *et al.* (2013) found that 'Family members' foremost concerns are often procuring basic care and ensuring patient safety, rather than higher level issues such as patient autonomy.'

Meanwhile in some areas there is a sense that safeguarding teams and the media are almost waiting for an accident to happen. Yet, as we have seen, for many older people, 'feeling safe' is about having freedom to take risks as as well as about preventing physical harm: it is as much about being able to get out as it is about others not being able to get in.

Owen *et al.* (2012) describe how one care home manager relates how he decided to support an older person's wish to walk down the stairs unaided, having discussed with them (and documented) the risks involved and helped them to reach an informed and positive decision. Sadly, the older person later died as a result of falling down the stairs. The manager described his profound sense of loss and guilt over what had happened. However, instead of being supported by the wider system to deal with these emotions and identify any organisational learning, he described how it 'felt as though the world was caving in on him', as various professionals intervened with their own statutory requirements to investigate from, as he experienced it, a position of mistrust towards him. His immediate reaction was to 'tighten the reins' in the care home: he told the staff to minimise any risks associated with the activity of older people within the home.

We discuss 'positive risk-taking' in more detail in Chapter 6.

7. Build resilience

From a commissioner and policy perspective, once an older person has been admitted to residential care, attempts to 'promote independence' are effectively deemed to have failed. Yet, as we describe in this chapter, the best care homes go to great lengths to build the resilience of their residents – enabling or re-abling them to stay mobile and maintain continence, or doing life story work with them to help them find peace, reframe and move forwards.

The 'wheel' of resilience we referred to in Chapter 1 (and is presented in Chapter 9 as Tool 1) can shrink dramatically as older people move into care homes, to the point where many segments can feel redundant. This, in itself, suggests that it may be all the more important to look at it again with the older person and their family to identify, assess and strengthen the resources of the past, present and future.

How do good homes create a good life?

How can attachment theory inform practice in care homes?

We are not expecting that care home staff will have the opportunity, skills or mandate to undertake in-depth therapeutic work with the older people they support. However, attachment theory can provide us with insight and new ideas for working with the minority of people with whom we feel really 'stuck'. Even if staff are not fully confident with the names and details of the different types of attachment strategy, a general awareness of the following key points can help to maintain empathy and an instinctive understanding of how to create an environment which is safer – emotionally not just physically – for residents:

- Be aware that moving into and living in a care home, receiving personal care from others, living alongside new people (many of whom behave strangely or are unwell) can all be experienced as threatening and stressful, especially for a person who has dementia.

- Understand that different people respond unconsciously and automatically to perceived threats in ways that are shaped by their earlier life experiences and relationships.

- Appreciate that these behaviours are not consciously intended to make our lives difficult; they are the person's best attempts to feel safe, comforted and connected to others.

- Even if we do not fully understand the previous life experiences which have shaped the development of a distressed person's ways of responding to threat, we can begin – instinctively, as one human being to another – to see ways in which we can help to make the world feel safer and more predictable for them.

Jane Price, nurse and health manager and her team in Nîmes use the sensorial approach known as 'snoezelen' to help meet the needs of residents, especially those with dementia, for safety, comfort, proximity and predictability. The team recognises that the home can feel like a bewildering and threatening place for a person at the advanced stages of dementia. Verbal communication can become challenging, people may not recognise care staff and they may become confused about the act of washing and its purpose. Meanwhile, staff are busy and can easily become focused on completing personal care tasks as quickly as possible. This can result in distress, anxiety and displays of aggression, which create a stressful environment for everyone.

The 'snoezelen' approach involves understanding and building residents' 'sensorial identity cards' to create a personalised multi-sensorial atmosphere in their bedroom or bathroom in order to stimulate feelings of wellbeing, security and pleasure. Each of us has our own 'sensorial identity card', drawn from life experiences which are unconsciously registered in our emotional memory. Positive memories may be linked to sounds – a certain piece of music, the sound of tinkling bells, rain or flowing water – a smell, texture or type of touch. When these senses are stimulated, pleasant memories can come back, helping us to feel safe, and connected to people and places we care about.

When creating a sensorial indentity card for someone, Jane and her team spend time with them, trying to understand their life history. If verbal communication is difficult, they will involve family members and/or build the information up step by step by observing the individual's reactions to different sounds, smells and textures. They explore favourite colours, music, hobbies, smells and whether or not the person appreciates touch. They consider the need for any modifications to take account of sensory impairments. The resulting sensorial identity card is then used to guide the use of certain coloured lights, music, essential oils or scented soaps, tactile objects and massage aids.

Corinne Sergent, one of the auxiliary nurses in the care home, decided to take a snoezelen approach to support one of the residents to take a shower. Marcel was refusing to be washed and was becoming angry with staff who tried to shower him. Corinne involved Marcel's family and found out from his wife that he enjoyed traditional French music hall type music; that he feels the cold; and that he has always liked the scent of lavender. His wife told Corinne that Marcel was popular socially but very difficult to live with at home.

The staff worked with him to identify his favourite music, colours and scents. Corinne was extremely attentive to the temperature of the bathroom and prepared hot towels. She diffused essential oils of lavender in the room and played music on a CD player.

A projector of blue, turquoise and white lights was used to create a peaceful atmosphere and Corinne encouraged Marcel to wash himself as much as possible and at his own pace.

Marcel explained to Corinne that they 'had lavender sachets at home' and started to tell her stories from his life history while relaxing after his shower. Corinne observes how he reacts and what he enjoys each time and records anything which might help other carers to recreate the same atmosphere in future. Bathing has become a pleasurable experience for Marcel and the carers now also enjoy this time spent with him, getting to know him better.

The care home uses snoezelen in a number of situations to soothe residents at times of stress – in end of life care, nursing care or to relieve chronic pain, or simply for the pleasure of appreciating the 'here and now'. Jane Price, the home's manager, has just finished a research project studying the impact of the snoezelen approach during bath time for people living with dementia or other similar conditions. The emerging findings of this study suggest that, where snoezelen is used, there is a reduction in aggressive behaviour (based on the Neuro Psychiatric Inventory) and it is therefore possible to reduce the use of certain types of medication.

Rethinking activities

Research consistently finds that the majority of older people living in care homes do not have enough to do and that, despite living in a communal setting, many can become isolated. One Norwegian study (Slettebø 2008) described the experience of nursing home residents as 'safe but lonely'. Although most of the participants in the study felt much safer than they had done living in their previous homes, many told the researchers that they felt isolated, lonely and disconnected from family and friends, from their local communities, and from staff who did not have enough time to connect with them.

Smith *et al.* (2017) suggest that around three-quarters of older adults living in residential care in England had 'unmet needs for activity and occupation' (Smith *et al.* 2017). In their study, these unmet needs were so severe for one in five of the residents they met that there was 'the potential for negative physical or mental health consequences' (Smith *et al.* 2017). As Bigger Boat (2014) puts it:

Cleanliness (getting people out of bed, washed and dressed) is prioritised over meaningful activities and social engagement. People can be impeccably groomed yet terminally bored. What is the point of getting someone ready for the day if the day contains nothing worth getting ready for? (Bigger Boat 2014, p.12)

Clearly, the shortage of staff and other resources in care homes does not help. However, when they interview care home staff, residents and relatives, Smith and his colleagues (2017) find other forces at work here:

- They hear widespread assumptions that activity will naturally decline in later life as physical and mental abilities decline. However, as they point out, if our ability to feed ourselves reduces, care home staff would not let us starve – they would offer us more support at meal times or find other ways to make eating accessible to us.

- They find that relatives often support this prioritisation of basic care needs and safety. In our own research interviews, we have met relatives of care home residents who feel reassured if they visit and find their mother is wearing jewellery and has had her hair done, and anxious about the quality of care if this is not the case.

- As a result of the prioritisation of basic needs, the day – certainly in larger homes – tends to be highly structured. Care workers focus on getting everyone up, washed, dressed, fed and toileted and there is little time to play games, do artwork or even have proper conversations. Although the inclusion of an activity coordinator on the team of a care home can be a great resource, Smith highlights the risk that 'activity and meaningful occupation in care homes is seen as something distinct and special, not part of everyday routine, and so requires the support of additional staff whose job it is to coordinate activities within the home' (Smith *et al.* 2017, p.15).

Within this context, strengths-based and relationship-based practice risks becoming the cherry on the cake – a luxury extra which is not always possible in a typical care home or other institutional setting. Finding out how to truly engage an individual becomes the responsibility of the activity coordinator – if there is one, and only if and when they can be spared from getting drawn into the rota of daily tasks and emergencies.

A key message of this chapter is that if we are to care differently in institutional settings and do this sustainably, this needs to become embedded in the everyday, in care practice, in the way we relate to and connect with people as we pass them in lounges and corridors, as we help them to wash and eat.

Everyday creativity

There is growing evidence that participating in the arts can benefit older people in a number of ways, for example by:

- increasing confidence and self-esteem by producing a sense of accomplishment

- helping them to embrace and express new and positive aspects of their identity as an older person

- improving their resilience to losses in their life

- promoting cognitive functioning and increased physical activity

- building new relationships and strengthening existing relationships – with peers, family, workers (Mental Health Foundation 2011).

In their 2011 survey of members, the National Care Forum found that arts-based activities were a regular feature in many of the care homes which responded. Examples of activities included drawing and craft sessions, film clubs, performances and music-based exercise sessions. This is undoubtedly good news. However, the survey also showed that, perhaps unsurprisingly, just 10 per cent of the activities were initiated by residents themselves. As Cutler, Kelly and Silver (2011, p.7) reflect, 'Who decides on the activities? 'Who defines them as art?'

Strengths-based approaches challenge us to consider how we can support the older people living in care homes to increase their sense of agency and control, and the evidence suggests that participatory arts may be one way of doing this. But how can we change the culture in older people's care settings from one in which residents wait passively to be entertained, corralled or organised into arts activities, to one in which creativity is everywhere and belongs to everyone – residents and staff, regardless of 'talent' or role?

64 Million Artists is a national campaign to unlock the potential of everyone in the UK through creativity.[2] It seeks to challenge the widespread perception that 'art is what artists do' and that some people 'aren't very creative' or 'aren't any good at art'. Jo Hunter, the campaign's co-founder argues that 'If we flex our creativity, we find a greater sense of agency: we get to see the world in different ways; we can transcend the rules' (interview with author to inform this book).

Creativity can provide a powerful (yet often quick and free) way for older people and those who care for them to break out of cycles of negativity and helplessness in which they can sometimes feel trapped. McGovern (2015) describes how couples and families affected by dementia are able to reconnect in 'shared moments' spent painting and watching movies – moments that focus on 'what remains, rather than what is lost'. In creative moments, people with dementia and those without can become truly equal again and can connect more deeply.

Hunter (in our interview with her) suggested a number of tips to those working in care settings about how to promote 'everyday creativity':

- Don't attempt to do something big! Find daily opportunities to do something creative for five to ten minutes.

- Start by doing this yourself – in work and/or outside of work.

- Don't try to do things well: it's about the quality of the process not the quality of what you produce.

- Challenge yourself and others to do things they feel they aren't very good at.

- Do things that don't have a set outcome and see how they turn out.

---

2   See the website http://dothinkshare.com for more information or to sign up to their current or next 'challenge' – these usually involve emailing out a daily creative challenge which will take just five to ten minutes to complete: everyone in your care home could commit to doing a daily challenge for a month.

- Follow this simple approach: do, think and share — *do* something creative, then *think* (reflect and observe — how did it feel? What did I notice?), then *share* the reflections and the output with someone else or perhaps a group.

- Find ways to build this into the life of the home or other service setting: do a creative challenge together at the beginning or end of mealtimes, or whilst you are helping someone to get dressed or get ready for bed; use the start of regular team meetings, noticeboards or social media to share your reflections and/or outputs.

Here are some examples of the sorts of mini-challenges you might do individually, one-to-one or in a group:

- Draw the view from your window.

- Write a poem about Mondays.

- Make a sculpture using the things in your room.

- Go for a walk without knowing where you are walking to.

- Arrange belongings or small objects to make a pattern — shells from the beach, buttons, medals, cutlery.

- Try doing something in a different order, in a different place, at a different time.

- Take black and white photographs of places, objects, views (not people) around the home and surrounding neighbourhood, and make an exhibition from them.

- Play a word association game (where you take it in turns to say the first word that comes to mind in response to the word the other person has just said) as you help someone to get dressed.

- Sit quietly for five minutes outside and really observe with all your senses.

Remember then to '*think*' (reflect on how this felt) and '*share*' with others.

Everyday creativity can be part of a wider approach within a care setting to provide opportunities for activity, connection and spontaneity.

Dementia Care Matters *Best Friends Approach*[3] argues that 'activities' can be as short as 30 seconds and can provide opportunities to stimulate the senses, connect with the person, evoke memories and have fun. They should be personalised for individuals and must respect people as adults (rather than treat them like children). Examples of 'activities' might include:

- pointing something out – a bird or a flower out of the window, vivid colours in an item of clothing

- asking for an opinion, advice or help (e.g. to fold a tea-towel, comment on a new tie or advise on a recipe)

- showing a photo of your children, grandchildren, pet, etc.

- evoking a memory from the person's life story – 'Tell me more about x... Did you/he/she really x?'

- something physical – blowing up a balloon and patting it around, a spontaneous dance with someone to music on the radio/television, stepping outdoors for some fresh air, etc.

- physical touch, which can be really important – giving a hug, shaking someone's hand or giving them a hand massage. People are comfortable with different levels of physical contact and this should, of course, be respected. (Best Friends Approach to Alzheimer's and Dementia Care 2018)

The College of Occupational Therapists has produced a toolkit,[4] which includes a booklet of resources for care home staff (Royal College of Occupational Therapists 2013). This contains lots of ideas for enabling residents to explore objects of interest – by displaying them in communal areas, creating 'rummage boxes' or 'treasure chests' (which could be a chest with drawers painted in eye-catching colours or left half open so as to attract attention and invite discovery). These could provoke sensory stimulation (e.g. different textured materials, a

---

3   Adapted from Free Best Friends handout resources, *30 Activities to Do in 30 Seconds* and *The Best Friends Approach to Activities* – both downloadable from http://bestfriendsapproach.com/products/handouts

4   *Living Well through Activities in Care Homes: The Toolkit* contains different resources for residents, families and friends; care home staff, managers and inspectors; and occupational therapists – all can be downloaded for free from www.rcot.co.uk/practice-resources/rcot-publications/downloads/living-well-care-homes

tube of scented hand cream, polished pebbles or worry beads) or could trigger reminiscence (e.g. old household items, books of photographs, shells and fir cones). Staff are encouraged to notice when residents touch or look at these objects and make conversation ('What does that remind you of?' 'How does that feel in your hand?').

A 'memory box' or 'comfort box' could also be put together for individuals, especially those with dementia. These could include personal photographs and keepsakes, perhaps as a result of – or leading to – life history work with the person and their family. (See Chapter 9, Tool 6 on life story work.) The family tree, introduced in Chapter 3 and included in Chapter 9, Tool 4 may also be useful here.

Promoting independence

One of Sarah Rochira's conclusions, following her review of care homes in Wales, was that:

> The culture of care homes is often built upon a dependency model, where it is assumed that people need to be 'looked after'. This approach often fails to prevent physical decline and does not allow people to sustain or regain their independence. (Older People's Commissioner for Wales 2014, p.8)

She heard that people were often pushed around in wheelchairs or lifted in hoists because it was quicker than supporting them to walk. This may be true of many homes, but it is not true of all. Hawkins *et al.* (2017) compared practice in two care homes: in one, they found a lot of resource was focused on supporting people to walk to the dining room as independently as possible; in the other, people tended to be wheeled to meals to maximise efficiency. Older people in the first home were less dependent on walking aids, were more active and were encouraged to go outside in the summer and take part in household tasks; whereas in the second home, residents were more likely to spend most of the day seated. There is a recognised trade-off here though: it takes a lot of time to enable people in this way and, in the home where this is prioritised, the mantra 'We've got to find ways of keeping them moving' runs throughout the culture, systems and communications.

George's story: 'You can't beat a nice cup of tea!'

George told the manager of the care home he lived in that he felt frustrated by the fact he was no longer able to make himself or others a cup of tea. The manager raised the idea with kitchen staff, but they were anxious about the prospect of residents accessing the kitchen and either 'getting in the way' when they were preparing food or being in there unsupervised at other times. George's daughter, who visited him regularly, was not convinced it was a good idea either: she was concerned that he might burn himself and she seemed to feel embarrassed that he was making a fuss about something so small. 'The tea trolley always seems to be coming around, Dad. You just need to wait and they'll bring you a cup.'

However, the manager could see that this was important to George: he was a keen tea drinker and his personal strapline was 'You can't beat a nice cup of tea!' More than this though, George remembered fondly how he had always enjoyed making tea for his wife and their guests in the past: it was his way of taking care of people and showing his gratitude. For George, being able to make tea or not being able to make tea felt like the deciding factor between feeling at home and feeling like he was in prison.

The manager decided that she needed the input and advice of an external specialist, partly to persuade George's family and her own team, partly to find the safest way of doing this, and also to reassure herself (and anyone looking at this from outside) that the risks could be managed. She asked an occupational therapist (OT) to come in and meet with George and give the home some advice on whether and how he could be supported to make tea.

The OT helped George to test out some different pieces of equipment, including a cordless kettle tipper, which supported the weight of the kettle while the boiling water was being poured out. This reduced the risks of scalding due to George losing his balance or his hand shaking. The OT, manager and George looked at whether, where and how a little tea-making station could be set up in his room. They looked at the placement of sockets and cables and the quality of the lighting, and they considered where and how George would carry the tea once he had made it. With a slight reorganisation of the furniture and expenditure of around £30, they set George up with the means to make tea, and the OT was happy to give her blessing.

George's daughter and the care home staff seemed reassured by this process and George is now able to make himself tea when he wants to. More importantly, he can make his visitors a cup of tea and he often invites staff and other residents to pop in and have a drink with him. This gives George a role and a way of taking care of others, and it means that his room is now the place to go for tea and a chat!

Leadership

John Kennedy has spent some time trying to understand the secrets of the 1 per cent of care homes in England which have been rated 'outstanding' by the Care Quality Commission (Kennedy 2016). He has reached the conclusion that there are three key ingredients of their success:

- They have an outstanding manager who is well supported and valued.

- They have sufficient resources to do the job well and these resources are invested in the service.

- The provider organisation's values and ethos are clear and effectively translated from the board room to the floor of the care home.

There is, however, still a long way to go across much of the sector:

- Kennedy estimates elsewhere that, at any time, half the care homes for older people in England are failing the regulatory test (Residential Forum 2017).

- Skills for Care estimate that care home manager turnover rates stand at around 20 per cent (Skills for Care 2016).

- Warmington, Alfridi and Foreman (2014) found that supervision in care homes is all too often a tick-box process to ensure Care Quality Commission compliance and care staff did not feel it was very useful in helping them to improve outcomes for older people.

- The Older People's Commissioner for Wales (2014) identified a clear need for effective support for care home managers, given the increasing demands and expectations placed on them.

In Chapter 8, we discuss in detail what good supervision should look like and propose a number of tools to support managers in this.

However, if this is to be sustainably achieved, care home leaders need wider support from the companies that employ them and from the systems that commission and regulate them. Kennedy describes how good care home providers try to create the conditions for managers to thrive and survive – they audit and check their managers, but from a position of confidence and trust (Residential Forum 2017). They recognise that systems and paperwork need to support, not prevent, relationship-based care and creativity.

The My Home Life Leadership Programme brings together care home managers from a local authority area and begins by asking strengths-based questions about what is already working well, how it could be made better and what can be done to move towards this. It promotes dialogue between local care home managers and the local authority performance monitoring team and creates a community of practice around improving relational care and improving outcomes. A key tenet of the programme is to build a shared vision which is owned by staff, residents and their families, giving them more power and responsibility to take the initiative and problem solve themselves.

Comments from participating care home managers include:

> Everything has a knock-on effect, people feel more relaxed – staff and residents – they take the initiative, feel safer to try things, residents appear to feel listened to and valued. It's hard to put your finger on what has changed... (Owen *et al.* 2012, p.53)

> One manager remarked on how older people in the home were taking greater responsibility for roles in the home (watering plants, flower arranging, feeding fish): like that our new relational approach has helped them feel more engaged and closer to the home, rather than ordering the staff around as if they were servants. (Owen *et al.* 2012, pp.53–54)

5
Maintaining Connections and Interests

Introduction

In this chapter, we consider loneliness: what can cause or exacerbate it, and how we might use strengths-based and attachment-informed approaches to support older people to maintain their connections and interests.

We recognise that, in the current health, social care and housing context, few professionals have the time and mandate to get involved in preventative work with older people in relation to their social networks. This is perhaps particularly true in England and may be less so in the rest of the United Kingdom. However, in some areas, there has been a recent emergence of roles such as 'community navigators' or 'connectors', 'befrienders', 'social prescribers' or 'local area coordinators'. Many of these posts are in the voluntary and community sector, though some have been commissioned by local authorities or are employed by larger housing associations.

We hope this chapter will resonate beyond this small but emerging sector: loneliness is often an accompanying (or even underlying) issue when older people come into contact with statutory services and ignoring it may simply speed up the revolving hospital door. We have tried to include examples, tools and ideas here which promote a more holistic and creative way of responding to individuals at the point of contact with statutory services. We also hope these materials will provide food for thought for those commissioning services – encouraging a wider 'place-based' vision, linking into resources from public health, leisure, libraries and the cultural sector. Finally, we hope these practical ideas will be useful to family and friends wanting to support an older relative maintain their social connections.

Loneliness: an overview

Loneliness is a key challenge for older people in Western societies.

Increasing numbers of older people in the UK are living alone: more than half of those aged 75 and over live alone, and this number has increased by 24 per cent in the last two decades (ONS 2017b). Some never had children (Institute for Public Policy Research 2014, p.14); others are living miles away from them.

On average, we are living longer, but we are living longer with health conditions, reduced mobility and other impairments: almost two-thirds of people over 80 have a disability (Age UK 2018, p.7).

Meanwhile, community life has changed over the past generation or two: there is a high turnover of residents in many urban areas (especially more deprived areas); and younger people have tended to move out of rural communities. In many households, both partners work; and technology has changed the way we connect with each other, shop and bank. These changes may play out slightly differently in some minority ethnic communities. However, it is dangerous to make assumptions: although some BAME older people live in multi-generational households, this is not true of all. There can also be high levels of hidden loneliness for those who do live with younger family members: language, culture and histories of migration can act as barriers between the generations (Khan 2014). Some South Asian older migrants – like their white British peers – face loneliness as their children have moved away for work and their own generation, both in the UK and back home, begins to die.

This sense of changing neighbourhood relationships is a recurring theme in qualitative research with older people in the UK and other parts of Europe (Blood *et al.* 2016b). Buffel interviewed older people in deprived urban areas in England and Belgium and many said the 'community spirit' of old had been lost. One woman summed this up by saying, 'I feel like a stranger in my own neighbourhood' (Buffel, Phillipson and Scharf 2013, p.97).

None of these social changes make loneliness in older age inevitable; and, despite the decline of 'community' in many neigh-bourhoods, other 'communities' (such as faith communities) have survived or are emerging (online communities, like DropBy, spring to mind). However, this changing community context does mean that, if we are to support older people to enjoy a good quality of life, we need to think about their social and emotional needs as well as their physical health and care needs. Loneliness not only increases the risk of depression and cognitive decline but also that of coronary heart disease, stroke (Valtorta *et al.* 2016) and high blood pressure (Hawkley *et al.* 2010). Being socially isolated is as damaging to our health as smoking 15 cigarettes a day (Holt-Lunstad *et al.* 2010).

Identifying lonely individuals

The Campaign to End Loneliness (which has produced a series of useful resources[1]) proposes the following definition: 'Loneliness is a subjective, negative feeling experienced where there is a discrepancy between the amount and quality of social contacts one has, and the amount and quality one would like to have' (Goodman, Adams and Swift 2015, p.1).

In other words, it is possible to be surrounded by people but to miss a certain depth of relationship or intimacy, and it is also possible to spend a lot of time on your own and not feel lonely. For example, one participant in our research with older people in Wales explained:

> I had a neighbour who I used to talk to over the garden fence – he didn't want any interference from anybody. I tried to interest him in U3A [University of the Third Age] and he said 'Oh no, no, no!' and as far as I was concerned he didn't meet anybody. He was only interested in his garden, making beer and that was about it; he was perfectly happy. (Blood *et al.* 2016b, p.18)

Loneliness is very personal and contextual – it can come and go at different times and, as the quote above shows, one person's idea of loneliness is another's idea of bliss. This means that the risk factors for loneliness – such as a recent bereavement, having dementia, living alone or not having access to a car – can inform those commissioning, or planning and designing services but they are less useful for those supporting individual older people. There is no quick substitute for taking a bit of time to understand a person's current 'world' – who

---

1   For a range of facts, films, guidance and case studies on loneliness and how to prevent and tackle it, see www.campaigntoendloneliness.org

they see, what they do, where they go – and how close this is to their 'ideal world'.

'My World' (Chapter 9, Tool 5) is a simple tool that can be used to map out the people, interests, places, pets and objects that currently form that person's world. This visual map can then be used to discuss aspirations and goals: what matters most to them? What would they like to be different?

Of course, not all lonely people are older and not all older people are lonely. However, as De Jong Gierveld and Van Tilburg (2010, p.121) point out, 'Some of the determinants of loneliness, such as the deaths of the partner and of peers, deteriorating health and financial pressures, are directly related to events and transitions in later phases of life.'

Older people may, therefore, be at particular risk of loneliness and their loneliness may have slightly different causes and characteristics, shaped by the stage of life they are at.

The Campaign to End Loneliness has developed a simple tool to help those who come into contact with older people in a professional capacity to identify loneliness. We have turned their survey-style statements into the following questions which could be included in an assessment or conversation:

- How content are you with your friendships and relationships? (Why is this?)

- Are your relationships as satisfying as you would want them to be?

- Are there people that you feel comfortable asking for help at any time? (Who are they? Or what gets in the way of this?). This question could be widened to think about who you relax with, who you call on in a crisis, who *you* support? (Adapted from the Campaign to End Loneliness Measurement Tool, in Campaign to End Loneliness 2015)

You may, of course, want to adapt the language so it feels more natural in some conversations, but an important principle is to retain the positive language. There can be a lot of stigma around loneliness (perhaps especially for men), so asking someone directly whether they feel lonely may make them close down rather than open up. You would also need to have established a certain level of rapport with a person to ask these questions.

Understanding an individual's loneliness

It is important to try and understand a person's loneliness in order to support them out of it (Jopling 2015). Some older people – through bereavement or house moves – have lost their 'inner circle' of relationships; others may have people in their lives with whom they would like to connect, but there are barriers getting in the way. These may include transport; living at a distance; caring for a spouse; lack of money; not being able to hear very well; being concerned about continence, memory or communication; or feeling that you do not fit into a social circle since your partner died: 'When my husband died, a lot of friends vanished, especially couples who found it strange now that I am on my own...you get a bit forgotten' (Blood *et al.* 2016b, p.22).

Some of these barriers may be practical: if someone gave you a lift, or you got your hearing aid fixed, you would be able to either connect with existing friends and family or meet new people. However, many of the barriers faced by those who feel lonely are psychological and emotional: anxiety about being rejected or stigmatised; rifts or tensions in relationships that have not been resolved; or a lack of confidence in socialising, especially without a partner.

In Table 5.1, we distinguish these different causes of loneliness as 'social', 'internal' and 'structural' and give examples of each.

Table 5.1: Different causes of loneliness

Internal	Social	Structural
Self-belief/confidence	Lack of relationships	Transport
Identity, e.g. being a 'widow(er)'	Type and quality of relationships	Discrimination: age, race, homophobia, etc.
Depression	Restoring and sustaining existing friendships	Poverty
Anxiety		Accessibility
Stigma: dementia, loneliness itself		Access to information – about resources
		Language
		Community – rural/high turnover urban
		(Fear of) crime and anti-social behaviour

Often an individual's loneliness will involve a mixture of internal, social and structural factors; sometimes these factors interact with each other. For example, issues with confidence or depression may well impact on the *quality* of a person's relationships and vice versa; poverty can jeopardise our sense of identity (if, say, we have always been the one who has bought the drinks, given the lifts and helped other people out); where the public world is inaccessible to us, this can increase our sense of being stigmatised. There can be a tendency to think of all these different causes of loneliness as individual; dividing them into these three categories should help us to recognise that there may be different causes and different types of solution – at individual, community and societal levels.

> *Person with dementia:* I often pull back from conversations with people because I'm worried about forgetting the words or it just being difficult. (Imogen Blood & Associates/Innovations in Dementia, unpublished, p.23)

> *Patrick (older gay man):* You just tried to lead a normal life as a 'bachelor'. People used to say about me, 'He's very shy!' I just closed off my sexual life. I would joke with other people and be a bit anti-gay myself, which I feel sad about now.' (Knocker 2012, p.5)

> I don't know many people – neighbours – it's more difficult because I'm Asian and Muslim, though I do know a few people. (Blood, Copeman and Pannell 2016b, p.19)

> Last time I went to my local theatre, there were no handles or rails or anything by the toilet and I got stuck which was embarrassing and I went to grab the handrail up the steps and it was just a wire, and the seats are very low backed so there is nothing to hold onto as you are walking along the aisle…it's a confidence thing really – you lose your confidence, when you worry you might fall or not be able to get to the toilet, or get stuck when you do. When I am out and about, I'm always thinking – where's the nearest loo if I need it? (Blood, Copeman and Pannell 2016b, p.39)

The marginalisation which these older people face is as much to do with racism, disabilism and homophobia as it is with age. However, these quotes remind us that there may be different barriers for older people trying to adapt to disability for the first time, or for older BAME people, for whom language is more likely to be a barrier than it is for younger BAME people.

Supporting older people out of loneliness using strengths-based approaches

In this section, we return to the seven principles proposed in Chapter 1 to consider what might it mean to take a strengths-based approach to tackling loneliness.

1. Collaboration and self-determination

Since loneliness is a subjective experience, loneliness interventions are not something we can simply 'do' to a person. A person could be referred to a lunch club, collected and taken there regularly; this will increase their social contact but it may or may not reduce their sense of loneliness, or the extent to which they feel that their relationships with others fall short of their ideal. In fact, the whole experience may make them feel even more lonely.

We can only support a person out of loneliness if we collaborate with them to find and action the right approach for them.

Cattan and her colleagues reviewed existing evaluations of loneliness interventions for older people in 2005 (Cattan *et al.* 2005) and highlighted the link between increasing self-esteem and personal control and reducing loneliness. They found that interventions which increased self-esteem and personal control tended to be more effective at reducing loneliness *in the long term*. It follows from this that our very relationship with the older person and the way in which we approach their loneliness together is a key resource for building lasting change. If we treat them as the experts in their own lives (rather than assuming to know best) and help them to take control, the resulting increase in self-esteem may, of itself, go some way to reducing their loneliness.

Collaboration may go wider than the one-to-one relationship between a worker and an older person; self-determination may take place at a group, family, network or community level. There are, for example, a number of approaches which aim to tackle loneliness at a *neighbourhood* level – such as Joseph Rowntree Foundation's Loneliness Resource Pack. Asset-based community development (ABCD) identifies and seeks to join up the skills, interests and networks of individuals, associations and organisations, with the aim both of countering an individual's isolation and also creating opportunities for a collective voice (IDeA 2010).

2. Relationships are what matter most

Loneliness is all about relationships and how we perceive them. Interestingly, there seems to be a gap in the research and good practice on loneliness regarding how we can support older people to maintain or rekindle their *existing* relationships – the primary focus tends to be on providing opportunities for them to form new relationships. Where services do seek to support existing relationships, the focus tends to be on practical enablers, such as transport or technology. Really important enablers can be: setting someone up with Skype, email or Facebook; giving them access to a phone which they can use; helping them to sort out their hearing aid; helping them to access a free bus pass or a community transport scheme. However, there seems to be less understanding or practical guidance on how we can support people to make *emotional and psychological repairs* to relationships which have become strained, broken or are not functioning as the person would like them to.

Repairing relationships

In our research with older people in Wales (Blood *et al.* 2016b), we were struck by the number of older people who had become estranged from close family members, sometimes remaining this way for decades. It was clear that some were feeling this loss increasingly with age. Attachment theory can shed light on ruptured relationships and how to achieve 'attuned repair', in which both parties heal a wound in a relationship so that they can reconnect and build a new relationship with each other:

- Falling out is usually about unmet needs – one or both parties not feeling valued, respected or listened to, or feeling that things are unfair or unjust.

- The emotional arousal surrounding falling out needs to die down to the point where both parties feel safe enough to consider repair.

- It is quite normal to read other people's signals incorrectly at times; it is easy to project our own emotions onto others and take things personally; however, sometimes we get locked into our own story.

- The aim of repair is to restore equilibrium: to listen to each other's stories, compare narratives and agree a common story. It is highly likely that both people contributed to the rupture, so fixating on it being either one person's fault or the other's is unlikely to achieve equilibrium.

With this in mind, the following tips may help you support a person prepare for and achieve repair:

- Validate their story and emotions surrounding the rupture.

- Help them to add an alternative or additional version: what do you think the other person might have been feeling at the time? How do you think they might feel about it now?

- Offer to act as a go-between: what if I contacted them to find out how the land lies?

- Consider using motivational interviewing techniques (Chapter 9, Tool 7) to help someone express their ambivalence and fears, consider what might help them to get in touch and build their own motivation to do so.

3. Everyone has strengths and something to contribute

Another significant finding of Cattan's *et al.*'s (2005) review is that older people emphasise the need for reciprocity in social support – they want (as do people of any age) to give back, to be part of a two-way, or three- or four-way relationship. This may be one of the reasons why Cattan and her team find stronger evidence for the effectiveness of loneliness interventions targeted at a *group* of people who have something in common than they do for one-to-one interventions or more general groups.

Focusing on an individual's interests, passions and strengths is often the best place to start tackling their loneliness. Helen Bown manages the Welcomers Team at Barnwood Trust, which meets with individuals who are typically very socially isolated and supports them to try and connect to their communities. She explains that the early meetings in a person's home are spent gradually building trust and keeping an eye out for clues about their interests, which might provide a 'way in' to connect the person to activities or other individuals in their neighbourhood.

Marjorie's story

Marjorie had become extremely isolated and depressed since the death of her son: she seemed to have withdrawn completely into herself. It took Marie several visits before Marjorie would even let her into the house and several more before she said anything much to her. One day, as Marie sat drinking her tea, she noticed that Marjorie was wearing a jumper with a picture of a dog on it – she commented on the dog and told Marjorie about her own dog Wesley. Marjorie seemed to come alive as she talked about some of the dogs she had owned over the years.

The next visit, Marie brought some photos of Wesley to show to Marjorie, and she asked if Marjorie would like to meet Wesley – they agreed that she would bring him with her on the next visit. After a few visits with Wesley, Marie suggested that perhaps they might like to take Wesley out for a short walk in the park around the corner. They did, and each time they went out for a walk, they walked a little further. Sometimes, they bumped into other local dog walkers and chatted to them while Wesley played with their dogs. Over the coming months, they regularly bumped into another older woman, Jean, who lived in the next street from Marjorie, walking her little dog Cyril.

One day, Jean explained that she had been given an appointment for her knee replacement operation. Marie and Marjorie asked what she planned to do about walking Cyril in the six weeks after the operation when she would not be able to walk. Jean was clearly anxious about this – she was hoping her son might be able to pop over some days in his lunch hour and let him out but, knowing how busy he was, she hadn't liked to bring it up with him yet. She knew of a few professional dog walkers in the area, but she couldn't afford to pay for this service regularly. Marjorie volunteered on the spot to walk Cyril – she asked Marie whether she might come for the first couple of walks just to give her the confidence. Everyone agreed to the arrangement.

For the entire six weeks after Jean's operation, Marjorie turned up at Jean's each day come rain or shine to walk Cyril and the two women gradually built a friendship. As Jean felt ready to start walking, they went out together with Cyril, and Marjorie provided Jean with a shoulder to lean on (literally!). Marie gradually reduced her visits as it became clear that Marjorie had built a 'natural' friendship and had found a reason to get up and go out. A year after she had first met her, she seemed like a very different woman from the one who had first talked to her on the door step.

In Marjorie's case, a shared interest in dogs gave rise – quite organically – to new friendships and local neighbourhood connections. However, sometimes relationships may need to be facilitated. Over time and very sensitively, the Welcomers team might ask whether a person would like to be introduced to someone else they know who shares their interest. If they agree, this would be arranged in a neutral place, such as a coffee shop. The Welcomers have introduced people who have a shared interest in crafts or playing the guitar; there is no pressure or expectation that these introductions will lead to ongoing friendships (though they often do) but this can be a really good starting point for someone who has become very isolated, and can be less intimidating than turning up as 'the new person' at a group meeting.

In an editorial called 'Seeing beyond the immediate', James Woodward describes how he supported an older woman who had just moved into supported accommodation to unpack her books (Woodward 2015). This provided a natural way of understanding the things that mattered to her, and chatting to her about her interests and her history.

Creating opportunities for people to make a contribution or volunteer – to help set up at the start of a craft group, to bake a cake for a coffee morning, to act as a buddy to someone else – can be a good 'way in' for some people. Using your skills and time to help others tends to be self-esteem boosting in a way that being a participant or recipient (especially of an intervention to tackle loneliness) may not.

4. Stay curious about the individual

As we have seen, loneliness is a complex and highly individual experience: it is a feeling which may come and go. What triggers or helps reduce loneliness in one person may not hold for another.

We heard in Chapter 2 how Rose's hoarding of cleaning products represented her best attempt to increase her social contacts and have a purpose within her neighbourhood. As she started to meet these social needs by volunteering at the local community café, she was able to let go of her cleaning products and find other ways of connecting with people. We heard in the last section how Marjorie's love of dogs helped to re-ignite her life and sparked her friendship with Jean.

Although there may be recurring messages from these stories which can inform our practice in supporting older people (or arguably people of any age), the 'keys' to a good life are clearly highly individual. There is no one size fits all here, but there are principles, based on our common desire to make a contribution and our human needs for comfort and proximity.

Attachment theory may help us to understand and find effective ways of supporting people with whom we feel really stuck. People using Type B strategies are – once a reasonable level of trust has been established – likely to be able to recognise their loneliness, talk about the reasons for it and begin to develop their own strategy to tackle it. Usually all they need from others is a sounding board, information and ideas, and encouragement, though this will of course depend on the extent to which their loneliness is shaped by structural factors, such as poverty, discrimination, rural isolation and/or lack of transport.

People using Type A strategies have often developed a self-reliant strategy; they may have withdrawn altogether on the basis that they 'don't do' people or emotions. This may beg the question as to whether and why we should seek to reconnect them. However, this strategy can sometimes result in behaviours that are viewed as 'problematic' or create very real problems. A person using a Type A strategy may, for example, seek to meet their needs for proximity through an intense attachment to an object, through hoarding, or through a fixation with rigid order and routine. Such people may only come to the attention of others when they encounter health crises and the likelihood of these may increase with age. Suddenly or gradually, they may no longer be able to continue their self-reliance: carers may need to come in and support them at home, or they may need to spend time in a hospital or residential community setting, such as a care home.

Loneliness – although not expressed as such – may be an underlying issue for people using these strategies; past hurt or trauma, or having their expressions of emotional need met with either dismissal or a negative response, may have caused their intense mistrust of others and reduced their ability to recognise their emotions. It may be helpful for those seeking to engage them to very gradually try and build trust and gently, over time, seek out any interests which may provide an opportunity for connection. This was the approach which Marie took in supporting Marjorie. Asking people at the outset to talk about their relationships or emotions, or to name the trauma which may have prompted them to withdraw from society, is likely to simply cause further retraction.

People using Type C strategies may similarly struggle to articulate their loneliness; some may express it as anger – they may phone services up on a frequent basis, complaining and leaving angry messages or become very emotional and threaten to harm themselves. As soon as they have someone's attention, they may then push them away, perhaps moving onto the next service. This is the strategy which Jakob, whom we met at the beginning of Chapter 1, was using in response to his feelings of loneliness. Some people using Type C strategies accrue a lot of very superficial connections with people, but these relationships can lack real intimacy or depth. This may become more of an issue for people as they age – perhaps reduced mobility or income makes it more difficult to get around and, say, have lots of different contacts with people in different pubs; it can be much harder to draw on those with whom we have very superficial relationships for practical or other forms of support.

In trying to enable those using Type C strategies to express and begin to address their loneliness, it is important to be very clear about what you can and cannot offer, and to coordinate with other agencies and individuals who may have been drawn in to help. Otherwise, there is a risk that a person using a Type C strategy ends up creating a service-based social life for themselves – and a mini-industry for different services – by bouncing from one worker to the next. Trying to support the person to map out their world and take control of it by thinking and planning can help them to get beyond a purely emotional response.

5. Hope

Hope has been defined as 'A belief that desired goals can be reached and that there were various pathways to meet these goals' (Brooks 2012).

Given that loneliness is a subjective state, it is perhaps unsurprising that hope has been found to protect people from it (Feldman *et al.* 2016). If we can see a way out of our loneliness and begin to see it as a temporary, circumstantial state, rather than a permanent state, we can begin to see and take ways out of it.

Where people have lost hope in their ability to change their relationships, motivational interviewing may offer some simple tools to help turn this around. This technique can be useful in supporting people to make changes that they want to make in their lives (see Chapter 9, Tool 7).

6. Permission to take risks

We have dedicated Chapter 6 to a consideration of risk; however, our focus there is more on challenging the risk aversion of professionals and family members. In some cases, older people choose to withdraw as a result of their own fears and anxieties. Fear of crime, fear of falling – especially in poor weather and fear of getting lost may all be well grounded, and a decision not to go out alone in the dark or in icy conditions may well be a sensible one. However, these fears can also be disproportionate, and some older people also describe feelings of generalised anxiety:

> I worry more – I don't worry about the future – I worry about stupid little things – it's hard to say – and I'm slowing down and I can't do the things I used to do and I think that worries me but there's not really anything to worry about. (Blood *et al.* 2016b, p.21)

Supporting people to talk more about what they are worried about and to balance this with the potential gains of continuing to get out and about may be helpful. This conversation may also highlight practical steps which could help reduce some of the risks and make people feel safer. Sometimes people perceive a social pressure that they shouldn't be doing something 'at this age', and simply giving them permission to take some risks can free them up. Often people feel quite conflicted, and some of the motivational interviewing techniques described in the previous section may help.

As professionals, we may need to overstep our traditionally defined roles to do this work effectively. Marie brought her dog over to Marjorie's house and all three went out walking together: what sounds like a natural human response may, in many organisations, in fact involve breaking several health and safety, professional conduct and risk policies. We will consider the implications of this more in Chapters 6 and 8.

7. Build resilience

Increasing and deepening our social networks is central to building resilience. A key message of this chapter is that those supporting older people to increase their social networks need to do so in a way that is sustainable: services should facilitate, stimulate and complement 'natural' networks, not replace them.

If we invest time and energy into listening and collaborating with an older person at the outset, and if we have the support of our organisations to take some risks and do things a bit differently, that person should be able to live better and with less need for professional help in future. Of course, Marjorie's friendship with Jean will not necessarily protect her from needing personal care at some point in the future, but it should reduce her loneliness, depression and the health risks that accompany it. If Marie had simply offered befriending visits to Marjorie with no attempt to engage her with her local community, the benefits of her support would probably have ended sharply at the point the funding ran out or the time-limited input came to an end. Marjorie may even have ended up feeling more lonely and depressed than she had been when Marie first met her.

Circles of Support can provide a simple model for facilitating and coordinating professional and 'natural' support around what really matters to an older person (see Chapter 9, Tool 8).

Supporting access to mainstream clubs and activities

Many older people understandably do not want to go to activities which target 'older people': some feel they will have little in common with those who attend; some do not see themselves as 'older people'; others want to continue doing the things that interest them alongside people of all ages who share that interest. This is not to undermine the value which some people get from mixing with their peers, or with others who share a diagnosis, are carers, are recently bereaved, and so on; but it does mean that we should not assume that being in the same age group or even sharing a diagnosis will automatically give people enough in common. Taking a strengths-based approach means that we should always explore opportunities to integrate people within their communities (whether that be a neighbourhood or a 'community' of music lovers or football fans) rather than jumping to segregate them.

Promoting access to the 'mainstream' — to football clubs, faith communities, arts and cultural venues, shops and services is partly about building knowledge of what is available in the local area; it is also about ensuring these places are accessible to those who may have reduced mobility, sight, hearing or continence. It may also be about challenging stigma and raising awareness about conditions such as dementia.

In many areas, there is considerable activity to create 'dementia-friendly' or 'age-friendly' communities. Such concepts have been criticised by some — for example, is it helpful to single out dementia? Surely this is about rights to inclusion, not just 'friendliness'. And what do we even mean by 'a community'? Sometimes, activity undertaken under the banner of 'dementia-friendly communities' risks the further segregation and stereotyping of people with dementia. The primary aim of these initiatives should be to make the public world — from buses to shops to swimming pools — more accessible to people with dementia, older people and, ultimately, everyone.

> In a 'Dementia Friendly Community', people with dementia are included and respected. Citizens, organisations and businesses work together to remove the barriers which stop people with dementia and their supporters from participating in community life. (Imogen Blood & Associates/Innovations in Dementia)

If you are supporting an older person with dementia, 'dementia-friendly communities' may create a number of opportunities for participation. In some areas, theatres, cinemas and swimming pools offer 'relaxed' or 'dementia-friendly' performances or sessions; pubs, shops and restaurants have taken steps to be more accessible to people with dementia; the police have set up schemes to help people with dementia who get lost. There should be opportunities for people with dementia and their supporters to get involved in these initiatives — perhaps by helping to identify local priorities, feed into awareness-raising training or audit the accessibility of public places and transport networks.

There have been a number of publications about how clubs, venues and places of worship might be made more 'dementia-friendly'.

Livebility's guide to *Developing a Dementia-Friendly Church* describes some of the different aspects of dementia and how these might affect a person's participation in church, such as:

- *day-to-day memory*: finding it difficult to recall events that happened recently

- *concentrating, planning or organising*: struggling to make decisions, solve problems or carry out a sequence of tasks (i.e. cooking a meal, finding the right passage of the Bible)

- *visuospatial skills*: problems judging distances (e.g. steps or stairs) and seeing objects in three dimensions

- *orientation*: losing track of the day or date, or becoming confused about where they are.

(Adapted from Livability 2017)

It also suggests various practical steps a church can take, including holding some shorter services, providing outreach to care homes and keeping in touch with members who are no longer able to attend. Many of these ideas could be translated to different settings.

The Australian publication *Your Shed and Dementia: A Manual* (Australian Alzheimer's NSW 2014) is aimed at Men's Sheds – leisure clubs where men come together to make and mend things – who want to include members with dementia. The no-nonsense guide contains tips for people with dementia on finding a club that feels right to them; discussing their abilities and what support they may need; and planning ahead for when their dementia gets worse. It also includes simple tips for other club members on language, how to involve people with dementia, and handouts for club members containing basic information about different types of dementia and how they may affect people.

Other resources include:

- how to make a performance or creative sessions dementia-friendly (West Yorkshire Playhouse, 2016)

- how to make a swimming pool accessible (Swim England n.d.)

- how to make an arts venue accessible (with lots of transferable learning for other types of venues) (Alzheimer's Society 2015).

6

Positive Risk-Taking

Introduction

In day-to-day life, we tend to associate 'risk' with excitement and uncertainty: we know there is danger here, but we decide something is worth doing anyway; sometimes the danger may even be the point. However, in social care settings, when we talk about 'risk', the focus tends to be on the possible harm that may result for a 'service user' and the accountability for that harm which we may face as a 'service provider'. As Alison Faulkner writes, 'In "Careland", there are different rules – you are not expected or allowed to do things that might hurt you or might risk your safety even if that "safety" means risking your own independence and wellbeing' (Faulkner 2012, p.11).

An overly cautious approach to risk can be one of the greatest barriers to working with older people in a strengths-based way. As Furedi (2011, p.14) argues, 'Once users of care are assessed through the prism of risk it becomes difficult to perceive them as individuals with a capacity for agency.'

Yet health, social care and housing professionals are increasingly being asked by the organisations they work for to conduct 'risk assessments' and to 'manage' risks. This is ultimately driven by the need to demonstrate that statutory duties and duties of care are being upheld and to protect organisations and individual workers from legal action where things go wrong. However, as local authority and NHS budgets – and the value of care contracts – shrink, this balancing act may become increasingly difficult and defensive.

In services, low-risk options are sometimes less resource intensive, so 'risk' can become an excuse for not meeting people's needs. The following example comes from the Alzheimer's Society (2012):

Mum was mobile and continent until spending three weeks in hospital. They kept her in bed with pads on during that time despite her shouting to get up and go to the toilet. When she moved into a nursing home they did the same, listening to the hospital staff rather than my mum or me. This caused her enormous distress – she had advanced dementia but still had sufficient awareness to feel trapped and humiliated. The day before she died she told me, 'I can't live like this.' (Alzheimer's Society 2012, p.9)

This story highlights the emotional, psychological and social harms that can arise when an older person is 'over-serviced', presumably partly for their own protection and partly for the convenience of staff and systems. The decision made by the staff in this example may appear callous and unthinking, but they will no doubt have been busily trying to balance the needs of lots of people, and worried about the woman's risk of falling if they were to encourage her to make her own way to the toilet.

In his *Care Home Inquiry* for the Joseph Rowntree Foundation, John Kennedy contrasts the care sector with the airline industry:

The expression 'skin in the game' was explained to me in relation to the airline industry. In aviation, everyone's 'skin is in the game' – passengers, pilots, crew, executives and regulators – no one wants a plane to fall from the sky. Consequently, not just one aspect of the industry is 'regulated' but the whole system is. The culture is also open and as 'blame-free' as possible. This encourages sensible analysis of risk/benefit. If something goes wrong, the first question is 'what went wrong with the system?' not 'who can we find to blame?' As a consequence, aeroplanes very rarely fall out of the sky.

So, what about the care sector? What of the current regulatory, safeguarding, commissioning environment? In my view, all the agencies surrounding the care home, although doing what they are *asked* to do, aren't doing what they *need* to do. The transactions are all one way. They don't have 'their skin in the game'. They don't share the risks or support the mission. What they do is stand on the sidelines and demand assurance without accepting some of the collective 'systemic' responsibility. We end up not getting better over time but being part of an endless circular firing squad. (Kennedy 2014, pp.48–49)

In this chapter, we argue that we need to move to a new way of looking at and working with risk, called 'positive risk-taking'. This does not mean that we should tear up the risk assessments and throw caution to the wind, but rather that:

- Decision making about risk should be *balanced*; in other words, we should look at the benefits of taking a risk (and the potential harms of not taking it) as well as the harms which might occur if something goes wrong. This needs to include considering the risks of putting a formal service in place as well as the risks of not doing so – for example, staying in hospital may seem on some level to be the 'safer' option but we must also weigh up the risks of losing mobility or confidence (as we heard in the example above).

- We should aim to make and record decisions which are *defensible* (i.e. well founded and justifiable) not *defensive* (i.e. which we can use to protect ourselves and our agencies).

- We should work collaboratively with older people, their families and across agencies to make decisions about risk: we all need our 'skin in the game'. Having 'skin in the game' means taking a risk to achieve a goal; in this instance, it means that each stakeholder needs to take a risk to support the older person's goal, collectively and through genuine engagement.

> Positive risk-taking is: 'weighing up the potential benefits and harms of exercising one choice of action over another. Identifying the potential risks involved (i.e. good risk assessment), and developing plans and actions (i.e. good risk management) that reflect the positive potentials and stated priorities of the service user (i.e. a strengths approach). It involves using 'available' resources and support to achieve the desired outcomes, and to minimise the potential harmful outcomes.' (Morgan and Andrews, 2016, p.128)

It is not easy to do this single-handedly in a risk-averse organisation; and working to persuade other risk-averse organisations to put their 'skin in the game' can feel like an uphill battle. But change can and must begin on the 'front line' because this is where the relationships with older people and their families happen. Once an older person has been viewed through the 'prism of risk' and this has been recorded and fed back to managers and colleagues, the direction of travel tends to become set. It can be hard to go back and have different, more balanced, strengths-based conversations.

How do attachment theory and strengths-based practice link to positive risk-taking?

There is considerable overlap between 'positive risk-taking' and strengths-based practice. Both seek to understand what matters most to older people and their families, and to enable them to identify and build on their existing resources and ways of coping. Both aim to work collaboratively with families and other professionals to reach solutions that promote the outcomes that really matter.

Attachment theory can be usefully applied here because the kinds of situations which call for the involvement of professionals in discussions about risk tend to be situations which involve a degree of uncertainty and potential threat. For example, these discussions could be the result of a person's deteriorating physical or emotional wellbeing, or because someone needs further support following the death of a partner, or because there is concern that someone is being abused by people close to them. These discussions touch on themes of illness, grief, mortality and loss, and as such, they are highly likely to represent threats to the attachment systems of the people involved and their loved ones.

This – as we saw in Chapter 2 – can trigger attachment strategies. People who use Type A strategies may suppress their emotions, withdraw from the situation or refuse offers of help. People who use Type C strategies may, unconsciously, be afraid that if the 'problem' is solved, then their supporters may become more distant, so they may find the prospect of a workable solution to their situation threatening in itself. Therefore, they may display heightened emotional responses and become angry or distressed, or perhaps alternate between demanding something be done and pushing away help when offered.

The attitudes to risk of each of those involved in a decision will inevitably be shaped by their own fears, experiences of loss, beliefs about how the world works and what kinds of solutions are possible, and the relationships they have with each other and the older person at the centre of the decision. There is no such thing as a totally objective risk assessment. If we are to work successfully with older people and their families (and with our colleagues) around risk, we need to tune into these underlying emotions, recognise where and how people can usefully be supported to name some of their fears and assumptions, and find better ways of expressing and meeting their needs for safety and comfort.

In this chapter, we will consider what it means to have conversations about risk in a strengths-based way. We will also highlight the emotional and social aspects of conversations and decisions about risk (as well as the physical ones which tend to dominate). How might the way the person feels about herself or himself and their situation impact on conversations about positive risk- taking? How might conversations about risk impact upon their relationships, in both positive and negative ways? We begin by exploring some of the reasons why older people, their families and professionals may have different perceptions of safety and concerns about risk.

Older people and risk-taking

We typically associate getting older with becoming more conservative and risk averse (whilst recognising that some people were risk averse to start with, whereas others have always lived their lives on the edge). However, the evidence from psychological research is complex and we know, of course, that 'older people' are as different from each other in their attitudes and behaviours as people of any other age group.

When it comes to *financial* decision making and gambling, psychological research suggests that older people – as a group – do seem to be less likely to take risks. There may be a number of reasons for this: it can be much harder to replenish finances and pay off debts through paid work or bank borrowing in later life, so this may be a very rational response. In some of the gambling-style experimental tests conducted by psychologists, researchers attribute older people's more conservative strategies to their slower mental processing speeds and poorer memory (Albert and Duffy 2012).

However, other psychologists (such as Rolison *et al.* 2013) have pointed out the importance of understanding how age might influence our decision making about risk in different areas of our lives and the need to look in more detail at what motivates that decision making (Rolinson *et al.* 2013).

Psychologists have identified what they call an 'age-related positivity effect'. Older people may be more likely to notice and process positive information than they are negative information – in psychology experiments, this might be about remembering a happy face but not remembering the sad face shown next to it. In research studies, younger people are more likely to do the opposite.

Carstensen and Mikels (2005) who have undertaken a number of such studies reflect that, as our cognitive (thinking, remembering) function deteriorates in older age, our emotional functioning (feeling) is usually preserved or even enhanced. They argue that older people typically use their relatively well-preserved memory for emotions, particularly positive ones, in order to maintain 'emotional equilibrium' – wellbeing and happiness. They do, however, warn that a reliance on feelings (instead of a memory for details) could lead either to good- or poor-quality decision making in different settings.

A key message from the research into age and risk-taking for those interested in supporting older people (rather than selling them financial products) is that older people tend to prioritise emotional goals. This tendency seems to be driven by how much of our lives we think we have left, as much as by age itself. As Carstensen and Mikels put it, 'When people perceive boundaries on their time, they direct attention to emotionally meaningful aspects of life, such as the desire to lead a meaningful life, to have emotionally intimate social relationships and to feel socially interconnected' (p.117).

This reflection also fits with the longitudinal Harvard Adult Development Study,[1] which has tracked a group of American adults over an 80-year period from when they were students. The study found that the people who were the most satisfied in their relationships at age 50 were the healthiest at age 80. Perhaps as we age, we know this instinctively, and use the strengths we have, including our gains in emotional functioning, to help us prioritise relationships and other things that matter to us emotionally. It also suggests that our decision making continues to be driven by our attempts to meet our emotional needs through our relationships – in other words, by our attachment strategies.

---

1   The Harvard Adult Development Study is described in an excellent TED talk given by Robert Walldinger, *What Makes a Good Life? Lessons from the Longest Study on Happiness*. www.ted.com/talks/robert_waldinger_what_makes_a_good_life_lessons_from_ the_longest_study_on_happiness

The value of 'independence'

A recurring theme in research with older people is how much 'independence' is valued (e.g. Blood 2013; Blood *et al.* 2016b). This means different things to different people but usually includes:

- having freedom and autonomy

- not being a 'burden' on others – feeling that there is a reasonable balance between what you are asking for and what you can offer

- having a sense of belonging and pride in your home

- being active, having purpose and staying connected

- trying to maintain 'normality' as far as possible.

Older people experiencing poor health or disability may try to find an acceptable balance between independence and risk in their everyday activities. Trying to do things for yourself without depending on others to do it is a key part of this and, where health worsens or fluctuates or other circumstances change, older people may find themselves having to continuously adapt and fine-tune this balance. This is what Mitchell and Glendenning (2007, p.25) have described as 'a complex and often lengthy process of redefinition and adaptation to physical and/or psychological changes arising from ageing and/or dementia'.

We can see this in the following conversation between Mrs B in her 80s (living alone and felt to be at risk of falling) and her daughter:

Mrs B: Last week, one of the bulbs went and I thought, I'll try with the steps. And then when I got on the steps...'

Daughter: I'm going to hide the steps (laughs). [...] You've got to accept you can't do what you used to do.

Mrs B: No, that's the trouble. You think to yourself, well, I'll try, and then sometimes it works. Sometimes I think, no, I'm going to fall off these steps. So I stop. I still have a bit of brain, not a lot. [...] It's wearing out, like me (laughs). Oh well, you've got to try, haven't you?' (Hamblin 2014, p.6)

In this short exchange, Mrs B explains how she does stop herself when she sees the risks are too high, though her daughter disagrees with her that this is a risk worth taking for the sake of a light bulb. Yet, for

Mrs B, attempting to change the light bulb is not just a one-off act of spontaneous defiance or misplaced determination. Rather, it needs to be seen as part of an ongoing process of balancing the pride she takes in her home and her sense of herself as an independent and capable person, with a recognition of her own reduced mobility and balance.

Family members' attitudes to risk

There is huge diversity in the attitudes of older people's families towards 'risk' and this is often apparent between different individuals in the same family. Some family members find it easier to tolerate higher levels of risk and uncertainty than others. Some intuitively understand the importance of 'independence' to their loved one whereas others find it harder to empathise with the (literal!) balancing act we have just described, and may interpret risky acts of independence as 'stubbornness' or 'recklessness'. In order to understand this and to help families to work together to agree a way forward, it is important to try and tune in to their underlying fears and uncertainties, which we introduced in Chapter 3.

In conversations with family carers, similar themes recur – or seem to be underlying, but are not necessarily articulated (Figure 6.1).

Figure 6.1: Family members' concerns

Often, how we behave in these situations depends on how we tell the story, and how we define our role in it. Identifying our worries and our conflicted emotions can be a first step in trying to negotiate a positive outcome.

Covert risk-taking/risk management in families

Where fears are not expressed and discussed in families, family members sometimes end up trying to 'manage' risks covertly, which can be counterproductive. If the daughter of Mrs B (who we met in the previous section, climbing on a step ladder to change a light bulb) simply hid the steps, we can imagine Mrs B trying to climb onto a table or the arm of a chair instead, thereby putting herself at even greater risk.

Similarly, Hamblin (2014) refers to Mrs Shepard, whose daughter-in-law had (on the advice of an occupational therapist) made a number of changes to her home while she was in hospital without consulting her. They included de-cluttering the lounge to reduce the risk of tripping over. Mrs Shepard was not pleased with the changes and said that her lounge no longer felt 'homely'. Over time, she began to move items of furniture back into the lounge. For example, she would drag a heavy coffee table into the lounge, only to drag it back out again if she was expecting her daughter-in-law; this strategy had created much greater risks than before.

The fear of losing independence and, perhaps being 'put in a home' can mean that older people sometimes hide the risks and challenges they are facing from their families:

> When they ask me how I am, half the time I'm telling lies – I've got this fear that if I tell them too much, they'll put me in a home – I want to die here. (Older person interviewed, Blood *et al.* 2016b, p.15)

A couple of older participants in Hamblin's research (2014) complain they are being treated like children. One describes being told when and where to wear her telecare pendant as 'like being at school again' (Hamblin 2014, p.19), and Mrs B (who was trying to change the light bulb) says that her daughter is 'worse than my teacher at school!' (Hamblin 2014, p.6). As discussed in Chapter 3, a degree of role reversal is part of the natural cycle in families, as parents age and need more support from their adult children; however, this sense that other people, including loved ones, may 'take over' in the name of protecting you and keeping you safe also reflects the disempowerment of older and/or disabled people in our society. Charlton describes this paternalism in his history of the disability rights movement, yet it applies equally – if not more so – to older people:

> Paternalism lies at the center of the oppression of people with disabilities. Paternalism starts with the notion of superiority: We must and can take control of these 'subjects' in spite of themselves... [they] must be cared for (for their own good)... Paternalism often must transform its subjects into children or people with childlike qualities... It is...the assumption that people with disabilities are intrinsically inferior and unable to take responsibility for their own lives. (Charlton 1998, pp.52–53)

We often see very similar attitudes to older people (many of whom are disabled). Older people are sometimes spoken to like children and professional responses often assume that they need protecting and rescuing.

How can we best support older people and their families in relation to risk?

The evidence we have considered so far in this chapter suggests that, if we are to support older people and their families effectively in relation to risk, we need to do the following:

- Support them all to articulate their fears and concerns about a situation or decision.

- Help older people to identify and express their 'emotional goals', what 'independence' means to them personally – or, put simply, what really matters to them now.

- Give family members the opportunity to bring the 'memory for details' to the table – what happened last time? Are there skills, learning and resources which the older person may have forgotten which could be useful here?

- Where family members are risk averse, we might usefully highlight what Clarke *et al.* (2011) has described as the 'silent harms' of boredom, frustration or losing the fulfilment of doing things for ourselves. We need to promote identity, meaning and purpose in life as well as physical safety.

- Take the time to hear and understand how the older person is already adapting and fine-tuning the balance between risk and independence as they go about their daily lives. How have they adapted the way they do things to reduce risks? What rules have they created for themselves? Do they feel this is working – or does it need to be looked at again? Could outside resources help to maintain the balance – a grab rail next to the bath, or a neighbour who might be happy to put out the bins?

- Consider whether 'covert' risk-taking/risk management may be going on here – if so, what is the impact? Is it actually increasing the risks? Can we plan and agree an approach that is acceptable to everyone, so we can be honest with each other moving forwards?

Professionals, risk and older people

There are a number of typical scenarios in which professionals are drawn into decision making about risk in relation to older people with high support needs, especially those with dementia and/or physical health conditions/ mobility issues. These are decisions about:

- where someone lives and how they are supported – often prompted by a period of hospitalisation and/or a fall

- whether or not someone should be supported to do a particular activity, especially where there is a question about their capacity to make the decision

- what to do in the face of puzzling, 'difficult' or 'risky' behaviour

- 'safeguarding'.

In this section, we will present case studies illustrating these decisions in order to explore the issues and introduce tools to support strengths-based practice. First though, let's remind ourselves of what the law tells us about mental capacity and decision making.

The Mental Capacity Act (MCA) 2005: Key points

- Assume people can make their own decisions unless proven otherwise – don't make assumptions just because they have a diagnosis of dementia or because of their age.

- Capacity to make decisions often fluctuates; decisions about capacity are specific to that time and that decision – 'lacking capacity' is not a permanent label.

- Everyone has the right to make unwise or unusual decisions – this, in itself, does not mean they lack capacity.

- Make every effort to support people to make the decision for themselves.

- A person lacks the mental capacity to make their own decision if one or more of the following conditions can be evidenced. (Note: the 'burden of proof' here is on the party arguing that the person does *not* have capacity, rather than on the party arguing they do – i.e. it is for us to demonstrate that someone lacks capacity, not for them to demonstrate they have it.) They are unable to:
  - understand information given to them
  - retain that information long enough to be able to make the decision
  - weigh up the information available to make the decision
  - communicate their decision (this can be by talking, sign language, muscle movement, blinking or squeezing a hand).

- If someone is assessed as lacking capacity, we must make the decision in their *best interests*. This does not mean that we automatically take the lowest risk option but rather that we must draw on their personal history, preferences and the sorts of decisions they have typically made in the past, and continue to involve them as much as possible in the process.

- If this decision involves a 'Deprivation of Liberty', for example in which a person will be subject to continuous supervision and control and/or is not free to leave a place, and the person is in a care home or hospital, the local authority must authorise this under the DoLS (Deprivation of Liberty Standards). The aim must always be to find the least restrictive option.

1. Decisions about where someone lives and how they are supported

Case study - Joyce's hospital discharge

Joyce has lived alone in the same house for over 20 years. She was diagnosed with dementia a year ago and recently had a fall at home, resulting in a month's stay in hospital. She fractured her wrist and her hip in the fall, and the doctors have diagnosed osteoporosis. She has now been deemed medically fit for discharge, but hospital staff are not convinced that she can return safely to living on her own. When the hospital staff have tried to talk to her about residential care, Joyce has become very distressed and said repeatedly that she wants to go home. She is particularly missing her cat, who is being fed by a neighbour.

Joyce has two sons – Eric and Michael. Eric lives about half an hour's drive from Joyce and has been able to visit her in hospital every other day; Michael lives at a distance but has been calling the hospital regularly to check Joyce's progress and is really anxious about the prospect of his mother going home alone. He has been researching care homes in the area and has ordered lots of brochures for Eric and is keen that Eric should try to encourage their mother to consider one of them. Michael has read negative stories in the press about state-funded care homes in the area and says he would be willing to contribute significantly to the cost of a private care home, since he knows his mother has limited financial means.

Eric has experienced his mother's reaction to looking at the brochures and feels really conflicted about the best course of action to take. He has teenage children and his own partner has a mental health condition, so he is conscious that there is only so much practical support he can offer his mother if she goes home; yet at the same time he knows how keen his mother is to get back to her own bed, belongings and cat.

Joyce's response when Eric and the hospital staff talk to her about residential care suggests that she is able to express a consistent view about what she wants, and that this involves going home as soon as possible. This may be an 'unwise' decision (as Michael believes) but it does not follow from this that she lacks the capacity to make it. It might be argued that she does not have sufficient accurate information about her options to make an informed decision, but again a lack of capacity does not follow from this.

So, assuming we are not in the territory of making a 'best interests' decision here, let us consider the different ways in which we might support Joyce and her family, drawn from the list above on how we can best support older people and their families in relation to risk.

First, we might support all of the family to articulate their fears and hopes about *both* the scenario of Joyce returning home *and* the scenario of her moving into a care home. If the focus is solely on concerns about a return home, Joyce's fears of going to a care home risk getting drowned out. As highlighted at the start of the chapter, it is important to consider the risks of putting in a service as well as the risks of not doing so.

Table 6.1 shows the key messages from the conversations with each family member. We include a blank version of this table in Chapter 9, Tool 9.

Table 6.1: Fears and hopes

Fears and hopes		Joyce returns home	Joyce moves into a care home
Joyce	Fears	Fear of falling again and ending up in hospital Not wanting to be a 'burden' on Eric, or for Michael to get stressed	Separation from cat, belongings and neighbours Won't be free to decide how I spend my time and with whom
	Hopes	That things can go back to normal	That I will die before I reach the point where I have to go in a home
Eric	Fears	Just how much support can I realistically give Mum, given my other responsibilities?	Have heard about poor practice in some care homes – how would you know you had found a good one? Will mum be miserable?
	Hopes	That she will be more open now to looking at how aids, adaptation and technology might help to keep her safe, and be honest with me about what she needs	If they did find a care home she liked, it would be nice to be able to just spend quality time together when I visit

Michael	Fears	It will only be a matter of time before another accident happens. If she goes back, I will be worrying about her a lot	That Mum ends up in a poor-quality home for financial reasons
	Hopes	That if she does go back home, Mum recognises that things will need to change radically and that she starts being honest about this and accepts help from others	That Mum settles into a good care home and I know she will be safe and well looked after

Since Joyce has such a strong preference for returning home, it seems we should focus on exploring this option. There is a risk that Michael's suggested approach of showing her brochures or taking her to visit care homes, in the hope of 'persuading' her, will lead to Joyce feeling railroaded into something she clearly does not want – she is unlikely to look at these with an open mind, simply because someone tells her to, even if it is her own son.

In our research into care homes (Blood and Litherland 2015), we heard of older people being 'tricked' into going into care homes or hurried into temporary placements which morph into permanent placements with little opportunity for them to choose or be supported to return home. The family members and professionals who set up such placements may sleep more easily in their beds knowing the older person is 'safe', but a move under such circumstances can be extremely disorientating, disempowering and upsetting for the person, and damaging to their relationships with people who they feel have lied to them. Care home staff also told us they felt they were left 'dealing with the fallout' in such cases.

We begin by sitting with Joyce and mapping out her world using the 'My World' tool (see Figure 6.2 and Chapter 9, Tool 5).

The 'My World' map helps the family place this decision in the context of Joyce's life and what matters to her; it makes it easier for everyone to see the trade-offs Joyce would be making by leaving her home.

We then consider how Joyce has coped up until now in her home and how she has adapted the way she does things since her diagnosis of dementia. Eric was able to prompt and remind her where she struggled to remember the details — he also has a conversation with her neighbours who add to the picture: they pop in to see her most days and provide bits of practical support, including the odd bit of shopping and DIY. They explain that Joyce — who is a dab hand at sewing — has done bits of mending and altering for them and some of the other neighbours. Joyce explains that she has a notebook in which she writes down everything she needs to do and remember — she often jokes 'I can't think without my book!'

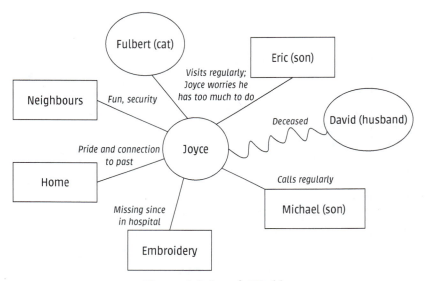

Figure 6.2: Joyce's World

The fall happened because Joyce tripped over and lost her balance — she is aware that her balance is deteriorating and has made a number of changes to her day-to-day life to compensate for this. For example:

- She either gets a lift or a taxi to the shops because she is worried about falling on the bus.

- A neighbour has helped her move everything to the lower cupboards in the kitchen so she does not have to stand on a stool to reach.

- She no longer carries anything heavy up or down the stairs.

Eric, Joyce and the neighbour agree that they will go around the house together when she is discharged from hospital and look again at the hazards, especially given that Joyce's mobility is further reduced following the fall. We give them a strengths-based risk assessment form (Table 6.2 and Chapter 9, Tool 9) and some advice about how to fill it in. We also tell them about some of the resources which may be available to support them – benefits; aids, adaptations and technology; specialist advice and support from dementia groups, charities and websites; and the sorts of care and support services that might be available either from social services or to buy in privately.

Table 6.2: Strengths-based risk assessment

Potential hazard	How do you feel about this item/ activity? What are the benefits you gain from it?	What are you already doing to adapt and reduce risks?	Does this reduce risk to a level everyone is comfortable with?	Can a better solution/ compromise be reached which reduces risks to a level everyone is comfortable with?
Rug in lounge – could be a trip hazard	It was a wedding present and has been in this location for decades	Joyce has changed her route around the lounge to avoid the part of the rug that curls up	No, others are concerned she might forget, take a 'wrong' route and trip	Rug could be rotated/ furniture moved so that the curled-up section is held down by the sofa
Could lose balance getting out of bath	Joyce prefers a bath to a shower and wants to continue doing this independently as long as possible	A neighbour has fitted a grab rail. She has stopped using bath oil to reduce the risk of slipping	It is going to be hard to get in and out of the bath since the fall and this seems too risky	Look at bath aids that would lower her into the bath and raise her back out. Only have a bath when Eric or the neighbour is downstairs – she can shout for help

There is no right or wrong decision here for Joyce and, as a result, we have deliberately not given the story a particular 'ending'. The three may generate lots of good ideas as to how resources can be drawn on and small – but acceptable – changes and compromises made so that Joyce can continue living independently in her own home. Joyce may decide that having paid carers to help her bathe is preferable to risking Eric or her neighbour having to help her out of the bath. It may be that, as they work their way around the house and think about her day-to-day life, Joyce begins to realise that it is just not going to be possible to make this work without putting herself at risk of another fall and/or asking more than she wants to of Eric and her neighbour. She may decide it is worth looking at care homes – or perhaps an extra care housing scheme – to see what the alternatives might be, preferring to make a move now while she can do so in a relatively calm and planned way, rather than waiting until she is less able to contribute to the decision.

The really important thing about this case study is the *process*, in particular:

- We assumed she had the capacity to make this decision and worked with her to try and find a way of making what she wanted work.

- We placed the decision within the wider context of Joyce's life by trying to understand – and help her express to those closest to her – what matters most to her.

- We worked with the whole family (including neighbours), not just the individual at the centre, and gave everyone the opportunity to voice their fears and hopes about the alternative outcomes.

- We avoided framing the decision in terms of someone 'being right' and someone else 'being wrong'. What's important is that everyone involved had the chance to express their thoughts and feelings, and to be listened to.

- We invested our (limited) time listening to Joyce and her family and explaining what is available to them. We then handed the risk assessment tool over to the Joyce and those closest to her: this is their solution to find, agree and action.

- Our risk assessment tool gives weight to the emotional and social gains and attachments as well as the physical risks; it identifies existing resources and coping mechanisms, and focuses on reaching levels of risk which the key players feel comfortable with (rather than the usual 'high', 'medium' and 'low', which assumes we all have the same attitude to risk and that this can be measured).

We give the family information about a range of external resources which they might want to draw on for support moving forwards, and how they might access them. Decisions about where a person should live and how they should be supported are inevitably made in the context of the resources that are available. Improving professional decision making about risk is therefore only part of the picture here: we also need more consistent and innovative commissioning of services which can provide a 'middle ground' between residential care and a return home, such as 'step-down' beds in extra care or sheltered housing, and services which support people's return home promptly, holistically and in a coordinated way.

In some areas, despite the best efforts of staff, older people typically face one of two scenarios on discharge from hospital: being rushed into a care home placement (often on a temporary basis but, for many, this becomes permanent) or being sent home with little support from the state and minimal communication with others who might provide support in the community, such as family, neighbours or housing staff. Healthwatch England (2015) gathered many stories of older people being discharged from hospital to high-risk scenarios at home. Without investment in services which can respond holistically to the needs of older people returning to or staying in their homes, the decision making of health and social care professionals – especially under organisational pressure to reduce delayed discharge – will always lurch between risk averse on the one hand and negligent on the other.

If short-term hospital-to-home services are to provide anything more than a sticking plaster at the point of discharge, it is essential that they work with older people in a strengths-based way to restore their confidence, (re)connect them with communities and families, and work collaboratively with older people and their 'natural helpers' to identify acceptable and sustainable solutions to the practical challenges of day-to-day living.

2. Decisions about whether or not someone should be supported to do a particular activity

If you want to prevent falls, start dancing!

The risk averse might argue that older people should be discouraged from dancing in case they should fall; but there is growing evidence to suggest that dancing can actually *reduce* the risk of falling. The pilot of the *Dance for Health* programme suggests that participants' risk of falls might be reduced by 55 per cent (Aesop 2017). The key factor here seems to be fun – people enjoy dancing, so they are more than twice as likely to stick to regular dancing than they are to traditional falls prevention programmes.

Manthorpe and Moriarty, in their *Risk Guidance for People with Dementia* (2010) produced for the Department of Health what they describe as a 'heat map'. This allows us to consider the level of risk of an activity against its potential benefits for a person's quality of life.[2] For example, where risks are high, we should not go ahead if the impact on quality of life is low; we might substitute an alternative activity if the likely impact on the quality of life is medium; but we would go ahead, managing the risks as much as possible, where there are likely to be significant gains for quality of life.

Dementia Adventure runs activities and holidays for people with dementia and their supporters, aiming to get them outdoors, connect with nature and retain a sense of adventure in their lives. An evaluation of their programme found that:

> During the holidays, a change in dynamics between husbands and wives was often apparent: the shared experience of an adventure seems to 'remove the dementia' from people for a little while. (Mapes 2017, p.159)

This reminds us that there is something inherently valuable about pushing the boundaries and having an adventure. Taking a risk is more than a calculation of possible benefit versus possible harm; it is also about reaffirming who we are and the power we have. These things are just as important to us as we age and, as we support older people to weigh up rationally the likely pros and cons of a course of action, we must also enable them – as far as possible – to follow their hearts.

---

2   Manthorpe and Moriarty (2010, p.52)

Only those who risk going too far can possibly find out how far they can go. (T.S. Eliot)

Case study – Fred and the pub

Fred has advanced dementia and has recently moved from one care home to another. His wife Sandra (who is herself at an earlier stage of dementia) arranged this move because Fred's previous care home would not let her take him out of the home during the day for short trips and he was becoming depressed.

The manager at the new care home is keen to find ways to improve Fred's quality of life. She sits down with the couple to talk about the things that matter most to Fred. They identify many things which Fred values but has not been able to do for some time, one of which is to go to the pub, another is to get some fresh air and have a short walk. Sandra suggests that she could take him out of the care home when he is feeling well enough for a walk and a pint.

Despite the concerns of some of her team, the manager is determined to find out if there is a way of supporting this to happen. She convenes a small group of people: Fred, Sandra, their daughter, an occupational therapist who assessed Fred when he moved into the care home, and a memory nurse who knows them both. Together, the group works through the following questions (see also Chapter 9, Tool 9):

- What exactly is being proposed?

- Does Fred have capacity to make this decision? Are we making a best interests decision or are we simply coming together to advise, support and problem solve?

- Why does/might this activity matter to him and his wife? How much is doing it/not doing it likely to impact on their quality of life?

- What are the specific risks? How likely are they to happen? What level of harm to Fred and Sandra is likely/possible if they do?

- What are the potential risks and benefits to family members, carers and the wider community?

- What are our own fears? These might be specific fears about harms or they might be general fears, for example about being blamed if things go wrong.

- Are there ways of doing the activity *and* reducing the risks? Are there alternatives – safer ways of meeting Fred's desire for fresh air and a pint?

- What's the bottom line?

    – What are the rules or conditions which we agree to follow?

    – What is the contingency plan (if things go wrong)?

- Which roles and responsibilities do each of us have? Is there anyone else we need to involve?

- Which changes should trigger a review of this decision?

After the discussion, they go out of the building to walk the potential route together. They take a scenic route through the park to an accessible pedestrian crossing, which takes them to the pub. The publican recognises Fred – he used to be his football coach. Sandra explains that she and Fred would like to come and have an occasional drink here, but that they may sometimes need a bit of support to do this.

They discuss the risks that they will drink too much alcohol. Sandra suggests that if the bar staff leave the glasses on their table it will help them remember how much they have drunk. The publican suggests that if they have had more than two alcoholic drinks he will point this out to them and suggest they switch to a soft drink. He asks what he should do if Fred or Sandra seem to be intoxicated or distressed. The care home manager gives him her number and says the home would be happy to pay for a taxi or that a member of staff could come out in an emergency. She also tells him that he and his team can request a free training course to explain the basics of dementia from the Dementia Friends scheme.[3]

Sandra and Fred agree that they will stick to this route and return to the home if the crossing is not working. The care home says they will ring Sandra's mobile phone once an hour while they are out, just

---

3   www.dementiafriends.org.uk

to check they are alright. Sandra also agrees to enable the GPS on her mobile phone so that her daughter can track her whereabouts if there are serious concerns.

They all agree that they will meet again to review the plan if Sandra's dementia symptoms get worse, if Fred's mobility and balance deteriorate or if there are any changes to the route.

Examples from case law

The following examples show the courts challenging decisions which have been made by local authorities and care providers on the grounds that they jeopardise older people's quality of life and wellbeing in the name of reducing risks.

Mrs P was living in a nursing home, following a second stroke. All the reports and assessments done before this move confirmed that her dog, Bobby, was the only living thing that mattered to her and that 'her face lit up when she saw other dogs'. The deputy managing her affairs had refused to arrange for Bobby to be brought in to visit Mrs P, despite her legal representative's requests. The deputy did not appear to have done a specific risk assessment but had simply said, 'it would seem irresponsible in the extreme to suggest that a dog visits a care home for elderly and frail people'. Yet the Court ruled that contact with Bobby was crucial to Mrs P's wellbeing and quality of life. (Mrs P v Rochdale Borough Council & Anor [2016] EWCOP B1)

Mrs Ross was living in a care home with a diagnosis of dementia. The Court of Protection was asked to consider whether Mrs Ross had the capacity to decide to go on a 16-day cruise with her partner of 20 years, which had already been booked. They had been on many cruises together and professionals felt she understood that she was due to go on a cruise and what this meant but that she 'cannot retain this information and does not have the ability to weigh up this information to make an informed decision'. The judge ruled that Mrs Ross should go on the cruise, and criticised professionals for focusing too much on what might go wrong and not taking sufficient account of the potential benefits of going on this cruise, for what might be the last time. He felt that Mrs Ross was sufficiently familiar with the layout and routine of cruising and that her partner was well placed to care for her while aboard. He concluded that:

...this is not a life-changing decision, or a choice between two evils or a decision over which an elderly person without Mrs Ross's impairment would be likely to agonise. It is a choice of whether to go on holiday or not, in familiar circumstances, with one's companion of the past two decades. (Cardiff Council v Peggy Ross (2011) COP 28/10/11)

3. Decisions about what to do in the face of puzzling, 'difficult' or 'risky' behaviour

We have seen throughout the book how risk assessments or responses to 'difficult' behaviours can easily fall into the 'quick fix' trap. When Mary lashed out at the carers supporting her to have a shower (Chapter 1), the care home doubled up the staffing to manage the risks, but in doing so they simply increased Mary's sense of threat and vulnerability, possibly resulting from childhood experiences of abuse. In Chapter 2, the initial response to Rose's hoarding of cleaning products was to remove the products, but it was only when the worker started to question the meaning and purpose of Rose's behaviour that a lasting solution was found.

In his excellent book *And Still the Music Plays*, Graham Stokes tells the stories of 22 people with dementia he has worked with. Many of them are displaying aggressive or perplexing behaviours that risk harm and/or carer breakdown. But Stokes asks, '...why do we degrade their behaviour to symptoms of a disease, rather than seeing it as evidence of efforts to survive in a world that resonates with fear, threat and mystery?' (Stokes 2008, p.54).

Stokes arrives on the scene – like Columbo or Sherlock Holmes – and assumes that there is a reason to be found for behaviour that has been dismissed as irrational, inexplicable or taken to be an inevitable part of dementia. He looks at the pattern of the behaviour: during which specific activities does the person become stressed? Are they banging on *all* the doors, walls and windows – or just the ones leading to the garden? Are there particular rooms the person becomes more agitated in than others (in one case, the *colour* of the room is evoking powerful memories for someone), or certain people – men, women, people in uniforms, and so on? When do they seem calm and contented – is there a common theme here? For instance, one man will sit contentedly (and not pursue his wife anxiously around the house) while the news is on.

He asks how people have coped with their dementia in the earlier stages to give clues about the function of their current behaviour and how it may be their best attempt to adapt to the erosion of their cognitive functioning, social anxieties or hallucinations. For some, aggression seems to be an expression of frustration where they are no longer able to use previous adaptive strategies. In the earlier stages of dementia, one man used to go out to work in his garden in order to avoid people. He becomes increasingly frustrated when this escape route outdoors is literally blocked in the care home he moves to.

Stokes tunes in to the dynamics of relationships – especially between couples where one partner is caring for the other with dementia. He hears the loss, the shame and the fear, as well as the love and the strength. He asks about the person's past life – their likes and dislikes, their fears and any traumatic experiences they may have had.

Just as a detective might, he explores and rejects different lines of enquiry and then begins to design and test possible solutions, supporting families and carers to put these into action. The wife of the man who only sits down and feels secure when the news is on records the news and plays it back to her husband when she needs to get jobs done or have a bit of time to herself. A woman who had lost her beloved youngest son and spent the rest of her adult life repressing her grief is brought a box of his belongings; her relentless compulsion to walk ceases, and for the first time in decades she is genuinely happy connecting with the photographs and objects that bring him back to life.

Stokes argues that dementia does not merely bring:

> ...neurological losses and dysfunctions to be understood in terms of dependency and care needs. As important is the emotional reaction to these debilitating, frustrating and frightening changes, an inner world of new feelings, chaotic and on occasions extreme. To the detriment of all involved, it is a world too often neglected by professionals. (Stokes 2008, p.64)

So, what does this mean for us as we think about risk and safety? The detective-like work around relationships and the attempts to identify the real reasons for a person's behaviour should not just be seen as a means to an end – a way of managing risks. The problem/behaviour triangle we introduced in Chapter 2 (Tool 3) is not just a tool to stop someone hoarding, walking off and getting lost, or lashing out at staff, critical though these things may be. It is a way of increasing people's emotional safety – of finding ways to meet their needs for safety, comfort, proximity and predictability. This reminds us that we need to take a more holistic view of safety and risk – one which reduces the risks not only of falling or getting lost but also those of feeling isolated, distressed, frustrated and afraid.

4. Decisions about 'safeguarding'

'Adult abuse' has been defined as 'A single or repeated act or lack of appropriate action, occurring within any relationship where there is an expectation of trust, which causes harm or distress to an older and/or disabled person' (Action on Elder Abuse 1995).

'Safeguarding' is the name given to the formal processes which seek to protect children or 'adults at risk of abuse or neglect'. In England, the Care Act 2014 has replaced the term 'vulnerable' adult with 'adult at risk of abuse or neglect', which is an important shift, since it challenges the idea that a person can or should be labelled as inherently 'vulnerable'. It recognises that vulnerability is contextual: all of us are vulnerable in *some* situations; and, short of being in a coma and on a life support machine, it is hard to imagine someone who is permanently vulnerable in *all* contexts.

Living in an institutional setting (including residential care and hospital) is one context in which all residents are potentially 'at risk'. That is not to suggest that abuse is endemic in these settings (there are fantastic care homes and hospital wards in which people are not only cared for well but also empowered). However, when you need care and when it would be difficult or physically impossible to leave a place, there is a built-in power imbalance between you and the staff – an imbalance which is present to a degree in all service settings.

Perpetrating abuse and neglect is often contextual too, and we know that people who would not normally dream of causing harm to another person can end up doing so if they are poorly managed and working within an institutional culture where maltreatment has become the norm.

Regardless of the language we use, the idea of seeking to 'protect' a person through a formal process sounds like the very opposite of strengths-based practice; yet adult abuse is real and it is – of course – the responsibility of everyone in the sector to identify it and respond effectively to it. So, is it possible to 'safeguard' someone in a strengths-based way? How can we protect and empower at the same time?

Many safeguarding concerns arise within older people's personal relationships – with partners, children, other family members, friends and neighbours. As at any age, an older person with high support needs may decide to continue seeing or living with someone who is abusing them, but – although (to use the language of the Mental Capacity Act) this may be an 'unwise decision' – it does not necessarily follow that they lack capacity to decide to do this. Where concerns about safeguarding have been raised, the complex, mutual and sometimes intimate nature of older people's relationships can sometimes be overlooked. For example, 'domestic violence' may be categorised instead as 'elder abuse' as couples get older (Blood 2004). The fact that those involved are or have been in an intimate relationship can be overlooked and, as a result, specialist domestic violence support may not be offered. Instead of seeking to understand the dynamics of the relationship, empower the partner(s) to leave, or to agree a safety plan, our primary response is to protect.

Making Safeguarding Personal (MSP) is a sector-led initiative, which has been running in an increasing number of English authorities since 2012 to improve safeguarding work with adults.

> MSP aims to facilitate a shift in emphasis in safeguarding from undertaking a process to a commitment to improving outcomes alongside people experiencing abuse or neglect. The key focus is on developing a real understanding of what people wish to achieve, agreeing, negotiating and recording their desired outcomes, working out with them (and their representatives or advocates if they lack capacity) how best those outcomes might be realised and then seeing, at the end, the extent to which desired outcomes have been realised. (Pike and Walsh 2015, p.7)

Like strengths-based practice, MSP seeks to work collaboratively with people to help them work out and work towards what matters most to *them*. It aims to move away from safeguarding being something which is done *to* adults, to something which is done *with* them. When asked what people do (or don't) want to happen as a result of the safeguarding process, most – perhaps unsurprisingly – say that they want to be safer; but interestingly, the next most frequent response (and one which sometimes conflicts with the first) is that they want to maintain key relationships (Pike and Walsh 2015). This reminds us how important it is to listen out for what is at stake emotionally and socially for the person – both if things stay the same and if they change. For example, an older person who suspects a friend is financially abusing them may be reluctant to challenge or report them if this is the only regular social contact they have.

Strengths-based and attachment-informed safeguarding involves:

- recognising that 'being at risk' depends on context and that we first need to understand the context better (i.e. the relationship or the institution in which the abuse is – or may be – occurring)

- focusing on what matters to a person and understanding how a relationship which includes abuse may also meet some of their emotional and social needs. If we are to enable them to become safer, a first step may be to help them find other ways of meeting these needs

- collaborating with the person to identify and achieve the outcome they want, rather than rushing in to 'rescue' them in a way which may further disempower them.

Conclusion

Figure 6.4 summarises the key differences between risk-averse practice and positive risk-taking.

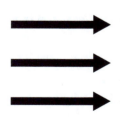

Risk aversion

'Risky/ vulnerable' people

Focus on worst case scenario

Focus on physical (someone getting hurt)

Medical problems, limitations, what's gone wrong before

A senior/ lead professional takes decision (and gets blamed if it goes wrong)

Positive risk-taking

Risk of specific situation

Consider benefits too

Also looks at social, emotional (including hidden harm/ benefits)

Strengths, resources (outside services), what's worked before

Person and supporters, range of professionals share responsibility for managing risks

Figure 6.4: Risk aversion vs positive risk-taking

What can your organisation do to support positive risk-taking?

Place greater trust in professional judgement

When Richards and colleagues (2007) present the findings of their study of social workers' decisions about risk-taking in older age, they argue that more standardised tools and guidance are needed to support such decisions. However, there seems to be a tide change in relation to this question, with writers such as Furedi (2011) and Finlayson (2015) calling for greater trust in professional judgement and in natural human relationships and conversations rather than yet more guidance. The evaluation of Making Safeguarding Personal finds that an 'increased emphasis on and confidence in professional judgement, especially around risk and decision making capacity' was a key success factor (Pike and Walsh 2015).

Build conversations with people about what matters most to them into processes and recording

If, at the very outset of our contact with a person, we start by asking them what they want from our involvement, what they want to happen, what matters most to them, this frames subsequent conversations about risk. If we see them first through 'the prism of risk', what matters becomes an afterthought. For this to happen consistently across an organisation, though, it needs to be reflected in paperwork and processes, and reinforced through induction, supervision and continuing professional development.

Clarify where professional responsibilities begin and end, through good supervision

The boundaries of our responsibilities are blurred and frequently shifting – sometimes we need to overstep our boundaries to do a good job, yet the risks – including to our own emotional wellbeing – must be clearly recognised when we do this. Good supervision encourages an honest and reflective discussion about the dilemmas here and an opportunity to reflect on the emotional impact of maintaining or overstepping a boundary.

For example, a care worker at an extra care housing scheme where the night cover had been removed due to funding cuts described to one of the authors the challenges of leaving the scheme when her shift finished late in the evening. She explained that there is no one to handover to at the end of this shift, and sometimes she goes home and cannot sleep for worrying about someone she left who was not well. She described how one night a tenant had got very drunk and she just could not walk away and leave him. She ended up staying on very late, even though this is someone who does not even receive a care package.

> It's hard because we are trying to balance their independence with keeping them safe – where does our responsibility begin and end? I suppose I could have just said the other night, 'It's the end of my shift, I'm off!' but I'm just not like that. (Conversation with author)

We discuss supervision in detail in Chapter 8.

Take a rights-based approach

In Chapter 4 on care homes, we looked at how practice can impact on residents' human rights to liberty and freedom. The Human Rights Act applies across the UK to all local authorities, health trusts/boards, housing associations, and private/charitable bodies delivering services on their behalf. The following articles may be particularly pertinent to older people:

- *article 3*: which protects us from 'degrading treatment', i.e. that which jeopardises our dignity or humiliates us

- *article 5*: which protects our right to liberty, and has been used successfully by families where a disabled family member has been deprived of their freedom, for example, by being placed in a secure setting unlawfully

- *article 8*: which protects our right to respect for private and family life – this means, for example, that public authorities should not stop you entering or living in your home (whether you own or rent it) without very good reason.

It is important to place our discussions about risk in the context of this framework. There are some good resources on human rights in health and social care produced by the Equality and Human Rights

Commission[4] and Care about Rights (a project focusing on older people run by the Scottish Human Rights Commission).[5]

Model and challenge the language used to describe older people

The language we use to describe older people and their actions can influence the way risks are perceived. When Vallelly and colleagues (2006) interviewed care staff in extra care housing schemes they described how tenants living with dementia would 'wander' and risk getting lost as a result. However, when Vallelly interviewed tenants with dementia, they explained that they were walking with purpose – for exercise and to get out of their flats and meet other people. The risks of getting disorientated may still be real, but 'enabling someone to go for a walk' (which we appreciate is important to them) is a very different conversation from trying to 'stop someone from wandering' (which we have judged to be both pointless and risky). After all, at what point in our lives do we stop 'walking' and start 'wandering'?

As we have seen in the section above about safeguarding, there is a big difference between labelling someone as 'vulnerable' or even 'at risk' and describing them as 'taking a risk'. 'Taking a risk' implies an active decision to do something risky, which someone should perhaps be talked out of; 'being at risk' suggests a permanent state of vulnerability in which someone needs to be protected. There are value judgements in comments like '*still* driving' (which suggests someone should probably have stopped by now) and '*fiercely* independent' (which implies someone should stop being so stubborn and start accepting their limitations). This is not about creating an environment of political correctness gone mad, but it is about recognising how much our language can shape and influence our conversations and our reports about risk and older people.

---

4   See the Equality and Human Rights Commission's webpage on human rights in health and social care to download a series of resources. www.equalityhumanrights. com/en/advice-and-guidance/human-rights-health-and-social-care

5   The Scottish Human Rights Commission has a number of excellent resources, including videos and training materials through its Care about Rights project, which aims to promote the human rights of older people using care and support services. www.scottishhumanrights.com/health-social-care/care-about-rights

7

End of Life and Bereavement

According to the General Medical Council, people are approaching the end of their life when they are likely to die within the next 12 months (General Medical Council 2010, p.8) However, the term is used widely, sometimes to imply the care given in the last few months, or even hours, of a person's life. In this chapter, we will consider how both attachment theory and strengths-based practice can help us to support people who are approaching the end of life, and those who are experiencing or anticipating bereavement.

The 'medicalisation' of end of life

In the past 70 years, average life expectancy in the United Kingdom has increased by around 15 years (ONS 2017a), although there is some indication that the rate of increase is beginning to slow down (Fransham and Dorling 2017). Whilst the overall trend towards increasing life expectancy is to be welcomed, Gawande (a surgeon and medical professor) has highlighted the price we have paid for this: what he describes as the 'medicalisation' of the end of our lives. In the push to prolong life, he argues, the caring professions have too often lost sight of 'the larger aims of a person's life' – 'Lacking a coherent view of how people might live successfully all the way to their very end, we have allowed our fates to be controlled by the imperatives of medicine, technology and strangers' (Gawande 2014, p.9).

This is borne out by the fact that hospital remains the most common place of death in the UK, with around a half of deaths occurring there. People who are single, widowed or divorced, and those with dementia are more likely to die in hospital; however, the medical reasons for death and the availability of community-based palliative care services also play a significant role in shaping place of death (Public Health England 2015).

Data from the National Survey of Bereaved People suggests that, from the perspective of family members, those who died at home, in hospices or in care homes were more likely than those who died in hospital:

- to have had their emotional and spiritual/religious needs met

- to have been involved in decisions about their care

- to have been afforded privacy.

Sixty-one per cent strongly agreed that the family was supported effectively during the process when the person died at home, compared with 38 per cent in hospital settings (ONS 2016b).

Although there has been a significant drive to reduce the proportion of hospital deaths in recent years, it is simplistic and unhelpful to typify hospital deaths as inherently 'bad' and home-based deaths as 'good'. As the survey confirms, many families do feel that their loved one was well supported at end of life in hospital, where access to pain relief and medical specialists can be better. Meanwhile, home deaths are not always characterised by the presence of close family and excellent support and symptom control: home 'can be the best place or the worst place to die' (Barclay and Arthur 2008, p.230). It seems that it is not so much the place but the environment which matters at the end of life; the priority should be to ensure that basic needs are met in all settings.

What do we know about what matters most to people at end of life?

More important than actual place of death is where people want to die, whether they are asked, and whether their wishes are met. The 2015 National Survey of Bereaved People (VOICES) shows that 34 per cent of people had stated where they wanted to die; of these, 82 per cent had said they wanted to die at home (ONS 2016b).

The evidence suggests that these preferences sometimes change as people's health deteriorates and, perhaps, they perceive that death is closer. However, the gap between preferred and actual place of death is still significant and the gap increases with age and with poverty (Public Health England 2015). Moreover, a significant majority of older people do not seem to have had a conversation about their preferences at all: this group are much more likely to end up dying in hospital (Howell *et al.* 2017).

An international study which explored people's priorities for treatment, care and information if faced with serious illness, found that most people would prioritise improving the quality of life for the time they have left over prolonging life regardless of its quality (Higginson, Gomes and Calanzani 2014). This seems to fit with Gawande's call to ensure that our interventions at end of life – as professionals, but also as relatives and friends – 'serve the larger aims of a person's life' (Gawande 2014, p.259).

How can attachment theory help us to support people at the end of life?

Death represents the final separation from our relatives and loved ones. The prospect of our own death, or that of someone we love, is very likely to evoke strong emotions, such as fear, anger, sadness and a need for comfort. In addition, there may be changes in the person's environment at the end of life – a move into hospital, or to a new room, for example – which may represent a move away from a familiar place or familiar people. Patterns of interaction with family and friends may alter, as people visit more, or less, and new kinds of conversations may occur. Physical deterioration may result in a person requiring more intrusive forms of support or care. All of these changes can add to increased feelings of vulnerability for the person who is approaching the end of life and for their family. As Bowlby wrote, 'Loss of a loved person is one of the most intensely painful experiences any human being can suffer. And not only is it painful to experience, but it is also painful to witness' (Bowlby 1980, p.7).

Our response to approaching death, or that of a loved one, will be influenced by the attachment strategies which we have developed across our lifespan. As outlined in Chapter 2, our attachment system is triggered in response to perceived threat or danger, in order to increase the likelihood that we will stay safe and to elicit care from attachment figures. These unconscious, self-protective mechanisms will play an important role in shaping how we respond to the prospect of our own approaching death, for example in relation to whether and how we display our emotions, and how we go about seeking support from professionals and family members.

As always, it is important to remember that human beings are complex, and our behaviour cannot be reduced to our attachment strategies; there is nothing deterministic or fixed about these processes. How we think, feel and behave when faced with the prospect of our own mortality will also be influenced by a range of external factors, including our spiritual beliefs, our family situation, where we are living, how much money we have, our race, ethnicity and culture, and our health situation and other resources. However, an increased understanding of attachment patterns can be useful to people who are involved in caring for those who are approaching the end of life. As Loetz *et al.* (2013) write, 'Attachment patterns play a crucial role in the way a patient copes with the situation of approaching death' (Loetz *et al.* 2013, p.4).

Responses to the end of life: Type A

People who use Type A strategies may approach the end of life from a cognitive standpoint: for example, they may be focused on understanding their symptoms and medical treatment and organising their financial arrangements, with little apparent display of emotions. Across their lifespan, the person has learned to inhibit their emotions, to the point where they may not be able to recognise that they are experiencing strong feelings. It's not necessarily the case that they are making a conscious decision to keep their feelings hidden – they may not even be consciously aware that they are experiencing feelings. Bowlby referred to this process as 'defensive exclusion' – information about emotions is blocked from awareness before it reaches our conscious mind.

On one level, inhibiting emotions and focusing instead on cognitive processes, like structures, plans and routines, may help a person who uses Type A strategies to feel safer and more able to cope in the face of illness and mortality. However, the risk is that the person may become isolated – if they are so cut off from their genuine feelings, how are they able to access support? People around them may truly believe that they are coping well, and may focus instead on people who are asking for help or displaying their distress. Another risk is that the unexpressed emotions may 'burst out' in the form of uncontrolled displays of anger, sadness or fear. This may be distressing for the person, and for those who are witness to this, but it may serve the purpose of releasing a build-up of emotions.

Type A: Anthea's story

Anthea lives on her own in a flat within a supported housing project. She is visited by domiciliary carers twice a day, to help with her personal care and meals. She has recently been diagnosed with inoperable cancer and has been prescribed strong painkillers. One of her carers asked her how she was coping with her diagnosis, and she said that she felt 'fine' and wished that people would stop fussing. The carer raised this a couple more times over the next fortnight. On the last occasion, Anthea snapped at her, saying that she was perfectly OK, and that it was other people who were having trouble coping with the news that she was going to die. The carer apologised and decided not to mention it again.

Responses to the end of life: Type C

People who use Type C strategies may share their emotional state with people around them in ways which can seem exaggerated. The emotions which they express may fluctuate between fear, anger and sadness. They may frequently seek support or reassurance from family or those who are caring for them, and then reject support when it is offered.

This strategy may help the person to feel safer, because their displays of emotion may succeed in eliciting care and closeness from other people, which reassures them that they are seen and heard by others. However, the risk of the strategy is that it may make it more difficult for them to focus on making plans for their end of life care or having important conversations about their wishes and hopes. Additionally, the person's expressions of need, and rejection of support when it is offered, may lead other people to feel frustrated by them and to withdraw their offers of support or to find it difficult to remain compassionate.

Type C: Connor's story

Connor was aged 79 and living in a residential care home. He was diagnosed with coronory heart disease, and his GP had advised that he was entering his last year of life. One some days, Connor experienced a lot of pain, but less so on other days. At night time, Connor began to ring his buzzer several times a night to call a member of staff, and then to tell them that he'd forgotten why he'd called them, or ask them to get him a glass of water, despite already having one within reach. During the day times, he would then complain that he was tired because staff were always bothering him during the night. The staff tried hard to be patient and to think about his underlying feelings about his chronic ill health. However, they began to lose patience and to respond less quickly to his calls. This in turn led to Connor feeling rejected, which made him feel less safe and cared for, and resulted in him using his call button more frequently.

Attachment-informed care at the end of life

Having established that our attachment strategies are very likely to influence how we respond to and cope with the end of life, we will now think about how we can use this knowledge to inform the way in which care and support are offered.

A key concept in attachment theory – as we have seen in Chapter 2 – is that of the 'secure base' provided by our attachment figures, and from which we feel sufficiently safe to be able to explore. Loetz *et al.* (2013) have argued that this secure base is essential as death approaches, that 'at the end of life, we face an unknown that frightens us and that we must confront, preferably from a secure base' (Loetz *et al.* 2013, p.12).

Loetz and colleagues argue that feeling held by a secure base at the end of life will support us to feel emotionally contained, so that we can focus on the various tasks which a 'good death' requires of us. There might be practical loose ends to tie up, reconciliations and farewells to make, but also inner 'spiritual' work to be done: reflecting on your life, its purpose and death. When the whole family is feeling secure, they are more likely to support the older person to die at home (if this is what they wish to do), calmly and surrounded by their possessions (rather than rushing them to hospital, which can be a stressful experience for all). They are also more likely to spend their time together talking, remembering and being together. A secure base might involve:

- feeling a sense of control

- inner peace and hope

- retaining a sense of identity

- being in a physical environment which meets our needs for safety, comfort and privacy

- being surrounded by people and possessions that matter to us.

Milberg and colleagues carried out a research study into the experiences of patients and family members using a palliative home care service in Sweden (Milberg *et al.* 2012). They interviewed the participants about how secure they felt during their experience of palliative home care and how confident they were that the service would support them. They found that by setting an explicit goal of providing a 'secure base', they were able to support patients and family members to feel safe, meaning that they were then able to feel more of a sense of peace and inner control. Patients were therefore able to focus on continuing some of their everyday activities, such as meeting friends and family, safe in the knowledge that the team could be relied upon to be available if needed. Family members reported feeling relieved that they were now supported by a professional team, and able to focus upon supporting their family member to be as comfortable as possible, and to remain at home until death, if that was their choice. In contrast, in the absence of a secure base, people described feeling afraid, hopeless and alone.

These points are illustrated well in this quote from a 62-year old man with prostate cancer interviewed by researchers:

> I feel a bit insecure when it is not the same staff members coming... I have good contact with the two regular carers. It is not the same with the others... The regulars sit down and talk to me...not only about me being sick...but about what I have done in my life, what I have been able to do...it is more personal. (Milberg *et al.* 2012, p.890)

Informed by this research study, it seems that we can draw some conclusions about how professional and non-professional supporters can contribute to the development of a secure base at the end of life:

- *Ensure as much continuity of carers as possible* – so that relationships can develop, based on trust, predictability, reliability and familiarity.

- *Communicate as part of a wider team* – including care workers, nurses, family members, doctors, so that information is shared in a consistent way.

- *Use familiar things to reduce the perception of threat* – radio, TV, music, smells, the feel of a soft blanket, religious or symbolic items can all offer soothing and familiarity.

- *Support people to do things for themselves* – to promote the sense of continuing to be a person of worth.

- *Invite family members to participate in the care* – to the degree that they feel comfortable, and with appropriate information and support, so that they do not feel alone with the responsibility.

- *Encourage connections with family, friends, pets* – most people find it soothing and comforting to be close to their attachment figures at the end of life.

- *Develop a plan together in advance of a crisis/the final days* – there is more on this in the section on advance planning below.

- *Recognise achievements and history* – it is as important as ever for the person who is approaching death, and for their loved ones, to continue to be seen and heard as individuals, yourself' and to feel that they have a valuable contribution to make.

Focusing on the promotion of a secure base at the end of life can support both individuals and their families to retain a sense of control, even in uncertain and painful moments. If professional supporters make it their goal to offer soothing and comfort in ways which are predictable and attuned, it will enable individuals and their loved ones to feel secure, even in the face of approaching death.

Supporting families and individuals through bereavement: an attachment-informed approach

John Bowlby, the originator of attachment theory, considered grief to be a natural feature of the attachment system, the function of which was to maintain closeness between an individual and their attachment figures (Bowlby 1980). Around the world, different cultures have developed a wide range of patterns and rituals which help people to express their grief. These rituals may differ, but what they share in common is a recognition of the universal pain caused by the loss of a loved one. A person's experience of loss and grief will be influenced by many different factors, including their age and life stage, the nature of their relationship with the person who has died, the nature of the circumstances surrounding the death, practical issues such as the impact of the death upon their financial position and housing situation, their support network, and their spiritual or religious beliefs (Cassidy and Shaver 2008). In addition, paying attention to people's self-protective attachment strategies may help us towards an increased understanding of their emotional reactions, and therefore enable us to offer appropriate support through bereavement and the loss of a loved one.

Bowlby's stages of grief

In his main writings about grief and loss, Bowlby described the stages of grief which he believed applied to adults who have experienced the death of an attachment figure (Bowlby 1980). The first phase is protest, characterised by intense yearning, and searching for the person who has died. When these efforts do not result in a reunion with the loved one, the grieving person may then be overwhelmed by despair and hopelessness, which marks the second stage. Bowlby initially called the third and final stage 'detachment' but later renamed it 'reorganisation'. This stage involves the bereaved person making adjustments to the way they think about themselves, and their new role in life, and considering how life might be without their loved one. This stage may involve adapting to the loss, whilst continuing to feel an emotional connection with the deceased person. Bowlby was clear in his writings that it is not necessary to completely sever the emotional ties with the deceased person in order to build a new life; human beings are capable of holding the relationship with the lost loved one in mind whilst at the same time adjusting to the new situation. It was not Bowlby's intention to suggest that every bereaved person goes through these stages in a set order; he recognised that people will go through the stages in different ways, and in different time frames, depending on their unique traits and circumstances.

An attachment-informed perspective on the grieving process

Bowlby and other writers who have been influenced by his work (Stroebe and Schut 2010) have proposed that people with a secure attachment style, Type B, will be more likely to experience a healthy grieving process – they will experience all the emotions of sadness, loss and yearning but will not be overwhelmed by them. People who use Type A attachment styles are likely to inhibit their feelings of sadness and loss, and display absent or delayed grief. Their buried emotions may burst out from time to time under particular stress but this will appear out of character. Or, they may suffer physical symptoms, such as headaches, pains, digestive problems, and so on, which can be understood, through an attachment-informed lens, as the body's way of reminding them about the unexpressed emotion. People who use Type C attachment styles are likely to display their whole range of emotions and appear preoccupied by the loss. This is in line with the notion that Type A strategies function by inhibiting emotion and Type C by exaggerating or hyper-activating the display of emotion. Researchers have found some support for this, although it is complicated by the number of different factors which can influence how a person experiences loss of a loved one (Stroebe, Schut and Boerner 2010).

The dual process model

Stroebe and Schut (Stroebe and Schut 1999) have outlined a model of coping with bereavement called the dual process model, which has many links to attachment theory. They identify two themes which a bereaved person has to deal with at the same time: loss-oriented stressors and restoration-oriented stressors. Loss-oriented stressors are to do with processing the loss of the loved one, including all the different stages of grief, and coming to terms with the events surrounding the death. Restoration-orientated stressors include all the changes which come about as a result of the death, such as changes in self-identity (e.g. from 'husband' to 'widower'), changes in financial situation and all the differences involved in getting used to everyday life without the loved one. They suggest that 'oscillating' or fluctuating between these two dimensions is a normal part of grieving – at any given point in time, a person will be focusing on either loss-oriented stressors or restoration-orientated stressors; both are important, but they cannot both be paid attention to at the same time. They argue that over time, there is usually a shift away from themes of loss and towards restoration, as experiencing positive emotions and finding meaning in a new way of life are a key part of coping well with bereavement. In a later paper, they write that:

> adaptation to bereavement is a matter of slowly and painfully exploring and discovering what has been lost and what remains: what must be avoided or relinquished versus what can be retained, created and built on. (Stroebe, Schut and Stroebe 2005, p.52)

Stroebe and colleagues argue that a person with a Type B attachment style would be likely to fluctuate, or oscillate, between loss- and restoration-orientated stressors. They would experience the intense emotions associated with grief, but over time they would manage to retain happy memories of the deceased person as well as missing them. They would both miss aspects of their previous life while also building a new life and getting used to new roles and activities.

People with a Type A attachment strategy would be more likely to inhibit their emotions, show little grief or sadness and focus instead on tasks associated with restoration, such as the daily activities of their new life. This could be seen as them paying more attention to restoration tasks than to loss-orientated stressors. They may find that they have somatic symptoms – physical symptoms to do with their unexpressed emotions, such as headaches and pains. They may benefit from being given permission, in a respectful and sensitive way, to express their feelings.

People with a Type C attachment strategy would be more likely to show intense grief and a level of preoccupation with thoughts of the deceased person. They may appear 'stuck' in this emotional state and pay little attention to building a new life. This could be seen as them paying more attention to loss-orientated stressors than to restoration tasks. They may benefit from being encouraged to build strategies for everyday living in their post-loss world.

Any model of grief is likely to involve simplifications and generalisations, as each loss is unique and each grieving process is individual and complex. It must be remembered that the context of the loss will play an important part; if the death was unexpected or traumatic, the impact can be expected to be magnified. The grief process will also be impacted by the social situation of the individual, and the support they can gain from relationships with the people around them. It is also unrealistic to expect people to exactly fit any model; the usefulness of such models is in helping us to organise our thinking and to guide our responses. The underpinning message of this model is that both loss-orientated and restoration-orientated work are important in order for a person to come to terms with the death of a loved one.

A strengths-based approach to end of life care

End of life where, for many, physical strength and energy are draining away and high levels of care are needed, can feel like an unlikely location for strengths-based practice. However, if we are to focus upon the quality of life and self-determination until the end and support the whole family at this profoundly challenging time, we will need – more than ever – to draw on those key principles: collaborating, nurturing relationships and promoting positive risk-taking from a position of hope.

If we are to counterbalance the medical approach to end of life, we need to support emotional resilience, create space for spiritual reflection and focus on people's relationships. This is not to downplay people's physical needs – maintaining comfort, offering hydration and nutrition and relieving pain form the cornerstone on which good end of life care must be built.

Practical ways of supporting a strengths-based approach at the end of life

Helping individuals and families to plan for a 'good death'

In a study in Melbourne, Australia, a group of patients aged over 80 were offered advance planning with a trained facilitator at the point of discharge from hospital. This involved assisting patients and their families to reflect on the patient's goals, values and beliefs, and to discuss and document their future choices about healthcare. Patients were encouraged to involve their families in these conversations and to appoint people who would speak for them if they no longer had capacity to do so.

Patients who received this service welcomed it and felt that it had increased their sense of control and, crucially, strengthened their relationships. Where family members were interviewed following the death of their loved one, those who had been involved in advance planning had fewer symptoms of post-traumatic stress, depression and anxiety than those who had not (Detering *et al.* 2010).

Quotes from this evaluation by those who had received advance planning included:

> No one has asked me before what I would want when I get really sick. It was really great. It made me feel relieved

> We had a clear plan so could just relax and enjoy time with dad

> We felt really comfortable making decisions because we had discussed it with him

By contrast, quotes from those who had not received advance planning included:

> They didn't speak to me and kept discussing everything with my family. I think they thought I was too old and couldn't understand

> He knew he was dying, and it was very hard for him. We should have talked with him about it

> They wouldn't let her go. They kept doing tests and things she would not have wanted

There are a number of advance care planning 'tools' and checklists, yet as Borgstrom has pointed out, building these tools into our procedures can be counterproductive by turning what needs to be a relational and very personal conversation into yet another task to be ticked off the list.

Here are some questions which can be used to kick-start or prompt advance planning, ideally between the person and their family:

- In the event that you became too sick to speak for yourself, who would you want to speak for you?

- Have you spoken to that person about what you would want?

Further prompts might include: Have you talked with them about where you would want to be as the end of your life approaches? Who you would like to be there, if possible? Any treatments you would/would not wish to receive? Financial, legal and funeral arrangements following your death? Have you recorded any of this formally or created anything legally binding, like a Power of Attorney? Would you like to share these plans with carers and healthcare staff, so that we would be clear about who to contact and what to do?

Identifying goals, priorities and preferences

Strengths-based practice calls us, not only to help families plan for death but also to support them to maximise quality of life right up to end of life. As Cecily Saunders, the founder of the hospice movement, said, 'You matter because you are, and you matter to the last moment of your life. We will do all we can not only to help you die peacefully, but to help you live until you die.'

A key message here from research and practice is that often seemingly little things can make a huge difference to quality of life.

Jane's story

Jane was admitted to hospital following a stroke at the age of 82. She was unconscious for several days, during which time her daughter and grandchildren visited her. Her daughter brought Jane's radio from her home and asked the hospital staff to have it playing by her bedside, tuned to Radio 4. During one visit, her grandson noticed that the staff were turning the radio off at 10pm, even though she was in a private room so it wasn't disturbing anyone else. He asked why and was told that the assumption was being made that she would have turned the radio off and gone to bed at about that time. He was able to tell the hospital staff that, for many years, his grandmother had been in the habit of going to bed at 3am and sleeping until noon! They then agreed to leave the radio playing overnight. Jane died without ever fully regaining consciousness, but her daughter and grandchildren gained great comfort from knowing that she had her beloved radio playing through the night.

Consider spiritual or religious needs

Health and social care services are often offered in a context which is secular and non-religious. However, as Saleeby (2005) writes, this may have a particular impact upon older people. As a group, a much higher proportion of older people have a religious faith than younger people. Additionally, for people approaching the end of life, their reflections on life's religious or spiritual dimensions may become greater.

But what does 'spiritual care' mean in a modern context? Allen (2010) defines spiritual care as:

> Primarily to be concerned with searching for an answer to the question: 'In my current state of health, just who am I?' Buried in this apparently simple question lie notions of identity, some awareness of a relationship with God or a life force, the context of one's own and other people's environments, and a feeling that life ought to have both meaning and purpose. (Allen 2010, p.7)

The National Council for Palliative Care (n.d.) conducted a study which involved sending notebooks to carers, for them to interview friends and family on the theme of, 'What does spiritual support mean to you?' The findings remind us that each individual's understanding of the meaning of 'spiritual support' will be unique to them and will reflect their experiences, beliefs and values.

> To have my beliefs listened to, respected and acted on.

> As an agnostic/atheist, I guess I would define it as anything in the emotional or psychological arena – emotional support is a form of spiritual support.

> For me, it's anything that makes the person feel themselves – whatever gives them meaning. Therefore, it should encompass anything that may be associated with the things that give an individual person meaning or a feeling of purpose.

As a Hindu, the word 'spiritual' carries a number of meanings for me. I see that very much as care for my soul, care for reincarnation, care for my spirit, not my body, meditation, calm reflection, inspirational verse, devotional verse and song.

My faith is important, and I would hope that someone would pray with and for me.

I think for me it's about care focused on the issues relating to an individual's sense of purpose and their own significance – basically, care of their spirit.

I would not want to have a minister around if I were dying. My mother didn't either, but the hospice assumed that she did. If a person does have a faith, then their beliefs should be taken into consideration.

These responses serve to remind us that 'spirituality' is an important part of end of life care, but that it means very different things to different people.

Using attachment- and strengths-based approaches to support people with dementia at the end of life

In England and Wales in 2016, dementia was the most common cause of death for women, and the second most common cause of death for men, with 15.4 per cent of women and 8 per cent of men dying due to dementia (ONS 2016a).

The World Health Organization expects that deaths due to dementia will rise by over 40 per cent from 2015 to 2040, so the care of people with dementia at the end of life is an area of increasing prominence (World Health Organization 2018).

People with advanced dementia may have a range of medical symptoms and physical needs as they approach the end of life, including pain, pressure sores, eating problems, lack of mobility and vulnerability to infections due to a compromised immune system. They may also be less likely than people without dementia to be able to communicate their needs and wishes regarding end of life care at the time when decisions need to be taken, and less able to communicate their physical and emotional needs.

Dementia erodes both memory and communication, and has a significant impact upon the person's ability to express their needs and wishes at the end of life. Tibbs argues that if you can no longer remember your own story you are 'living in a place which undermines our very humanity' (Allen 2010, p.37). We become dependent on others to hold on to our story for us, which 'depends on other people caring enough about us and having enough time and skill to tell our own story back to us' (p.37). We also depend on others having the time, knowledge and motivation to 'decode our fractured and fragmented language' (p.37).

Tibb (Allen 2010) argues that this is most likely to happen in a context where:

- there is love and outstanding kindness well beyond legal requirements

- the atmosphere is accepting and non-punishing of their limitations

- there is a clear value system – where right and wrong are clear and where questions of meaning (which are of great interest to people reaching end of life) are on the agenda.

From a strengths-based perspective, she concludes that:

> People with dementia need us to acknowledge and encourage their attempts to seek meaning as they try to make sense of their experiences. It is clear that they are making strenuous efforts to sustain their own well-being, and these need to be supported. (Allen 2010, p.39)

The majority of deaths of people with dementia occur in settings such as hospitals and care homes (Lawrence *et al.* 2011). However, there is evidence that staff involved in the care of people with dementia may not always recognise the signs that a person is approaching death. For example, in one study, staff in a nursing home were asked to indicate whether they thought that newly admitted people had a life expectancy of less than six months. The staff rated only 1.1 per cent of people as likely to die within that time frame; however, 71 per cent of them did (Mitchell, Kiely and Hamel 2004). Therefore, people with dementia who are approaching the end of life may not receive the support they require because they are viewed as 'having dementia' rather than 'approaching the end of life'.

Lawrence and colleagues (2011) carried out a study which involved interviewing professionals and bereaved family carers about the quality of life of their relative with dementia in the last six months of their life. One finding was that people with dementia who died in general hospital wards often experienced a poor quality of care, without enough assistance with eating, drinking, pain management and personal care. Given that only a small proportion of people with dementia die at home, this highlights the need for improved care in hospital settings. The study found that the elements of good end of life care for people with dementia were routinely identified by family members, but not routinely provided.

Using dementia expertise to support meeting physical care needs

When staff lacked knowledge about dementia care, they often failed to meet basic physical care needs, such as managing pain and making sure that the individual's needs for food, fluid and personal hygiene were met. Family carers often expressed concern that staff didn't know the individuals well enough to recognise facial and bodily signs that they were distressed or in physical discomfort.

Going beyond task-focused care

Care staff all recognised how important it is to offer holistic care at the end of life, including meeting physical, social, cultural and emotional needs. However, there was little evidence that this was offered in a consistent way. Staff often spoke of care being reduced to a series of basic tasks, mostly focused on physical needs. Family members spoke with gratitude about the occasions when they felt that a staff member had empathised with their relative or showed them warmth – for example, by talking to them to help soothe them during a wash or by knowing them well enough to dress them how they would have wished to have been dressed.

Prioritising planning and communication

Both relatives and professionals lacked knowledge about undertaking advance planning at a point in time when the person with dementia could contribute as fully as possible to the process. The issue of whether a person with dementia should be transferred to hospital during the final stages of their life proved a particularly difficult decision for family carers to be involved in. The study found that family members often felt that transfers to hospital were inappropriate and unsettling for their relative, but felt unable to challenge the process. Professionals noted that there was often an unwillingness to withdraw active treatment in the absence of explicit advance planning.

As the researchers concluded, 'If end of life care does not take into account the unique circumstances and needs of people with dementia, it is likely to fail them' (Lawrence *et al.* 2011, p.420).

Supporting families through bereavement

The death of a family member can lead to many painful or unresolved issues being raised within a family. These issues may be directly related to the death of the loved one, or there may be long-standing disagreements and tensions which resurface. For example, there may be conflicts about who makes decisions about end of life care — there could be differences of opinion about life-extending treatment, which can be more complex if the person who is approaching death is unable to communicate their wishes. Some family members may feel that they are shouldering more of the care responsibilities than others and may feel resentful. Family members who are only able to visit the dying person infrequently may feel guilty. Some family members may wish to speak about what's happening, but others may prefer to avoid difficult conversations. Long buried conflicts about money, or family loyalties, may be reignited. There may be painful secrets within a family, which some people may fear will be revealed. Therefore, most families will experience the end of life period as characterised by intense emotions and potential conflicts. Those supporting families will need to be prepared to offer time and patience, and to support open communication and the sharing of information.

Zaider and Kissane have reviewed the research on family resilience in palliative care (Zaider and Kissane 2007). 'Resilient families' are able to maintain their integrity during the crisis and 'bounce back' through successful adaptation. The key features of such families include:

- *cohesiveness or 'togetherness'*: the family's ability to work together as a team, their inclination to spend time together and to provide each other with mutual support

- *conflict management*: the presence of conflict is not in itself a negative, provided the family is cohesive and can resolve these conflicts

- *communication and expressiveness*: readily sharing feelings and thoughts with each other.

Where families exhibit these strengths, professionals can serve them best by 'affirming their strengths and reinforcing their successful teamwork' (Zaider and Kissane 2007, p.75) as they prepare for and come to terms with the death of their loved one. However, where families are fractured, distressed and have difficulty working together, they may need a lot of support to plan palliative care and cope with their bereavement.

Where the existing resilience of families is low, there is some evidence to suggest that a course of family-focused grief therapy (typically between four and eight sessions) can help to reduce distress and depression during palliative care and bereavement (Kissane *et al.* 2003). The key principles of this approach include:

- bringing the family together for routine meetings, which initiates a sense of teamwork (or 'cohesiveness')

- inviting the family to share and reconstruct their story, the story of their loved one's illness and of how their family has experienced and dealt with loss over the generations

- asking the members of the family during these meetings together to voice their fears, expectations and wishes and to express their grief, which encourages expressiveness and communication.

This will not be necessary for the majority of families, but it may be a useful approach with families who do not have the interpersonal resources to resolve these issues between themselves, or for whom the death has raised complex issues.

Considering the needs of staff members

An approach to end of life care which embodies both strengths-based practice and attachment-based practice must include paying attention to the practical and emotional needs of staff. Medical staff, domiciliary carers, care home staff and staff in older people's housing schemes all need to feel properly equipped to support people and their families at the end of life if they are to be able to offer consistent and attuned support and care. If staff and carers feel that their strong emotions of anger, sadness, fear or a need for comfort are activated in the course of their work, then they need to be able to rely on their professional support networks, or the quality of care will suffer. Themes covered should include factual information about symptom management, advance planning and legal issues, alongside more interpersonal themes such as communication skills, values and ethics, and personal support. In addition, it is important that the culture of each organisation promotes discussion about the issues raised by providing end of life care. The theme of attachment and strengths-based supervision and leadership is returned to in Chapter 8.

Resources

- NICE published guidelines in December 2015, *Care of Dying Adults in the Last Days of Life* (www.nice.org.uk/guidance/ng31), which includes references to many sources of support and training, including an e-learning package from e-learning from Healthcare, in association with the Association for Palliative Medicine (www.e-lfh.org.uk/programmes/end-of-life-care).

- The Social Care Institute for Excellence has good practice examples of staff training and support, with other later research findings available elsewhere on their website (www.scie.org.uk/publications/guides/guide48/practiceexamples/index.asp).

- Death Cafe is an international organisation, which aims to promote community conversations about death. They aim to hold events where people have guided conversations about death and dying, in a safe, informal setting, always accompanied by cake. It is a social franchise, so anyone can download a 'how to' guide, and organise a Death Cafe if they sign up to the organisation's aims (http://deathcafe.com).

8

Reflective Supervision, Staff Wellbeing, and Strengths-Based Leadership

Introduction

One of the implications of the UK's ageing population is that the demand for long-term care is increasing rapidly, along with the demand for people to work in this labour-intensive sector. Skills for Care estimated that over two million people were employed in the delivery of long-term care in the UK, split across the domiciliary (49%), residential (38%) and day/community (13%) sectors (Skills for Care 2015). Eighty-five per cent of the workforce is female. The provision of care to older adults is heavily reliant on the human contribution of the workforce, offering emotional as well as practical support and building relationships with the people they are caring for.

Morrison writes about the impact of bureaucracy and budget cuts upon the care sector. He argues that if we strip away all of the human processes from an organisation, we remove fundamental opportunities for people to interact authentically and are left with a dehumanised workplace (Baim and Morrison 2011). For example, many domiciliary carers speak of their frustration at having very short time slots during which they have a set series of tasks to complete (e.g. check medication, prepare a quick meal, help a person to bathe or get dressed). If the focus is heavily weighted towards tasks and processes, the person at the heart of the service can be overlooked, and the human relationship can be undervalued (UK Homecare Association 2012).

In this chapter, we will explore the way in which both individual care workers, and those who lead the organisations in which they work, have shared and mutual responsibilities to contribute to healthy workplaces and better outcomes for the people who are being cared for. We will begin by examining the nature of employment within the long-term care sector.

Low pay in the care sector

Shereen Hussein completed an analysis of the long-term care sector in the UK (Hussein 2017), based upon national workforce pay data and interviews with workers and other stakeholders. She found that it is common practice to pay workers at the level of the National Minimum Wage. However, her analysis found that 10–13 per cent workers receive an hourly pay rate which is below the national minimum wage, once unpaid travel time and unpaid breaks are taken into account. She also found that many workers were finding it difficult or very difficult to manage their finances, were living in households with a low income, and were claiming some form of welfare benefit to 'top up' their wages.

Hussein identified three themes which contribute to continued low rates of pay in the care sector:

1. *Care work is seen as a vocation.* Many employers justified low rates of pay by describing care work as a vocation and as a form of employment which offers many non-monetary rewards, which are seen to 'compensate' for the low wages. Some carers seemed to agree with this, stating during interviews with the researchers that they accepted that low wages were part of the landscape of the care sector and that they valued the non-monetary aspects of their work, such as the relationships they formed with the people they care for and feeling that they were making a positive contribution to society.

2. *Age discrimination within society.* Discrimination towards older people, who are often portrayed as vulnerable and weak, can also affect those who work with and for them. This can impact upon the value placed by society upon the work done by carers.

3. *Marketisation and outsourcing.* Care providers, both public and private, are operating within an increasingly tight funding structure. Staffing represents the largest cost of providing care, and so wages and employment conditions come under pressure when agencies are looking to cut costs.

Hussein concludes that it is very important to address the issue of low pay and employment conditions in order to protect the rights and welfare of workers, and to continue to be able to attract enough workers to this vital sector. Influencing to improve pay in the sector is essential. However, it is also important to consider wider working conditions.

The nature of roles in the care sector

Most roles in the care sector involve a variety of tasks and responsibilities. These include the practical tasks associated with meeting the physical care needs of the people being cared for, such as assisting with personal hygiene requirements, dressing, feeding, and supporting physical health and wellbeing. There will also be administrative tasks connected with the care home or agency, such as filling in care plans, other forms and records, or tasks associated with the professional training or specialism of the individual worker, such as encouraging mobility, carrying out assessments and dispensing medication. Additionally, all roles involving the provision of care require the 'softer' skills of building rapport and forming relationships with people and their families.

Manthorpe and colleagues asked a group of people who received care services and their families what kinds of qualities they most valued in the people who were employed to provide care (Manthorpe *et al.* 2017). All of the people who took part in the study appreciated an approach which was based on a recognition of 'shared humanity' and a sense of moral integrity. Qualities which were valued included being respectful, kind, compassionate, warm and genuine. A strong work ethic and trustworthiness were also valued, perhaps because they are connected with the person turning up on time (which is especially relevant in domiciliary care environments) and behaving with honesty. Friendliness was identified as particularly important to people who lived alone and who may have had few social contacts other than the care worker. However, this was not seen as a quality which was characteristic of all carers.

For example, one woman who participated in the study indicated that she felt more connected to some carers than to others.

'I think one of the things really is that usually you feel as if you can talk to them, they understand. So they seem to be that type of person, as a rule that you can talk to. You can't talk to everyone, can you?' (Manthorpe *et al.* 2017, p.88).

Most people believed that, whilst it was important for the care workers to have some knowledge about specific issues, such as dementia or other illnesses associated with older age, it was at least equally important that the person had human qualities of respect and compassion for the people they were working with. There was also a sense that these qualities are innate, rather than teachable through training.

The point was emphasised by one man, whose wife had dementia. 'I think there should be a tremendously high standard of training… to understand the nature of Alzheimer's and dementia…for instance somebody could be kicking off and having a screaming match and they say, "Oh, she's awful," but it's the illness… You need that as well as the general compassion. They're talking about nursing now and teaching them compassion. You can't teach anyone compassion, they've got to have it haven't they?' (Manthorpe *et al.* 2017, p.87)

This study suggests that 'softer skills' associated with relationship building, such as respect and friendliness, are valued by those who receive care and their families, at least as much as being proficient at the tasks involved in the work. This has important implications for the ways in which staff working in care environments are supported, and how organisations which provide care are managed and led.

Emotional labour, relationship-based practice and 'burnout'

Working in an organisation which offers care to older people in a domiciliary or residential setting can offer an employee a sense of achievement and fulfilment, and an opportunity to make an important contribution. However, these roles are likely to present challenges as well as rewards. Those challenges may include:

- working alongside people who are approaching the end of life

- bearing witness to physical and cognitive decline, and eventually death

- working with families who are grieving or in conflict

- working with people who are distressed, whose behaviour can be difficult to understand

- managing conflict within teams and organisations.

We have seen above that a worker's ability to use their 'soft skills' in forming relationships is rated by people receiving care and their families as being just as important as their practical skills. A worker's capacity to form compassionate working relationships is affected by their own sense of wellbeing and their capacity to cope with the practical and emotional stresses of the workplace.

The term 'burnout' is used to describe a set of responses to emotional stresses at work. A model has been developed by Maslach, Jackson and Leiter (1996), which identifies three aspects of burnout:

- feelings of emotional exhaustion and reduced emotional capacity to cope with work stresses

- depersonalisation – an increase in negative thoughts and feelings about the people who are being cared for

- a reduced sense of achievement and negative evaluation of oneself.

The consequences of burnout can include negative impacts on the wellbeing of staff, low morale and a reduction in the quality of care provided. It is likely that levels of burnout may influence the ability of staff who are working with older people to form compassionate relationships with them. One study found that, among staff working with older people, those with higher levels of burnout were more likely to respond angrily to residents who were displaying aggressive behaviour (Macpherson et al. 1994). This may, in turn, lead to the residents feeling less secure and therefore more vulnerable to emotional outbursts. We can see that it is very important, for the welfare of both staff and those being cared for, that emotional wellbeing is paid attention to.

Miesen (2006) has studied the relevance of attachment theory and relationship-based practice to working with people with dementia. People with dementia may experience strong feelings of loss, fear and confusion, and a sense of being alone. This may lead them to engage in attachment behaviours, such as calling out for people who are not present, following staff and displaying strong emotions, in an attempt to regain a sense of safety and comfort. Miesen has suggested that the way in which professional caregivers respond to the attachment-seeking behaviours of people with dementia is likely to have a significant impact upon the quality of their working relationships and their ability to offer attuned care. This means that supporting staff to remain emotionally balanced is likely to have a positive impact upon the wellbeing of both staff and those receiving care.

Tony Morrison, writing about social work, focused upon the importance of emotional intelligence in shaping a worker's ability to form working relationships (Morrison 2007). He believed that the worker's capacity to be aware of their emotional responses to their work has an important impact upon:

- their ability to 'tune in' to the people they are working with, through accurate listening and paying attention to non-verbal communication

- their capacity to empathise with others and be aware of the impact of challenging work upon themselves.

Supporting staff to form positive working relationships with the people they are caring for is complex and involves both individual and organisational processes.

Supporting relationships at an organisational level

The challenges of working in relationship-based ways are intensified if a person's job role is carried out in a working environment which is characterised by low wages, long hours, hard physical work and low levels of autonomy, as is the case in many roles in the care sector. High-profile abuses of power within care settings, which have involved staff behaving physically and emotionally abusively towards people who they were employed to care for, are sometimes thought of as being due to 'a few bad apples' within a staff team (Equality and Human Rights Commission 2011; The Mid Staffordshire NHS Foundation Trust 2013). It may seem superficially appealing to blame individuals for these abuses of power, as the solutions seem very straightforward – remove the abusive individuals and the problem is solved. However, this is too simplistic; of course, there are some individuals whose value base and beliefs make them unsuited to care work, but it is the responsibility of an organisation to create an environment where compassion and emotional intelligence are promoted and valued.

Killett and her colleagues carried out interviews and observations in 11 UK care homes (including both residential homes and nursing homes) in order to investigate the ways in which the working culture in different care homes affected the ways in which individual care workers coped with the demands of their jobs (Killett *et al.* 2016). They found that although all but one of the homes had a document which outlined the person-centred values of the organisation, this did not automatically translate into the provision of person-centred care. For care to be of a consistently high standard, it was important that staff at all levels found ways of dealing with the everyday demands and conflicts of their role in ways which brought these values to life. For example, in one care home, the manager noticed that the staff were focusing upon getting all the residents up and the beds made by 12 noon, at the expense of paying individual attention to the needs and preferences of the residents. The manager spoke with the staff and encouraged them to spend time meeting the needs of individuals rather than getting through a list of jobs which needed to be done, explaining that outstanding tasks could be handed over to other staff when they came on shift. The manager said, 'think of the person, not that you've got to wash them…' (Killett *et al.* 2016, p.174).

The researchers found that if, as in this example, managers became directly involved in supporting staff to deal with the conflicts and pressures of their roles, then person-centred ways of engaging with residents could be promoted, and in this way, policy documents which described the values of the organisation could be brought to life. In homes where this was the case, researchers observed behaviours such as managers stepping in to cover tasks if the team were short-staffed, thinking creatively about how care plans could be completed in a way which was more time-efficient and considering how to support family members better in order to enable positive risks to be taken.

However, if managers and the wider organisation did not step in, groups of workers found their own solutions to the conflicts which they faced, which often involved a lack of emotional engagement with the residents and a reliance on rigid routines. If these behaviours were not challenged, then they became part of the fabric of the home and reinforced unconscious assumptions about the workforce's inability to challenge poor practice, or to make a positive difference to the welfare of the residents.

The researchers concluded that person-centred values become translated into person-centred practice only when organisational culture promotes these values through everyday problem solving. Managers need to support staff to find solutions which fit with person-centred values, and staff need to communicate with each other and their managers about their everyday problems and challenges. In this way, a culture which promotes reflection and positive practice can be supported.

Hawkins and colleagues carried out a study involving detailed observations and interviews in two care homes, with a particular focus upon how the staff promoted physical activity among residents (Hawkins *et al.* 2017). They were interested to see how the interactions between the physical environment (how space is used in the home), the social relationships between staff, families and residents, the needs of individuals, and the organisational aspects of the home influenced the home's ability to support the physical mobility of residents. The researchers called one home Hebble House and the other Bourneville (neither of which is the real name of the home), and they noticed some very significant differences between the ways in which routines were managed in each home.

In Hebble House, residents were encouraged by care staff to move independently where possible, even if that took longer than pushing them in a wheelchair. The staff regularly shared their observations about the changes in individuals' physical capacities, and revised care plans accordingly. Leisure activities were promoted and workers were present in the lounges, encouraging residents to be active, such as by taking a walk in the grounds or contributing to the running of the home by helping with tasks. In Bournville House, staff tended to either push residents in wheelchairs or observe them walking from a distance, while undertaking other tasks. In the times between meals, many residents sat in the lounges, where staff tended to discourage independent movement in case of falls. Those residents who were able to move about independently were not prevented from doing so, but there was little encouragement or support available. In Bournville House, the researchers observed that residents were generally sedentary, with short bursts of movement focused on daily routines around personal care and mealtimes.

Both of the care homes shared broadly similar organisational values and aims; however, these were translated into practice very differently. Hawkins and her colleagues concluded that one of the factors which contributed to this difference was that the manager at Hebble House was very active in walking around the home and intervening in practical ways to both support and challenge staff to deliver care which was focused upon promoting mobility. There was an acceptance that it takes time to support an individual to do something for themselves, rather than doing it for them, and teams were encouraged, in team meetings, to reflect upon the conflicts of their role and to problem solve.

In contrast, the managers at Bournville House were less able to support their staff to translate values into concrete practice. Staff meetings were spent discussing new residents, or changes to routines and practices, rather than in reflective problem solving. Managers at Hebble House invested in training for their staff, and reinforced this through immediate feedback, both positive and negative, in response to practice they observed in the home. This enabled the staff to feel confident in taking small positive risks and choosing to spend time engaging with an individual rather than taking a quicker or more straightforward option, and in that way, it helped them to put values into action. The manager at Bournville House also spent time on the floor of the home, but she saw her role as offering the residents her attention in a way which staff members were unable to because they were busy with routine tasks.

These two studies, by Killett and Hawkins, emphasise the importance of managers and staff working together in practical ways to bring person-centred values to life in ways that improve the quality of life of the residents. Supporting staff, through collaborative problem solving and through giving immediate feedback, was seen in both studies to make an important contribution to the culture and daily practices of the home in ways which seem likely to improve the quality of life of the residents. What these studies also emphasise is the importance of a positive organisational culture in supporting staff members to truly engage with residents by forming positive working relationships with them.

Sometimes our organisational policies and procedures actually create barriers to relationship-based work. The DEEP project (Developing evidence-enriched practice in health and social care with older people) (Andrews *et al.* 2015) included work to revise an organisation's professional boundaries policy, which provides guidance to staff on how they should relate to service users (Andrews *et al.* 2015). Both those delivering and receiving services were frustrated by the fact that existing policies often:

- prevented older people making a contribution (like making a worker a cup of tea or letting them offer some emotional support)

- got in the way of building a genuine two-way relationship (like a worker bringing in their children and pets, or at least photos of them, or giving or receiving small gifts)

- meant that if workers wanted to go out of their way in their own time to support an older person to do the things they want to do, they would end up doing this 'behind the service's back' (this might include bringing an older person along to sell some of their belongings at a car boot sale, or taking them to visit a friend or special place on their day off).

Service users, their families, frontline workers and managers were all involved in deciding how the revised policy should support the things which older people said they valued and enable staff to do simple acts of human kindness, whilst ensuring a level of safety and accountability which was acceptable to all stakeholders.

Impact of financial cuts upon the provision of care

Burns, Hyde and Killett (2016) did a study looking at the response to cost pressures in 12 UK care homes. All of the homes introduced similar money-saving measures, mostly focused on the cost of staff, such as making shifts longer, cutting numbers of staff, removing pay for breaks and cutting other staff benefits. Whilst these changes meant that workers bore the brunt of the cuts at every care home which was studied, there were important differences in the ways in which the cuts affected the *quality* of care offered at different homes. In some homes, staff adopted what the researchers called 'work-arounds', such as working through breaks, swapping shifts when staff needed time off for personal reasons and being flexible about role boundaries. This meant that the residents were insulated from the impact of the cuts and the quality of care was largely maintained through the efforts of the staff. At homes where quality of care fell as a result of the cutbacks, the researchers noticed that the focus of care shifted towards meeting the residents' physical needs; care was perceived as a series of physical tasks.

The researchers concluded that cost pressures can impact upon the dimensions of care which matter most to the quality of care received by residents – the social and relational aspects. However, it is encouraging that they found that teams of staff could work together in flexible ways to ensure that residents were protected from the worst impacts of the cuts. This study also supports the view that how the organisation is run on a daily basis, and the way the staff team at all levels put their values into practice, will have a considerable impact on the welfare of the residents.

Supporting relationships at a personal level: attachment theory and wellbeing

As outlined above, jobs which involve caring for older people can offer the potential for a great deal of professional satisfaction and reward, but also present a wide range of practical and emotional challenges. Working alongside people who may be facing physical illness, cognitive decline and the end of life is likely to evoke strong emotions in staff members. If the organisational culture does not support relationship-based practice by helping staff to speak about the day-to-day conflicts and challenges they face, there is a risk that the staff will solve these challenges by relying upon rigid routines. They may also, unconsciously, protect themselves from the emotional conflicts by becoming detached from the people they are working with. This results in residents receiving care which is less personalised, and in staff members feeling disempowered, unable to make changes and at risk of burnout.

Attachment theory can help us to understand how these processes may operate at the level of the individual worker. It is a useful framework for considering how adults may respond to perceived stress and pressure, and how they may activate their emotional responses in order to stay psychologically safe, by either inhibiting or exaggerating the ways in which they express their feelings in relationships with others.

Kokkonen and colleagues (2014) did a study involving 77 staff over nine inpatient wards for people with dementia, exploring the connections between attachment styles and burnout. The majority of staff who participated were healthcare assistants and staff nurses. Their main finding was that staff with secure, Type B, attachment styles were less likely to suffer from burnout than their colleagues with Type A or Type C insecure attachment styles.

Staff with Type A attachment styles were more likely to emotionally distance themselves from the distress of the people they were caring for, but when levels of stress and threat reached a high point over a long period of time, their emotional inhibition broke down and they were vulnerable to outbursts of emotion, such as distress or anger. This is in keeping with the concept of an 'intrusion of negative affect', as outlined in Chapter 2.

Type A: Anita's story

Anita has been a domiciliary care worker for five years. Her manager, Miranda, describes her as an excellent worker, who never causes any trouble and gets on with the job. Anita's own mother has recently been diagnosed with dementia. She lives with Anita's sister, but Anita is worried about how long she will be able to stay there, as her sister is struggling to cope at night times.

Recently, Miranda, received a complaint from a client, Desne. She reported that Anita had been increasingly impatient with her and that she shouted at her when she lost her glasses.

Miranda asked Anita to explain what had happened. Anita began to cry and was full of apologies for losing her temper. She felt very ashamed, and also felt ashamed of crying in front of Miranda. Miranda was calm and reassuring, reminded Anita that she had valued her as a worker for five years and that this episode was out of character for her. Anita was then able to tell Miranda about the stresses she was facing due to her mother's ill health. Miranda helped Anita to apologise to Desne for shouting at her, and she and Anita arranged to meet monthly to discuss how she was coping. Anita began to trust that it was OK to talk with Miranda about her emotions.

In the same study, staff members using Type C attachment strategies were more likely to suffer from emotional exhaustion, and to adopt depersonalised attitudes to the people they were caring for. They showed a tendency to become overwhelmed with personal distress when faced with the distress of others, which could reduce their ability to respond in attuned and balanced way to others.

Type C: Christine's story

Christine has worked in a residential care home for three years, where she is a valued member of staff. Recently, she has begun to enjoy talking with a resident called Brian. He has been talking to her about how unhappy he is that his son, Roger, does not visit more often, and that he does not bring his children to visit more often. Brian tells Christine that he would love to see more of his son and his grandchildren.

On the next occasion that Roger visits, Christine bumps into him in the corridor. She tells him that he should bring his children more often because his father is lonely. Roger tells her not to interfere and to mind her own business. He then makes a complaint to the manager of the home.

Christine's manager asks her to explain the reasons why she approached Roger. She explains that she was very affected by listening to Brian speak about his loneliness, and about how much he missed his family. She says that she can't imagine how sad it must be to be alone in a home, and she feels strongly that Roger should make more of an effort. Christine's manager asks her to reflect upon the kinds of reasons that Roger might have for not visiting more often, and reminds her that there are often many things going on in families which we don't know about. She reminds Christine to stay more neutral in conversations about families, and to pay attention to her own emotions, which are separate from those of the residents.

It is important to be clear that it is certainly not the case that only staff with Type B strategies are suitable for caring roles. The use of Type A and Type C strategies can offer benefits in certain situations; sometimes, it can be useful to be able to distance yourself from your own distress, or alternatively to be able to display it for others to see. People who use Type A and Type C strategies are likely to make really important contributions to their teams. It can, however, be helpful for a team manager to be mindful of the different ways in which team members respond to their strong emotions, in order to help them use their strengths and to notice their emotional tendencies when their attachment strategies are triggered.

Managers should bear in mind that attachment strategies can also influence a staff member's willingness to seek help or support at work when they are under stress. People using Type A strategies are less likely to acknowledge their distress, and are likely to prioritise the needs of others, and to aim to solve their own problems. People using Type C strategies are more likely to ask for support but are less likely to be able to act upon it because of their tendency to be preoccupied by their emotions (Adshead 2010). It can therefore be helpful for a manager to recognise how different staff members behave under stress, in order to offer appropriate support.

Supervision

A worker's ability to be aware of their own coping styles and emotional responses can be enhanced by a supportive and attuned management style, which encourages them to be self-aware, and to take their share of responsibility for continuing to reflect on their experiences in the workplace. This is certainly not the same as therapy – paying attention to emotions does not mean that the worker needs to disclose their life story and past and present struggles to their manager. This would be inappropriate and risky, and it is important that boundaries are respected.

Tony Morrison defines supervision as '…a process by which one worker is given responsibility by the organisation to work with another worker(s) in order to meet certain organisational, professional and personal objectives in order to promote positive outcomes for service users' (Morrison 2005, p.32). This definition highlights the idea that good supervision benefits the staff member, the organisation and the people who are using the service. In England, an employer's responsibility to properly support and supervise staff is outlined in the Care Quality Commission's regulations:

Health and Social Care Act 2008 (Regulated Activities) Regulations 2014: Regulation 18

The intention of this regulation is to make sure that providers deploy enough suitably qualified, competent and experienced staff to enable them to meet all other regulatory requirements described in this part of the Health and Social Care Act 2008 (Regulated Activities) Regulations 2014. To meet the regulation, providers must provide sufficient numbers of suitably qualified, competent, skilled and experienced staff to meet the needs of the people using the service at all times and the other regulatory requirements set out in this part of the above regulations. *Staff must receive the support, training, professional development, supervision and appraisals that are necessary for them to carry out their role and responsibilities* [emphasis added]. They should be supported to obtain further qualifications and provide evidence, where required, to the appropriate regulator to show that they meet the professional standards needed to continue to practise.

Good supervision in the care sector will balance paying attention to how a person is fulfilling their role with encouraging them to reflect upon the emotional impact of the work. In the long-term care sector, there is little tradition of reflective supervision, and this can be hard to achieve in a high-pressure environment, with a focus on efficiency and processes. However, as we saw from the study which compared Hebble House and Bournville House earlier in the chapter, a brief conversation between a manager and a staff member about specific interactions with residents can have a big impact upon the way the staff member feels, and upon their ability to self-reflect. Supervision does not only have to mean a structured one-to-one conversation in an office. Meaningful supervision can happen in more informal ways, such as a brief reflective conversation, on-the-job coaching and handover meetings which focus on emotions as well as tasks.

Tony Morrison identified four important functions of supervision:

- *management*: ensuring that the tasks and functions of the role are being performed well

- *development*: encouraging self-reflection, and building professional skills and confidence

- *support*: acknowledging the emotional demands of the role

- *mediation*: helping the worker to be clear about their role, and how it fits in with other people's roles.

Any individual supervision session may focus on one or more of these functions, but over the course of a period of supervision sessions, they should all be paid attention to in order to make sure that the needs of the worker and the organisation are met. The supervision relationship should be outlined in a supervision policy and a supervision contract, and each session should follow an agenda, and be recorded accurately through written notes. Workers should be clear about the organisation's supervision policies, what is expected of them, and what they can expect from others.

Over time, it is likely that the focus of supervision will change, as the worker becomes more experienced and competent. In the early stages of a role, the focus may be upon ensuring that the worker is clear about the organisation's policies and procedures, and about the elements of the job which they have to carry out. They may work alongside a more experienced worker, for example. As they develop, supervision may focus more upon helping them cope with the emotional demands of the role or helping them identify further learning opportunities to help maintain their career development and job satisfaction.

One of the aims of supervision conversations, whether formal or informal, and at all stages of a worker's development, is to promote a worker's capacity to reflect on their work, and to consider their own emotional responses as well as those of the people they are caring for. Kolb's model of experiential learning is commonly used as a framework for promoting reflective practice (Kolb 1976; see Figure 8.1).

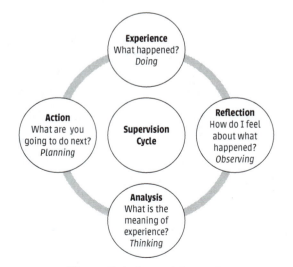

Figure 8.1: Supervision cycle

This cycle describes the different stages in helping a worker reflect upon an experience in the workplace. For example, a worker might notice that they are beginning to feel irritable with a resident, or might be concerned about a mistake they made. A manager using what Tony Morrison described as a 'short circuit' cycle might move from the Experience stage, straight to the Action stage, missing out the Reflection and Analysis stages, like this:

Worker: I'm starting to lose my patience with David. He keeps calling for me to help him, and then when I go to him, he can't remember why he called me. It happens four or five times a day.

Manager: Well, that's all just part of the job, and it's to be expected. You need to carry on doing what you're doing, in line with his care plan.

The worker in this example is not very likely to feel properly listened to or empathised with — it sounds like the manager has brushed away their concerns. This is likely to result in the worker becoming more frustrated with David over time, and in the loss of an important opportunity to reflect and learn.

Asking questions which follow each stage of Kolb's experiential learning cycle gives the worker the best chance of being able to safely reflect upon his or her full range of thoughts and feelings. Importantly, it also enhances his or her ability to self-reflect in future situations; if the supervisor helps the worker to reflect fully upon difficult thoughts or feelings in supervision sessions, the worker is more likely to learn how to do this independently in the future, as they become a more reflective practitioner.

Here is an example of how the conversation might sound if the supervisor was using each stage in Kolb's cycle:

Worker: I'm starting to lose my patience with David. He keeps calling for me to help him, and then when I go to him, he can't remember why he called me. It happens four or five times a day.

Manager: (Experience stage) Let's talk about this for a few moments. Can you give me an example of a time when you felt this way with David?

Worker: Yesterday, he called me into his room twice in 15 minutes, and each time he looked confused and a bit lost. The first time he said that he needed his glasses, which he was already wearing, and the second time he said he couldn't remember why he called me.

Manager: (Experience stage) What had you been doing when he called you?

Worker: I had been with Elizabeth, who needed help to wash, and I felt annoyed that I'd been interrupted.

Manager: (Summary) So, you felt annoyed that you'd been called away from Elizabeth, who you thought really needed your help, to answer David's call, when he didn't seem to need you?

Worker: Yes, that's about right.

Manager: (Reflection stage) How do you feel about it now?

Worker: Now that I'm talking about it, I can see that I was feeling bad because I couldn't be in two places at once.

Manager: (Analysis stage) When David called you into his room twice, without a clear reason, what else do you think might have been going on for him?

Worker: I suppose he might just have wanted a bit of company. His family haven't visited for a while, and he spends a lot of time in his room on his own.

Manager: (Analysis stage) That sounds possible. What do you think about him wanting some company?

Worker: I think it's very normal for him to want to chat. The part of my job that I really like is spending time getting to know the residents. Now that I'm talking about it, I think I feel guilty that he felt so alone in the first place.

Manager: (Analysis stage) I can understand you feeling that way, but it's important to be clear about the limits of what we can offer. You do have lots of tasks to do during a shift, but maybe we could think about how you, and other people, could spend more time with David.

Worker: I'd like to do that. The problem I face is that when I go to start a conversation with him, it's hard to get away, because it feels like he's not going to stop talking. So maybe I do avoid him a bit.

Manager: (Action stage) I understand, and it's good that you've been able to notice it and talk about it with me. I think it might be a good idea if you took responsibility for reviewing his care plan with him. Perhaps you could ask him what kinds of activities he might like to get involved in, so that he spends longer out of his room and gets to make some more connections with other residents.

Worker: That sounds like a good plan. It's really helped me to realise that my frustration with David was actually more to do with me feeling guilty about not spending enough proper time with him. I'd like to talk with him about his care plan, and about how he spends his time. I think he'd like that too.

In this example, the manager asks questions which help the worker to move through the stages of the experiential learning cycle, paying attention to the worker's thoughts and feelings. They make a plan together which balances the worker's job role, his emotional needs and David's needs. The worker is able to reflect upon how his avoidance of David has left him feeling guilty, and the manager is able to hear this without making him feel ashamed. They are then able to translate this into a plan, which focuses upon helping David to feel less isolated. (See Chapter 9, Tools 10 and 11 for a seried of tools to support reflection.)

Strengths-based leadership

Although our focus throughout this book has been on strengths-based and attachment-informed practice, we recognise that it is very difficult to practise consistently in this way in organisations and systems which do not support this approach. Despite the increasing rhetoric of strengths-based practice, if services are commissioned, performance managed and inspected in a way which is risk averse and which values outputs over outcomes and short-term costs over long-term savings, then anyone trying to work in this way will find themselves constantly swimming upstream. Given the pay and conditions of most people working directly with older people, and the wider lack of understanding and devaluing of social care by politicians and the media, it will require enormous tenacity and resilience at the frontline to create and sustain the transformation which is needed.

A detailed discussion of system change, exploring commissioning, performance management and regulation is beyond the scope of this book. There are other publications which explore these important questions, such as John Kennedy and Des Kelly's proposals for transformation of adult social care in Northern Ireland (Kelly and Kennedy 2017) and a toolkit for Social Care Wales on commissioning for older people's wellbeing (Blood and Copeman 2017). Our priority here has been to start and support transformation by articulating what it might look like in practice. Surely it makes sense to start with what it might actually mean to work in a strengths- and attachment-based way with older people and seek to build the processes and structures around that? To do this requires leadership which not only understands and can model strengths-based practice, but which is itself strengths-based in its approach.

This has been described by De Jong *et al.* (2012) as a 'parallel process'. This recognises that leadership and practice *both* need to apply strengths-based approaches, that workers, as well as people who use services will do better in the long term if they can be helped to identify and use the resources they have in themselves and in their environment.

We would like to end the chapter with an example of how this might be done.

Reviewing assessment processes in an adult social care team

Belinda is an older people's service manager in an adult social care department. Her authority has recently produced a vision statement regarding working with people in a more strengths-based and outcomes-focused way. However, she is concerned that many of the assessments conducted by the teams she manages offer little insight into what actually matters to the older people they are assessing.

With the blessing of her director, Belinda decides to review assessment processes and training needs so she can make some changes in her service area and feed back the learning to her seniors and peers. She plans a series of discussions at team away days. She creates a presentation which sets out all the values and aspirations included in the organisational value statement, then lists all the examples she has of how current assessments are falling short of this. Once she has presented this, she will launch a team discussion to explore what is driving this poor practice, and what the barriers are.

On the way to the session, she has an epiphany. She thinks to herself, 'If I want my teams to work in a more strengths- and outcomes-focused way, I should surely introduce these ideas in a strengths-based way! How can I expect them to do it as workers if I can't model it as their leader?' She decides to ditch the presentation; instead she comes up with a series of strengths-based questions for the team to discuss:

- When you do an assessment, what is it that you hope to accomplish? What difference should it make?

- What are the key features of a good assessment?

- What supports you to do a good assessment?

- What are your ideas about how we can do better assessments?

It takes the team a while to warm up; at first most of the answers they give relate to other processes: good assessments are about convincing the panel there is an eligible need; they are about recording risk assessments; they result in referrals to voluntary sector befriending or welfare benefits advice services. Someone even says cynically that good assessments are done quickly because you know you've got half a dozen more to get through. Belinda writes all these points down on the flip chart, but keeps prompting the team to think wider and deeper about the underlying purpose and values of what they are hoping to accomplish. Someone shouts out, 'Assessments are about promoting older people's independence'. Belinda agrees and writes this down, but then asks what this might actually look like: what does 'independence' mean? Eventually, people start saying things like:

'The purpose of assessment is to find out about what people can do and what they can't.'

'Really we are trying to understand the resources they have available already and what – if anything – we might be able to put in place to support that.'

'It's about helping an older person and their family reach a decision – ideally one they agree on, though that isn't always possible – about where and how they should live and how and by whom they should be supported.'

'Our job is to facilitate and empower.'

'But we also need to be accountable and consistent: it is our job to make sure that the limited public resources we have are used effectively.'

Belinda asks the team, 'Bearing these objectives in mind then, what are the key features of a good assessment?'

Where people get stuck, she goes back to the points she has just recorded on the purpose of assessments and prompts them for a corresponding feature – for example, if the purpose of the assessment is to find out what people can do and what they can't, both of these things should be clearly recorded in a balanced way in the write-up.

The team goes on to identify some of the things that support them to do good assessments, for example:

- having enough time to build trust and have conversations with the older person and their family (and not feeling judged on the basis of the quantity of these assessments rather than their quality)

- being in a setting that is conducive to this (e.g. ideally the person's home, rather than a hospital ward)

- feeling clear about what the organisation and the law expects from them in relation to questions of accountability, risk, rationing of resources, mental capacity, and so on.

- feeling supported by their manager and their colleagues when assessments are particularly difficult – both to decide what to do, but also to reflect on their emotional response.

She then asks the team for their ideas: 'How can *we* (i.e. not just *you*) do better assessments?'

This provokes a lively discussion and Belinda is really surprised by how much energy and innovation there is. There is a lot of discussion about paperwork – how the assessment forms are far from balanced in terms of asking about what people can do and what resources they already have (as well as what they can't do and what they might need from services). People also suggest ways of incorporating the voice and perspective of older people into assessment paperwork. One idea is to include a 'My world' (see Chapter 9, Tool 5) visual on each person they assess so anyone else reading the assessment gets a clear view of that world and what matters to the person – this would be quicker than having to write this up in prose. They also suggest various ways in which they could support and learn from each other in a more structured way, not just in one-to-one hierarchical supervision sessions and general moaning in the open plan office.

She realises that, in recent years, she has begun to see many of these workers as a *barrier to* rather than a *force for* change – 'they are too stuck in their processes', 'they've had enough of change, they'll resist this as just another initiative' are comments she made in senior management meetings when the introduction of the new strengths-based approach was being discussed. On reflection, she wonders whether this perception has been fuelled by the fact that she only gets involved where things have gone wrong and so her focus has been on putting in place processes to try and prevent things going wrong in future. Ironically, many of these processes are now getting in the way of workers doing good assessments and achieving the service's wider purpose and values.

After the session, a number of people come up to Belinda and tell her how excited they feel about having the opportunity to shape this, and that the session has reminded them why they came into social work in the first place.

Graybeal's article (2001) on how we can do strengths-based assessment within the dominant processes of a medical, deficit approach gives some useful pointers for Belinda and her organisations. First, he argues that 'assessment' must be seen as part of the intervention, not as a distinct and neutral exercise to decide whether and which intervention should follow (as in case management approaches). Helping someone to identify their strengths and aspirations and facilitating them to decide how to use available resources to overcome the challenges they face is an intervention in its own right. He then highlights opportunities to build and record strengths-based questioning into assessment, for example:

Where forms ask us to describe presenting problems and needs:

- Include the language of the older person and the language their family uses to describe them.

- Present exceptions to the problem (times when they are able to cope or when the 'problem' behaviour was not evident).

- Describe resources available (outside of services) to support the person and tackle the problem.

- Set out what the older person and their family see as the ideal solution (clearly there may be different ideas here).

If – as in Belinda's service – there is an opportunity to rewrite the forms and recording systems, these headings could be built in from the outset.

In this chapter, we have explored the importance of strengths-based and attachment-based practice at all levels of the organisation: managers, workers and the people we work with. We recognise that this can be difficult to achieve in organisations which are judged and inspected according to their compliance with performance measures, but it is nonetheless important to have the conversations.

Resources
Internet-based tools and reports

Health and Safety Executive (2017) *Tackling Work-Related Stress Using the Management Standards Approach: A Step-by-Step Workbook.* Available at www.hse.gov.uk/pubns/wbk01.pdf

SCIE (2013) 'Narrative Summary of the Evidence Review on Supervision of Social Workers and Social Care Workers in a Range of Settings Including Integrated Settings.' Available at www.scie.org.uk/publications/guides/guide50/files/supervisionnarrativesummary.pdf

Skills for care (2015) *Greater Resilience, Better Care: A Resource to Support the Mental Health of Adult Social Care Workers.* Available at www.skillsforcare.org.uk/Document-library/Skills/Mental-health/Greater-resilience-%E2%80%93-better-care-WEBv3.pdf

Skills for Care (2015) *Effective Supervision in Adult Social Care: Free Summary Edition.* Available at www.skillsforcare.org.uk/Documents/Learning-and-development/Effective-supervision/Effective-supervison-in-adult-social-care-Summary.pdf

Books

Baim, C. and Morrison, T. (2011) *Attachment Based Practice with Adults.* Brighton: Pavilion.

Morrison, T. (2005) *Staff Supervision in Social Care.* Brighton: Pavilion.

9
Tools

Tool 1: Using the resilience wheel

Figure 9.1: The wheel of resilience

Mapping a person's supportive resources

Where a person is experiencing a challenge in one or more areas of the wheel of resilience (Figure 9.1), it can be helpful to look at the remaining segments to understand the *supportive* resources a person has. An older person may, for example, experience a challenge in relation to their *physical health* or the loss of a partner (*relationships*); but they may be supported to stay strong by a close-knit *community* or by their personal beliefs and sense of humour (*internal resources*).

You can support someone to 'map' their resources in this way in order to identify the areas that could be strengthened to promote resilience, either during a crisis, ahead of a crisis (prevention), or reflecting back on a crisis to plan what they would do differently if things became difficult again.

Making sure that someone has *information* about benefits and how to access support or facilitating them to build relationships with people in their *community* should mean that they are better equipped to adapt when their health condition flares up, or their partner's dementia worsens.

Working positively with risk

Sometimes, different segments may be in conflict with each other: a beloved *home* may be worsening a person's *physical health* because of damp or inaccessibility; a beloved grandchild (*relationships*) may steal money (*financial*).

Giving people the opportunity to express and explain these conflicts can be a first step in working positively with them around risk, since it highlights the positives that come from taking risks as well as the negatives, and sets the risky scenario within the context of the whole of a person's life. We discuss 'positive risk-taking' in detail in Chapter 6.

Ideally, if we have helped an individual to identify and strengthen the supportive resources they have, they will be in a much stronger position to manage risks and challenges in future. By understanding their own ways of coping more consciously, they should be in a better position to prevent and adapt to challenges.

Practical tips for using the wheel

There are a number of ways in which you might use the wheel:

- *As a conversational prompt*: look at the wheel together and encourage the person to select the segments from it which *they* want to talk about – this allows them to prioritise the agenda rather than working through set assessment questions in order.

- *You could do the strength mapping exercise outlined above in a number of different ways*: writing notes in or by each segment; you could support a person to give each segment a rating (with high scores representing the strongest resources); or by drawing a line in the centre of the wheel, which is closer to the outer edge where resources feel strongest and closer to the centre where they feel less strong.

- You could do this:

  - collaboratively with an older person, a family member, or both together – this is the ideal, but may not always be possible in practice

  - by leaving a copy of the wheel and a key question (see below) with an individual or family to reflect on before you meet them again

  - as an exercise on your own, soon after you leave the person (and before you start writing any formal notes)

  - about an individual in a meeting with colleagues and/or a case (or family group) conference type meeting – you may find you all have very different views about someone's strengths and the challenges they face.

Some suggested questions to ask people

The key is to move away from asking about needs and areas in which someone is facing challenges and instead to ask questions like:

- What has helped you to stay strong so far?

- Are there areas which you would like to build on or change to help you stay strong in future?

Tool 2: The art of asking questions

We met with Social Services and my mother-in-law then answered the questions that were being asked: 'Are you ok?' 'Yes.' 'Can you do this?' 'Yes.' 'Can you manage?' 'Yes, no problems at all.' And I'm sitting there thinking, 'No, she can't!' Because people from that era are that proud they don't want anyone to know that they can't do this and that.' Family member interviewed in Blood *et al.* (2016b, p.55)

Being able to ask good questions is a core skill for anyone working in the caring professions, yet it is often overlooked in training courses and guidance. Often the questions we ask – as in the example above – offer little space for the responder to expand, explain, explore or clarify. The standard questions we have been trained to ask typically steer people into 'problem-talk', which many service users have learned as the best way to elicit a response where resources are limited. For example:

'So, what seems to be the problem?'

'What has triggered this crisis?'

'What are the main needs and concerns that have prompted you to get in touch?'

'Which daily tasks do you need help with?'

'For how long have you been struggling to cope?'

'What's stopping you from getting out and about more?'

Strengths-based practitioners instead seek to ask '…meaningful questions that will combat the relentless pursuit of pathology, and ones that will help discover hidden strengths that contain the seeds to construct solutions to otherwise unsolvable problems' (De Jong *et al.* 2012).

Some key principles:

- Ask open questions which invite the person to think and express themselves freely rather than yes/no and either/or questions which restrict or lead the response.

- Work together to develop solutions using available resources. Explore what a person wants – their ideal scenario – and identify opportunities, knowledge and skills which are taking them or could take them in this direction – for example, 'What can you do or say next time your son calls to take you one step closer to the ideal relationship with him that you just described?'

- Try and let go of the need to analyse or diagnose the problem! You do not need to know the answers – the aim is to facilitate the person to take responsibility. You might opt to develop the 'discipline of curiosity' (Burnham 2017) where you ask a question even though you think you already know the answer.

- Work with the person to understand what is happening when things go well: What does a good day look like? What is different about it?

- Find out about the people in their lives – the 'natural helpers' – family, friends, partner – and neighbours, hairdressers, shopkeepers, and so on who offer support, even if it is only low level.

- Use your questions to facilitate the 'meaning-making' we discussed under principle 7 (Build Resilience) in Chapter 1: asking them to reflect on their learning from and interpretation of their experiences.

Saleeby (2005) has identified a number of different types of strengths-based question (Table 9.1).

Table 9.1: Strengths-based questions

Question type	Examples
Survival	How have you managed to cope independently so far, given all the health challenges you have faced?
Support	Who supports you now – or has in the past? What support do you give/have you given to them?
Exception	When things were going well, what was different? Which parts of you/your life would you like to recapture/relive?
Possibility	What do you like to do? What now do you want out of life?
Esteem	What is it about your life, yourself and your accomplishments that give you real pride? When others say good things about you, what are they likely to say?
Perspective	What sense do you make out of your recent experiences and struggles?
Change	What are your ideas about how things might change? What's worked in the past? How can I help?

Clarke and Dembkowski (2006) distinguish problem-orientated questions (Table 9.2) from solution-orientated questions (Table 9.3).

Table 9.2: Problem-orientated questions

What's causing this problem?	Presupposes a cause (linear), rather than a series of interactions (systemic)
What's stopping you/What's the barrier?	Presupposes difficulties
Why did you do that?	Asks about motivation and can provoke defensiveness
Anything else?	Invites premature closure

Table 9.3: Solution-orientated questions

How did you do that?	Presupposes agency – that the client had an influence on the outcome
How did you know to do that?	Presupposes knowledge
How did that make a difference?	Presupposes awareness and observational skills
What did you learn from that?	Presupposes reflection
What helped?	Presupposes something was helpful!
What else?	Presupposes that the client could say more
What might you do differently next time?	Presupposes choice and decision making ability

Practice example

You receive a referral to go and visit Michael, who was discharged from hospital yesterday having fallen down the stairs a few days ago. Michael is 88 and has lived alone since the death of his wife a few years ago. Following his fall, he is able to walk using a walking frame; however, staff in the hospital made the referral because they were concerned that he may not be coping well at home.

A problem-/deficit-focused conversation

'So, Michael, what happened to you?'

'Well, I was carrying a box of stuff down the stairs and I just had a moment where I went dizzy. I lost my footing and fell down the last half a dozen steps and landed heavily on my arm, which I've broken.'

'Why were you carrying a box down the stairs?'

'I was just having a sort out of my tools.'

'Do you think that's a good idea?'

'What?'

'Carrying boxes around on your own when you're here on your own and you aren't that steady on your feet?'

'I'm usually OK.'

'How long have you been having these dizzy spells?'

'I don't...I don't know...not very often...this was the first...or certainly the first like that, in a while anyway.'

'Have you had it checked out with the doctor?'

'No.'

'What's stopping you from getting it checked out?'

'I didn't think it was such an issue really.'

'Have you considered getting a pendant fitted so you could call for help if you fell again?'

'No – I don't fancy wearing one of those.'

'While your arm is in plaster, will you need some help around the house or getting dressed?'

'No, I should be fine – I can manage thanks.'

'OK – well here's the number to call if you get to a point where you can't cope.'

A strengths-based/solution-focused version of the conversation

'So, Michael, how have you coped so far since you got out of hospital with your broken arm?'

'I'm getting by – very slowly! I can just about get dressed if I wear these tracksuit bottoms and my slippers and just take my time. My neighbour popped in last night and got me a few bits of easy food from the local shop – stuff I can make myself – toast, some of those cheese slices and a few microwave meals.'

'It sounds like you are doing a great job of adapting – and there are people around here that support you?'

'There's a few of us who've been here living here for years so we all keep a bit of an eye out for each other.'

'What sort of support do you give each other?'

'You know – bits and bobs – like putting out bins, keeping an eye on each other's houses. I was helping out the woman next door with her lawn but I don't suppose I'll be doing that for a bit! If one of us is ill or is having a difficult time, people will knock now and then and see if you want something fetching. When Rosa died, a few people brought over food they'd made.'

'And how have you coped since your wife's death?'

'I miss her a lot, but you just have to get through each day. I have learned to enjoy my own company and, in the last year or so, I have set up a little workshop and I make bits and pieces out of wood. That keeps me occupied.'

'So how will you keep occupied now, when I'm guessing it'll be hard to do much in the workshop?'

'Yeah, that's the one thing I'm going to miss most I reckon.'

'Have you had any ideas of other things you might do until your arm is better?'

'Not really. I like doing crosswords, but I'll have to see whether I can write the answers with my left hand... I also thought I might try and do some sorting out and decluttering, going through all the old boxes – but I'm a bit anxious 'cause that's what I was doing the night I fell down the stairs.'

'OK, so what might you do differently this time?'

'Well, I guess I won't be carrying any boxes around anyway with this arm – just set myself up as comfortably as I can in one place and leave the stuff I've sorted out for my son to move when he next visits. It's not like I'm in a rush...'

Tool 3: The behaviour, pattern and function triangle

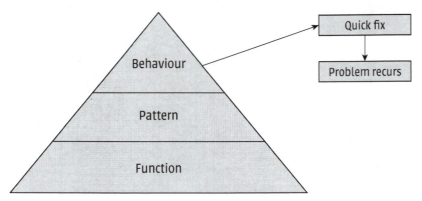

Figure 9.2: The behaviour–pattern–function triangle
Reproduced with kind permission of Baim and Morrison (Attachment-based Practice with Adults). Pavilion Publishing and Media.

This triangle (Figure 9.2) offers an attachment-informed way of reflecting upon a person's patterns of behaviour, by focusing upon the *meaning* of the behaviour rather than the behaviour itself. If possible, involve the person in this conversation.

Behaviour

What is the person doing which is causing difficulties for them, or for others?

Quick fix

What attempts have been made to 'solve' the problem or to reduce the frequency or severity of the behaviour? Has this helped, or not helped?

Pattern

By reflecting on the underlying patterns and trends, we may be able to learn more about what motivates and sustains the behaviour. Helpful questions include:

- When did this behaviour start?

- Are there times when it is better or worse?

- Can you see any patterns to the behaviour: days of the week, anniversaries, times when particular people are nearby or far away?

Function

What are your ideas about the meaning of this behaviour to the person? These processes can be more or less conscious. A useful question to ask is, 'Which basic needs does it represent their best attempt to meet, given their social context and the resources available to them?' Common underpinning psychological needs include the need for safety, comfort, proximity (physical or psychological) and predictability (or, what is familiar to them).

Tool 4: Family tree

Drawing a family tree – sometimes called a genogram – can be a very useful way of finding out more about a person's life and history. This exercise can be done with an individual person, with a couple or with a family. If the older person who you are working with is not able to do it for themselves, then it can be a useful exercise to do with family members or other people who are close to them.

The exercise involves drawing a diagram representing the people in the person's immediate family, going back in time as far as they can remember. This can be a prompt to further conversations about what relationships were like between family members, and what life was like for them at different points.

Doing this exercise can encourage people who work with an older person to reflect on them across their whole lifespan. Who may they have given and received care from across their life, and what roles might they have occupied – as a child, student, worker, partner or parent? This can also be a prompt for discussions about the person's current experiences of life and of their important relationships. Are there people they would like to see more of, or to reconnect with? What support, assistance or encouragement might they need in order to do that?

How to do a family tree

Start with the person and their current family situation. Using the symbols below (Figure 9.3), draw a diagram to represent the people in their immediate family. Then extend the diagram as far back in time as they want to go. The commonly used symbols are attached as a guide, but there is no need to feel restricted by them – use any symbols which make sense to the person you are working with! Feel free to include pets as well, as they can be important members of the family. Let the person you are working with take the lead in the exercise and let them set the tone of the conversation.

You can take as many sessions as you need to work on the family tree, and the sessions should only be as long as the person is comfortable with. You should also discuss who will keep the final diagram, and who it may be shared with. Figure 9.4 shows a worked example of a family tree for an imaginary family.

Depending on your relationship with the person you are working with you could ask questions such as:

- When in your life did you feel most happy? Or most sad?

- What was it like being a child in your family?

- How did you cope with life's difficulties? Who helped you?

Try to end each conversation on a positive note – such as identifying a strength which the person showed, or a person who cared for them, or an experience about which they have happy memories.

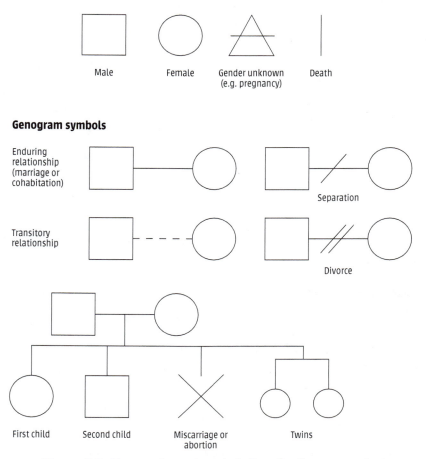

Male   Female   Gender unknown (e.g. pregnancy)   Death

Genogram symbols

Enduring relationship (marriage or cohabitation)

Separation

Transitory relationship

Divorce

First child   Second child   Miscarriage or abortion   Twins

Figure 9.3: Commonly used symbols for a family tree exercise

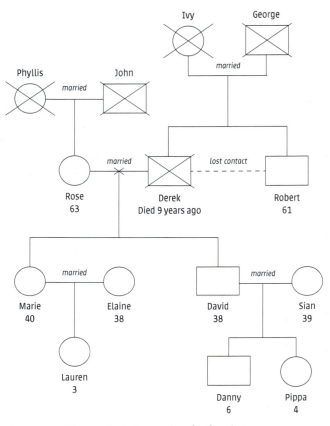

Figure 9.4: Example of a family tree

Tool 5: My world

A 'My world' diagram – sometimes called an eco-gram – can offer a person an opportunity to speak about what matters to them in their life. The focus is upon their most important connections and links, which can include people, pets, interests, beliefs, hobbies, places and anything else which they value. It differs from a family tree because it is not restricted to family members.

Working on this together can help you and the person you are working with to build a stronger relationship. It also encourages them to say more about what brings colour and value into their life, and makes it worth living, from their point of view.

How to do a 'My world' diagram

Start with the person in the centre. They can choose a symbol to represent them or write their name. Then ask them to draw the other elements of their world around the symbol which represents them. Things which matter most to them should be closest to them, and things which matter less can be further away. Then draw lines between the symbol representing the person and the other symbols. For example, a solid line represents a firm connection, a wobbly line represents a shakier connection and a dotted line represents a connection which isn't strong any more.

Let the person you are working with take the lead, and set the tone and pace of the conversation. Encourage them to use their creativity and imagination. To make it more colourful, you could use coloured pens or images from magazines. Each person's diagram will be unique to them.

This conversation can be a springboard into other conversations about things which would enrich the person's life, such as being able to spend more time out of doors, or making contact with an old friend or going to see a football match again. You could use this exercise to represent a snapshot of a person's world at different moments in time, either 'how things were in the past' or 'how I'd like things to be in the future.'

This exercise can also support people to make difficult decisions, by helping them to say more about what really matters to them and gives their life value.

Example of a 'My world' diagram

This is Joyce's 'My world' diagram (Figure 9.5) from Chapter 6.

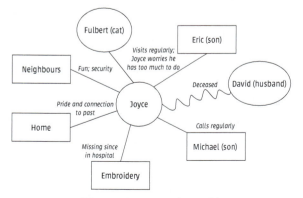

Figure 9.5: Joyce's world

Tool 6: Life story work

Life story work involves supporting a person to remember, develop and communicate their life story. It can happen in a number of different ways, ranging from gathering items, photos or written pieces for a memory box, board, folder or album to filling in a template with a person and/or their family, to one or more conversations which do not need to result in a particular output.

A number of studies (e.g. Clarke, Hanson and Ross 2003; Kellet *et al.* 2010) have found that life story work in care settings can help care workers to understand and connect with an older person better, and can also bring families and care staff closer together. From a strengths-based perspective, life story work can be a way of understanding what matters to someone and helping them to identify their strengths.

There may be particular benefits of life story work for people with dementia. Kitwood wrote:

> As we go through life we build up a personal history with its unique mixture of joys and pleasures, sadness and pain. Our sense of who we are is linked to that history and if we lose that history, we lose something of ourselves. For a person with dementia who is losing their memory and trying most of the time to make sense of who they are, a life story book can be an atlas, the compass, the guide to finding their self. (Kitwood 1997, p.56)

In care settings, life story work is often prompted either by a desire to record and share the learning about a person across or between teams, or by a desire to understand and better manage (or prevent) puzzling or 'challenging' behaviour.

Some people with dementia will find it difficult to order events in their lives chronologically, to communicate their 'life story', and to remember facts and names – the place they were born, the names of their parents, siblings or children. However, long-term memory for stories, experiences, senses and feelings from the past is often preserved, even in the more advanced stages of the condition, and there is evidence to suggest that 'individual reminiscence therapy' of this kind can provide cognitive stimulation and reduce depression (Subramaniam and Woods 2012).

Kindell *et al.* (2014) identified a number of resources which have been developed to support life story work with people with dementia.

However, they noted a lack of practical advice regarding how the life story book or other product might be used when completed. They critique the structure (at times chronological) of many of the available templates and resources and argue that — especially in the case of people with dementia:

> a more flexible and naturalistic encounter might allow the worker to follow the lead of the person with dementia in conversation... [this] begins with the stories the individual with dementia wants to share, rather than the questions the worker wishes to ask. (p.157)

Gridley *et al.* (2016) warn us of the importance of agreeing at the outset what the purpose of the life story work is. If the plan is to create a resource, how will that be used, who will have access to it and who has editorial control? It helps to be clear about whether our primary aim is to enable the person to build a collection of photographs and objects to help *them* to remember, or to build a resource which care workers can share and use to guide their care and support planning. If it is the latter, then we need to think about how we will apply the learning from the life story work to improve the quality of care and commit to doing this. For example, this might be through:

- offering a range of personalised activities and encouraging the person to lead or initiate these wherever possible (e.g. if it turns out they have been a keen painter, we might encourage them to show others some techniques)

- selecting relevant images and objects for display in the home (including the person's room and perhaps communal areas too)

- using elements of the life story so that staff can connect and engage people in day-to-day contact (as we saw in the 30-second activities in Chapter 4)

- identifying strengths and interests so we can think of roles which a resident might wish to play in the home or connections we might encourage with other residents, volunteers, and so on.

- developing a multi-sensory approach to comfort, stimulating people with more advanced dementia, especially during times of stress: this might, for example, include recordings of familiar voices, music or smells which have positive associations

- sharing a summary of the life story – or perhaps a memory board – with others working at the home (provided the person seems happy to share these details or photographs) so that they can get to know them better. This avoids the need to repeat the work and means that others can effectively pick up where you left off.

Tips for doing life story work

- Many people have painful memories, and the experience of remembering may be distressing. This should not put you off attempting to do life story work; sometimes those with painful memories have the most to gain from this sort of approach. However, workers should be prepared for the possibility of distress. This means doing life story work:

  - in a safe and private space

  - when you have time to stay with someone for a while and can give them your focused attention

  - when someone seems calm and in the mood to talk

  - only if someone wants to talk about their past

  - at a pace and covering topics led by them

  - when you know you will have the opportunity to debrief and get support yourself, ideally from your manager or a trusted colleague.

- Find a non-threatening and open-ended way of starting the conversation (rather than a series of direct, personal or factual questions) – e.g. 'I don't feel as though I know very much about you and your history, John – I'd like to listen, if you feel like telling me.' This allows a person to begin where they want to begin and does not put them on the spot if they cannot remember the name of the school they attended or a close member of their family.

- If and when someone decides to tell you about their past, find out from them how much of this – if any – they would be happy for you to share with other members of staff. If a person seems to have enjoyed talking about their life story, you could ask them whether they would be interested in making a book, or a box – either for their private memories or to share more widely. You could ask if they would like to involve family or friends in this process.

- Avoid making assumptions – for example that people had children, were married, are heterosexual, had a career.

- People do not want to be 'set in stone' by a particular version of their story (Gridley 2017); if you think about telling your own life story (or parts of it), you might do this very differently for different audiences or in different moods. Do not imply that someone's life story is finished and make sure that new photos or stories can be and are added.

Life story work with people who have more advanced dementia

If a person has advanced dementia or other communication difficulties, you will probably need to involve their family or others who know them well in building a life story but keep looking for ways in which you can involve the person with dementia. For example, once you have identified a few 'clues' from someone's past, you may find you can 'unlock' their memories using a favourite song, a photograph or an object. Sometimes, people who have barely said a word will begin to talk once a memory has been triggered in this way.

Do not get too hung up on factual accuracy or chronology – do not dismiss everything they are telling you because it does not completely stack up or because they contradict themselves later. The important thing is to tune into the feelings, the people and the passions. When someone's eyes light up as they tell you they used to be a famous dancer, the key thing is that you now know they have a passion and talent for dance.

If someone has advanced dementia, or other communication difficulties, and there is no family member available to consult, you could try to use a selection of photographs to prompt people's memories. For example, in our care homes research, we compiled a set of photographs depicting various activities from swimming to painting, from abseiling to reading the newspapers. We made sure that the images were clear and unambiguous (so, for instance, one image showed two people walking in the countryside but the shot was taken from behind so that people with dementia would not be distracted by thinking that they should be able to recognise the faces). There would always be a couple of photographs from the set that brought a person to life and prompted them to tell us a story or at least a fragment of a memory, which could form starting point for the next session of life story work.

There has been some promising practice in supporting people with advanced dementia to build 'sensory life stories' (Leighton *et al.* 2016). These might consist of a life story pared down into around eight to ten key events or a shorter snapshot story of one event. A sensory experience which triggers memories is then matched to each event. A couple might play the music they danced to or rub sun cream on each other's arms to bring back memories of summer holidays. Retelling these 'sensory life stories' can bring comfort and connection, especially where the words to say, 'I remember dancing with you' can no longer be found.

Tool 7: Motivational interviewing

Motivational interviewing (MI) is a skilled way of supporting people to build on their motivation to make changes in their lives. It was developed by Miller and Rollnick (2002), based upon their observations of the ways in which the most effective workers had conversations with people who were trying to reduce their alcohol use. MI is now used very widely across health, social care and criminal justice settings.

The MI approach is particularly useful when supporting a person who has some motivation to make a change but is in two minds about doing so. Most people who are considering making a change in their behaviour or lifestyle will spend some time weighing up the pros and cons of changing or staying as they are, and may feel torn between these options. This state of mind is called ambivalence and is a normal human response to thinking about making a change. This is because it is a difficult process to change our behaviour, even when we know it is in our best interest – just ask anyone who has tried to give up smoking, for example!

Motivational interviewing is described by Miller and Rollnick as 'a client-centred, directive method for enhancing intrinsic motivation to change by exploring and resolving ambivalence' (2002, p.25). MI is not about using fancy techniques to 'trick' people into making changes; it is based on the belief that each person is the expert in their own situation and is ultimately responsible for the choices that they make. A person using MI skills will work with a person to help them consider and reflect upon their personal motivation to change. It is a guiding style, which sits in between a counselling position ('make whatever decisions you want, at your own pace') and a directive position ('I know what's best for you – you need to follow my advice').

How is MI relevant to work with older adults?

MI can be used to support older adults who are considering making changes to aspects of their lifestyle, which can be linked to their goals and wishes about their physical health, or their social relationships and activities. For example, some of the physical challenges which can be associated with older age can be linked to issues of diet, physical activity, smoking and alcohol use – all of these are topics which can be discussed using MI skills. Other challenges of old age may relate to loneliness and boredom, and MI skills can also be relevant here. If an adult is keen to expand their social network, or to join in with activities with friends, then they may have some concerns or worries, which could be discussed with a trusted person using MI skills. There is support from research that using MI skills with older adults who are aiming to improve their diet, have more physical activity and to give up smoking can be effective (Cummings, Cooper and Cassie 2009).

How does MI work?

MI is more than just a set of skills – it involves a specific approach to change, and a way of being with a person and expressing empathy with them. This is often described as the 'spirit' of MI and involves three elements:

- *Collaboration*: workers are not experts, but guides – they work alongside the client in order to understand the client's aims, views and concerns in a respectful way.

- *Evocation*: it is the role of the worker to draw out of the client more information about their thoughts and feelings about making changes, about their motivations and about their goals. The client is seen as having important strengths and resources, rather than as needing to be 'fixed'.

- *Autonomy*: people will only make and maintain changes if they believe that it's right for them to do so. It's never effective, or ethical, to try to force a person to make changes. So, we might not always agree with people's choices but we need to resist our impulse to cajole or persuade them to do what we'd like them to do as it's likely to result in them being less willing to talk openly with us.

Common skills of MI

The core skills of MI are often referred to using the acronym OARS.

O: open-ended questions

A: affirmations

R: reflective listening

S: summaries

Open-ended questions

Open-ended questions are those which invite the speaker to say more about their thoughts, feelings and experiences of the world. Instead of asking a person, 'Do you understand why your daughter is worried about you?' we could instead ask, 'What do you think your daughter is worried about?' or 'Which of her concerns do you agree with, or disagree with?' Open-ended questions do not limit the speaker to having to answer 'yes' or 'no', and tend to result in a more collaborative conversation where the power to set the agenda is shared between the speaker and the listener.

Affirmations

Affirmations are statements of support for the strengths, achievements and qualities of the people we are working with. Affirmations can be helpful as they focus the conversation on the speaker's strengths and resources, both past and present, which can help build motivation to make changes. Affirmations are not the same as praise. 'I think it's amazing that you are still doing the gardening' puts the focus on the speaker and implies a value judgement. An affirmation would be, 'It's really important to you that you keep up with your gardening, even though it can be painful sometimes.'

Reflective listening

Reflective listening involves the listener repeating back parts of what a speaker has said. This can feel awkward at first but has the effect of showing the speaker that you are truly listening to them. It's important to make a distinction between a question and a reflection. Questions involve the voice going up at the end of the sentence and invite the other person to reply with an answer. Reflections are offered without the voice going up at the end, so they are heard as statements rather than questions. There are different types of reflections:

A *content reflection* involves repeating back the same or similar words to those used by the speaker:

Speaker: I know that something needs to change. It can't go on like this.

Listener: You know that something needs to change.

A *feeling reflection* involves reflecting back the listener's understanding of the emotional content of the speaker's words. For example:

Speaker: I never thought I'd need help with looking after my wife, but I think it's time to face the music. I don't like it though.

Listener: You feel sad about having to ask for help.

Speaker: Yes, I do feel sad, but also I feel like I'm breaking my promise to my wife. I promised to look after her.

Even if the listener doesn't quite reflect the emotions accurately, the speaker is likely to hear it as a genuine attempt to understand the meaning of their words and will often correct the listener if needed.

A *meaning reflection* involves the listener reflecting their understanding of the meaning of the speaker's words. Again, even if the listener isn't wholly accurate in their reflection, the speaker is likely to correct them and explain more about their meaning.

Speaker: I'd like to be able to offer visitors a pot of tea and biscuits. But the staff all seem so busy. I don't like to bother them.

Listener: It's important to you that you can welcome your visitors in the same way as you would have done when you lived in your own home.

Speaker: Yes, that's right. I have always been a very hospitable person. I was brought up that way.

A *double-sided reflection* involves the listener mirroring back to the speaker their understanding of the speaker's ambivalence, so that the speaker has a chance to hear it and think about it again. So, if we continue with the example above:

Listener: On the one hand, it's important to you to be able to welcome your visitors and be hospitable. But on the other hand, you don't want to give the staff another job to do by asking for a pot of tea and biscuits.

Speaker: Yes, I feel really torn. I suppose I could speak with Marie about it before it happens again and see what ideas she has. I really would like to sort it out.

Summaries

Summaries can be very useful every now and then in a conversation because they allow the speaker to hear that the listener has truly been listening. They can be used strategically, by pulling together many different aspects of what the speaker has communicated and giving them the opportunity to reflect further.

Listener: Let me see if I have understood correctly. It's very important to you that you are able to take a walk outside to the newsagent to buy treats for your grandchildren. But you agree that you are beginning to find the walk more difficult. You really don't like using the wheelchair, as you think that once you stop walking independently you are unlikely to start again. You'd be keen to talk about the different things we could put in place to support you to keep walking for as long as possible.

With all of the OARS skills, it's very important that they are used in way which is consistent with the spirit of MI – collaboration, autonomy and evocation.

Example of using MI skills

Winston was born in the Caribbean, and now lives alone in a big city in England. His daughter, Vanessa, works long shifts as a doctor in a hospital on the other side of the city. She visits him when she can, but not as often as she'd like to. Winston had a good friend, Derek, who was also born in the Caribbean, and they used to enjoy playing dominos together and sharing meals. However, Derek has now moved to live with his son and daughter-in-law in another part of England, and it's hard for him and Winston to meet up. Winston is feeling isolated and would like to get out of his flat and socialise with other people who share his cultural and ethnic background.

With his permission, Vanessa calls the local African Caribbean Centre. Joy from the centre comes out to meet Winston and tells him that a group of older Caribbean people meet regularly at the centre to play dominos and share food together, and that he would be very welcome. He feels torn – he would really like to go, but he has some concerns that he won't like it, and that he won't know what to say to anyone.

Joy: (*summarising*) So, Winston, let me check that I understand you correctly so far. You are missing Derek and Vanessa. You'd like to make some more connections with people from a Caribbean background so that you can share food and play dominos. Part of you likes the sound of the cultural centre and would like to give it a try, but part of you feels nervous about going.

Winston: That's about right. Yes, that's how I feel.

Joy: (*open question*) How much, out of ten, do you want to meet some new people?

Winston: About a seven. It's important to me – I don't like feeling lonely. I think that it might be good for me to go to that centre. But I have worries about walking through the door for the first time.

Joy: (*reflection*) You think it might be good for you to go to the centre.

Winston nods.

Joy: (*affirmation*) It's important to you that you have some social ties with people who you share a cultural background with.

Winston: Yes, it is. I miss talking with Derek, and Vanessa can't visit as often as she used to.

Joy: (*double-sided reflection*) On the one hand, you would like to make some more social ties with people you share a cultural background with. But on the other hand, you have some worries about walking through the door for the first time.

Winston: Yes, that sums it up well.

Joy: (*open question*) How confident do you feel, out of ten, about arranging to go to the cultural centre?

Winston: Oh, to be frank, I have worries about that. I'd say I'm only about four out of ten on confidence.

Joy: (*reflection*) So, Winston, it's seven out of ten important to you to go, but you are four out of ten confident about doing it.

Winston nods.

Joy: (*open question*) Where does that leave you now?

Winston: That's a good question. I think I need to make a plan! Maybe we could work something out together?

Joy: Yes, let's do that.

So, rather than simply giving Winston the information about the cultural centre, or giving him the advice that he should go, or indeed offering to accompany him to the group, Joy uses MI skills to help Winston reflect upon the ambivalence he feels – part of him really wants to go, but part of him feels nervous. Having a motivational conversation about this ambivalence is more likely to help him go through with a plan.

Resources

Motivational Interviewing Network of Trainers (MINT)
www.motivationalinterviewing.org
The website offers a catalogue of resources and information.

Rosengren, D.B. (2009) *Building Motivational Interviewing Skills: A Practitioner Workbook.* New York: Guilford Press.
This book contains a review of the theory, plus many exercises to develop your MI skills.

Tool 8: Circles of support

A circle of support brings together people who want to support a person with the person who wants their support. The circle might contain a mix of family members, friends, neighbours, volunteers and paid workers, but the focus is on mobilising community support or 'natural helpers'. Although paid workers can play an important role within the circle, especially at the outset, the circle should not simply become a multi-agency professionals' meeting, though it can be a good way to bring professionals and non-professionals together and might involve workers from outside the health and social care setting – from shop owners to hairdressers. In one story gathered by the Dementia and Neighbourhoods Programme,[1] one person living with dementia told researchers that they always walked to the newsagents at a certain time and, on the second day they did not come into the shop, the newsagent had knocked at their house to check they were alright.

A circle works together to achieve the goals of the person and may also support their partner or close family members as they care for them. This might include creating a network to help out in emergencies or supporting an older person who wants to continue living in their own home. A circle approach can also be used to reduce social isolation and loneliness – either as its primary aim or as a by-product of people coming together to provide practical support. Although the idea of a 'meeting' is often core to the model, there is no reason why those who are less likely to attend a 'meeting' (like the newsagent in the example above) cannot play a part in the circle.

The National Development Team for Inclusion (NDTI) has piloted circles of support for people with dementia (Macadam and Savitch 2015) and has found that this approach can really help people to maintain or increase their personal and social networks. However, they also warn that larger meetings can be stressful for a person with dementia. A flexible approach may be needed, perhaps involving people remotely, or having a separate meeting in which a couple of members of the circle support the person to identify their goals, then represent them to the larger circle.

---

1   Personal correspondence with researcher, www.neighbourhoodsanddementia.org/work-programme-4-description

Circles of support in action: Sue and Frank

Sue was diagnosed with dementia a couple of years ago – she lives with and is supported by her husband Frank. Their daughter, Lynn, has been getting increasingly worried about how they are coping. The house seems fine and they are clearly managing to eat and wash and dress, but Lynn can sense warning signs that her parents are not coping so well emotionally, and she is concerned that they have become very isolated socially. Her father looks exhausted and has lost the sparkle, humour and energy that has always been his trademark, and her parents are continually bickering. Sue seems to resent Frank's attempts to 'protect' her and says she feels like a 'child' or a 'prisoner in her own home'.

Lynn wants to help, but feels she doesn't know where to start, so she contacts a local dementia charity for advice and meets up with Mark, a carers' support worker. Lynn feels that her parents need some support, but she can't quite imagine what form it might take. Both are quite proud and she can't imagine them wanting strangers coming in to help with practical tasks – Mark is doubtful that they would be eligible for care and support from adult social care anyway, at this relatively early stage in Sue's condition. Mark asks who else is involved in Sue and Frank's lives and might want to support them. Lynn mentions a couple of long-standing friends and her nephew who lives fairly nearby – she's not sure who else. Mark tells her about circles of support: it's a simple and flexible way of bringing together the people who care about Sue and Frank and planning how they can best support the couple.

Lynn speaks to her parents – she explains that she is worried about them; she is really impressed with how well they are both coping, but she would like to try and help them bring back the 'sparkle'. She thinks that others who care about them would feel the same but suspects that – like her – no one quite knows where to begin. She tells them about the circle of support. At first, they dismiss it as 'hippy nonsense', but Lynn explains that she imagined simply inviting around a few of their friends, their grandson, the neighbour and anyone else they want to invite, for a bite to eat and an informal 'meeting' about how they can do this. They mull it over for a bit and eventually agree.

Lynn contacts the people her parents agree to invite and explains the idea to each of them – they are all up for taking part. She asks Mark if he might consider facilitating the first meeting – she feels a bit unsure about how it should work, she doesn't want it to just turn into general chat, but she is also anxious about seeming 'bossy'. Mark comes over to meet Sue, Frank and Lynn and they plan the 'meeting' together.

On the day of the meeting, Lynn makes one of her famous stews and everyone sits around in her parents' house and shares a meal. Mark explains what a 'circle' is and asks Sue and Frank one at a time what they think would make their lives better. Sue says she really misses spending time with her friends – she feels her life has become really boring and dominated by her diagnosis. She feels like dementia has become a prison and Frank is her jailer, though she feels awful saying it because she knows he is just trying to keep her safe and that he is working really hard around the house. Frank says he is worried sick about Sue wandering off or getting lost, he misses the fun they used to have together, and he hasn't been able to go fishing – which was always his 'release valve' – since she was diagnosed.

Mark reflects that the couple would like some time apart, reconnecting with other people and hobbies, and perhaps also that they would like to do something fun together? Sue points out that they used to go ballroom dancing together at a local social club in their early retirement – Frank reminds her that they stopped going because it just all got a bit awkward after Sue's diagnosis. She forgot the names of people she'd known for years and they got offended. The last time they went to the club, she lost her balance and knocked over a few drinks and neither had felt like going back after that. Their grandson, Dean, said that his girlfriend kept trying to persuade him to learn ballroom dancing – he suggested that perhaps they could try going as a foursome. Sue and Frank could show them a few tips on the dancefloor and it would mean they would have a bit of support when they were there. His girlfriend could go to the ladies with Sue to make sure she didn't get confused finding her way back.

Sue's friend, Brenda, explained that she and a couple of other women who Sue knew but hadn't seen for a while meet up regularly. Sometimes they go for a walk, sometimes for a coffee, sometimes they go to the cinema together. She hadn't invited Sue because she wasn't really sure whether she'd want or be able to join them and what sort of support she might need to do this. They discussed some of the things that Sue may need support with – like paying for things – and how she can sometimes get disorientated, and finds it easy to get 'overloaded' with noise and lots of lights. Brenda said she would go off and explain all of this to the other women and do a bit of research to plan a 'dementia-friendly' outing. Mark told her about a few local resources which might be worth checking out, such as the local theatre, which offers 'relaxed' performances in the afternoons. They all agreed this needed to be built up gradually so that everyone felt comfortable but that, if all went well, Frank could at least get a couple of hours to himself now and again – perhaps not enough yet for fishing but certainly long enough to enable him to get out for a walk or pop down to the local pub to watch the football. Lynn said that, if the friends were able to meet up at the weekends, she would be happy to give Sue a lift there and back and wait with her at home till her father returned, which would buy him a bit more time.

Clear about their respective roles, the members of the circle agreed to meet back in six weeks' time to find out how they had all got on.

Resources

For further information on circles of support, see:

Wisdom in Practice
www.wisdominpractice.org.uk/hints-and-tips-resources

National Development Team for Inclusion (NDTi)
https://www.ndti.org.uk/our-work/areas-of-work/ageing-and-older-people/circles-of-support-for-people-with-dementia
If safe and appropriate, you could suggest using this exercise to represent a snapshot of a person's world at different moments in time, either 'how things were in the past' or 'how I'd like things to be in the future'.

Tool 9: Positive Risk-Taking
Fears and hopes

Write the names of family members – including the older person themselves – in the column on the left, adding more rows if needed. Summarise option 1 and option 2 (you could add further columns to the right if there are more options to be considered). Write down the hopes and fears which each option raises for each family member. See the worked example for Joyce and her family (Table 6.1, 130). You could also use this simple tool (Table 9.4) within teams and multi-agency meetings.

Table 9.4: Fears and hopes

Family members	Fears and hopes	Option 1	Option 2
	Fears		
	Hopes		
	Fears		
	Hopes		
	Fears		
	Hopes		
	Fears		
	Hopes		

Strengths-based risk assessment

This simple tool (Table 9.5) might be used when assessing and managing risks around the home or in public, service or community settings. See Table 6.2, (page 133) for a worked example.

Table 9.5: Strengths-based risk assessment

Potential hazard	How do you feel about this item/activity? What are the benefits you (would) gain from it?	What are you already doing to adapt and reduce risks?	Does this reduce risk to a level everyone is comfortable with?	Can a better solution/compromise be reached which reduces risks to a level everyone is comfortable with?

Ten questions to guide shared decision making about risk

1. What exactly is being proposed? What are the options we are considering?

2. Does the older person have capacity to make this decision? (Remember to test this using the key principles of the Mental Capacity Act (see Chapter 6), not just to assume they will not have capacity because of their diagnosis!). Are we making a best interests decision here or are we simply coming together to advise, support and problem solve?

3. Why does/might this matter to the older person and their family? How much is doing it/not doing it likely to impact on their quality of life?

4. What are the specific risks? How likely are they to happen? What level of harm is likely/possible if they do?

5. What are the potential risks and benefits to family members, carers and the wider community?

6. What are our own fears and the fears of other professionals? These might be specific fears about harms or they might be general fears – for example, about being blamed if things go wrong.

7. What ideas do we have for doing what (we think) the older person wants *and* reducing the risks?

8. What's the bottom line?

   a. What are the rules or conditions which we all agree to follow?

   b. What is the contingency plan (if things go wrong)?

9. Which roles and responsibilities do each of us have? Is there anyone else we need to involve?

10. Which changes should trigger a review of this decision?

Tool 10: Tools to support supervision: writing a contract and setting the agenda

The supervision contract

A supervision contract helps both the supervisor and supervisee to reflect upon the processes which support their supervision. This will ensure that they are both clear about what is expected of them and what they can expect of each other. It is helpful to do this at the start of a supervision relationship, as it offers a safe base for the relationship to develop. It is a good idea to get this clear at the start, as then it is already in place if difficulties arise. The contract should cover the following aspects of supervision.

The functions of supervision
For example:

- to ensure that the supervisee carries out their responsibilities to the agency's standards

- to ensure that the supervisee fully understands their responsibilities

- to assist with the professional development of the supervisee

- to offer support to the supervisee

- to provide regular, constructive feedback to the supervisee, covering both things which they are doing well and areas for development

- to offer the supervisee the opportunity to offer feedback about the organisation.

The structure of supervision
For example:

- Frequency.

- Length.

- Location.

- How will it be recorded?

- Who is responsible for keeping records?

- How can supervision records be used?

- If supervision needs to be rescheduled or postponed, what is the procedure?

- If either the supervisor or the supervisee wants to make a complaint about supervision, what is the process for doing so?

The process of supervision

Supervision can be made more effective if, from the contracting stage onwards, there are conversations about the process, not just the content, because this will strengthen the relationship between the supervisee and supervisor, and support them both to be clearer about how they can work together effectively. These statements can help to structure that conversation.

For the supervisee:

- What I would like from you as the supervisor…

- What I am willing to contribute as a supervisee…

- The things I have responsibility for as the supervisee…

For the supervisor:

- What I would like from you as the supervisee…

- What I am willing to contribute as the supervisor…

- The things I have responsibility for as the supervisor…

The supervision agenda

A supervision agenda can be helpful in order to make sure that enough attention is paid to all the competing aspects of supervision. If there is no agenda, there is a risk that pressing issues, such as difficulties with a particular topic, or concerns about a particular person, will dominate the supervision. The supervisor needs to strike a balance between following the structure and being responsive to particular issues which arise. The agenda for the session should include:

- matters the supervisee wants to include

- the supervisee having the opportunity to talk about their welfare

- matters arising from previous sessions

- reviewing the supervisee's work, through discussions, reports, observations

- positive and constructive feedback

- agreeing future action plans

- discussing the development of the supervisee's skills, knowledge base and value base

- identifying the supervisee's developmental needs and setting goals

- offering the supervisee time to reflect on their experiences and feelings about the work

- an opportunity for the supervisee to give feedback on their experience of supervision.

Tool 11: Tools to support supervision: promoting reflection in supervision and team meetings

For more information about the supervision cycle and an example of a conversation between a supervisor and a worker, see Figure 9.6 and Chapter 8.

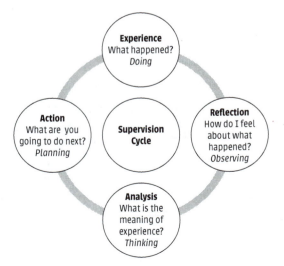

Figure 9.6: Supervision cycle

1 Sample questions to promote reflection in individual supervision, based upon Kolb's experiential learning cycle (Kolb 1988)

These are some ideas about the kinds of questions a supervisor could ask to help the worker move around the experiential learning cycle.

Questions to ask at the Experience stage

These questions focus on helping the worker to give a detailed account of what took place.

- What happened?

- What did you expect to happen?

- What happened just before? Or just after?

- What did other people think/see/feel?

- What took you by surprise?

- What information didn't you have?

Questions to ask at the Reflection stage

These questions focus on helping the worker to consider their feelings, and the impact of their previous experiences.

- What feelings did you have?

- What did this event remind you of?

- How do you think the other people involved were feeling?

- How do you feel about it now?

Questions to ask at the Analysis stage

These questions focus upon the meaning which the worker has made of the experience.

- What assumptions were you making about the people involved?

- What was the impact of issues of power (such as gender, race, culture, religion, etc.)?

- What do you understand about your professional role in this situation?

- Do you have any training needs in this area?

- What are the current strengths and risks in this situation?

Questions to ask at the Action planning stage

These questions help to translate the reflection into an action plan, focused on outcomes.

- What is it going to be important to do next?

- How would you prioritise your actions?

- Do you need any support from anyone?

- How will you let me know what you do next, and what the outcome is?

2 Framework for reflective team discussion, using the experiential learning model

Here are some ideas to prompt team discussions during team meetings. It may not be possible, or desirable, to have this kind of conversation every time the team meets. But building in reflective conversations where possible can help to encourage individual staff members to work in a more reflective and self-aware way. It can also encourage mutual understanding and cooperation within the team.

Experience

- What is the issue, or the particular incident, which we want to discuss?

- What happened? What did you see? What did other people see?

Reflection

- What feelings did you have at the time? What feelings do you have now?

- What feelings does the adult being cared for have?

- What feelings might their family or relatives have?

- How were other people affected (e.g. other residents)?

Analysis

- What issues or themes are raised by this discussion?
- What information might we be missing?
- What is going well, or not going well?
- What other help or support might we need?
- What is the impact of issues of power (race, class, money, age, etc.?)

Actions

- What plan can we make?
- Who can support us?
- How will we know that we are making progress?
- When should we talk about this again?

3 Schwartz Rounds

Schwartz Rounds were developed in the US, with the aim of promoting compassionate care with teams working in health and social care. They can be defined as:

> a multidisciplinary forum designed for staff to come together once a month to discuss and reflect on the non-clinical aspect of caring for patients – that is, the emotional and social challenges associated with their jobs. (Goodrich 2012, p.118)

A group of staff meet to discuss one person who is receiving care, with the discussion focusing on exploring the emotional challenges, rather than finding solutions. A study in the UK (Goodrich 2012) found that the introduction of Schwartz Rounds into two hospitals improved teamwork, empathy between staff with different roles and empathy for patients. People who participated in the discussions appreciated the opportunity to reflect upon the emotional impact of their work and felt that the organisation was acknowledging their emotional challenges and conflicts.

Implementing Schwartz Rounds is relatively low cost and may have benefits for organisations which offer support and care to older adults.

References

Action on Elder Abuse (1995) 'New definition of abuse.' *Action on Elder Abuse Bulletin* May–June, 11.

Adshead, G. (2010) 'Becoming a caregiver: attachment theory and poorly performing doctors.' *Medical Education 44*, 125–131.

Aesop (2018) *Dance to Health: Evaluation of the Pilot Programme.* Accessed on 28 February 2018 at https://issuu.com/aesopartsandsociety/docs/aesop_final_e

Age UK (2018) *Later Life in the United Kingdom.* Accessed on 28 February 2018 at www.ageuk.org.uk/globalassets/age-uk/documents/reports-and-publications/later_life_uk_factsheet.pdf?dtrk=true

Ainsworth, M.D.S. (1979) 'Infant–mother attachment.' *American Psychologist 34*, 10, 932–937.

Albert, S.M. and Duffy, J. (2012) 'Differences in risk aversion between young and older adults.' *Neuroscience and Neuroeconomics* 15 January 2012(1).

Allen, B. (2010) 'Remembering the Cost – A Theological Reflection.' In J. Woodward (ed.) *Between Remembering and Forgetting: The Spiritual Dimensions of Dementia.* London: Mowbray.

Alzheimer's Society (2012) *Challenges Facing Primary Carers of People with Dementia: Opportunities for Research.* Accessed on 28 February 2018 at www.alzheimers.org.uk/download/downloads/id/1416/challenges_facing_primary_carers_of_people_with_dementia_opportunities_for_research.pdf

Alzheimer's Society (2015) *Dementia-Friendly Arts Guide: A Practical Guide to Becoming a Dementia-Friendly Arts Venue.* London: Alzheimer's Society.

Andrews, N., Gabbay, J., le May, A. *et al.* (2015) *Developing Evidence Enriched Practice in Health and Social Care with Older People.* York: Joseph Rowntree Foundation. Accessed on 28 February 2018 at www.jrf.org.uk/report/developing-evidence-enriched-practice-health-and-social-care-older-people

Australian Alzheimer's NSW (2014) *Your Shed and Dementia: A Manual.* Accessed on 28 February 2018 at www.dementia.org.au/files/NATIONAL/documents/Mens-Shed-Dementia-Manual.pdf

Backhouse, T., Penhale, B., Gray, R. *et al.* (2017) 'Questionable practices despite good intentions: coping with risk and impact from dementia-related behaviours in care homes.' *Ageing & Society.* https://doi.org/10.1017/S0144686X17000368

Baim, C. and Morrison, T. (2011) *Attachment Based Practice with Adults.* Brighton: Pavilion.

Barclay, S. and Arthur, A. (2008) 'Place of death – how much does it matter?' *British Journal of General Practice 58*, 549, 229–231.

Best Friends Approach to Alzheimer's and Dementia Care (2018) Accessed on 28 February 2018 at http://bestfriendsapproach.com/products/handouts

Bigger Boat (2014) *A Bigger Boat for Ageing and Dementia.* Accessed on 28 February 2018 at http://biggerboat.org/wp-content/uploads/2014/10/A-Bigger-Boat-for-Ageing-and-Dementia-Final-Report.pdf

Blood, I. (2004) *Older Women and Domestic Violence.* London: Help the Aged/ HACT.

Blood, I. (2013) *A Better Life: Valuing Our Later Years.* York: Joseph Rowntree Foundation.

Blood, I. and Copeman, I. (2017) *The Anatomy of Resilience: Toolkit.* Cardiff: Social Care Wales.

Blood, I. and Litherland, R. (2015) *Care Home Whispers: Listening to the Voices of Older People Living in Gloucestershire Care Homes.* Age UK Gloucestershire. Kitwood, T. (1997) *Dementia Reconsidered: The Person Comes First.* Buckingham: Open University Press.

Blood, I., Copeman, I. and Pannell, J. (2016a) *How to Spend the Day? Community-Based Approaches to Providing Daytime Activities for Older People with High Support Needs.* Cardiff: The Barnwood Trust.

Blood, I., Copeman, I. and Pannell, J. (2016b) *Hearing the Voices of Older People in Wales: What Helps and Hinders as We Age?* Social Services Improvement Agency.

Blood, I., Pannell, J. and Copeman, I. (2012) *Findings from Housing with Care Research: Practice Examples.* York: Joseph Rowntree Foundation.

Boss, P. (1999) *Ambiguous Loss: Learning to Live with Unresolved Grief.* Cambridge, MA: Harvard University Press.

Bowers, H., Clark, A., Sanderson, H., Easterbrook, L. *et al.* (2009) *Older People's Vision for Long Term Care.* York: Joseph Rowntree Foundation.

Bowers, H., Mordey, M., Runnicles, D., Barker, S. *et al.* (2011) *Not a One Way Street: Research into Older People's Experiences of Support Based on Mutuality and Reciprocity: Interim Findings, October 2011.* York: Joseph Rowntree Foundation.

Bowlby, J. (1980) Attachment and Loss: Volume III. *Loss, Sadness and Depression.* New York: Basic Books.

Bowlby, J. (1982) *Attachment and Loss.* New York: Basic Books. (Original work published 1969).

Bradley, J.M. and Cafferty, T.P. (2001) 'Attachment among older adults: current issues and directions for future research.' *Attachment & Human Development 3,* 2, 200–221.

Breheny, M. and Stephens, C. (2009) '"I sort of pay back in my own little way": managing independence and social connectedness through reciprocity.' *Ageing & Society 29,* 1295–1313.

Brodaty, H. and Donkin, M. (2009) 'Family caregivers of people with dementia.' *Dialogues in Clinical Neuroscience 11,* 2, 217.

Brooks, R. (2012) 'Loneliness, self-efficacy, and hope: often neglected dimensions of the LD learning process.' Accessed on 28 February 2018 at www.ldonline.org/article/51177

Buffel, T., Phillipson, C. and Scharf, T. (2013) 'Experiences of neighbourhood exclusion and inclusion among older people living in deprived inner-city areas in Belgium and England.' *Ageing & Society 33,* 89–109.

Burnham, J. (2016) 'Is it (Aspergers) or isn't it (Aspergers)? Is that the (only) question?' *Context 144,* 29–31.

Burnham, J. (2017) 'Problems, Resources, Possibilities. Restraints – A Versatile PPRRactice Map.' Presentation delivered at the Centre for Systemic Social Work.

Burns, D.J., Hyde, P.J. and Killett, A.M. (2016) 'How financial cutbacks affect the quality of jobs and care for the elderly.' *ILR Review 69,* 4, 991–1016.

Byng-Hall, J. (1995) *Rewriting Family Scripts. Improvisation and System Change.* New York: Guilford.

Campaign to End Loneliness (2015) *Measuring Your Impact on Loneliness in Later Life.* London: Campaign to End Loneliness.

Carstensen, L.L. and Mikels, J.A. (2005) 'At the intersection of emotion and cognition: aging and the positivity effect.' *Current Directions in Psychological Science 14*, 3, 117–121.

Cassidy, J. and Shaver, P.R. (eds) (2008) *Handbook of Attachment: Theory, Research, and Clinical Applications.* New York: Guilford Press.

Cattan, M., White, M., Bond, J. *et al.* (2005) 'Preventing social isolation and loneliness among older people: a systematic review of health promotion interventions.' *Ageing & Society 25*, 1, 41–67.

Charlton, J. (1998) *Nothing about Us without Us.* Berkeley and Los Angeles, CA: University of California Press.

Chen, C.K., Waters, H.S., Hartman, M. *et al.* (2013) 'The secure base script and the task of caring for elderly parents: implications for attachment theory and clinical practice.' *Attachment and Human Development 15*, 3, 332–348.

Clarke, A., Hanson, E.J. and Ross, H. (2003) 'Seeing the person behind the patient: enhancing the care of older people using a biographical approach.' *Journal of Clinical Nursing 12*, 5, 697–706.

Clarke, C.L., Wilkinson, H., Keady, J. and Gibb, C.E. (2011) *Risk Assessment and Management for Living Well with Dementia.* London: Jessica Kingsley Publishers.

Clarke, J. and Dembkowski, S. (2006) 'The art of asking great questions.' *The International Journal of Mentoring & Coaching IV*, 2 (September).

Crittenden, P.M. (2008) *Raising Parents: Attachment, Parenting and Child Safety.* Cullompton, Devon: Willan Publishing.

Cronen, V., Johnson, K. and Lannaman, J. (1982) 'Paradoxes, double binds and reflexive loops: an alternative theoretical perspective.' *Family Process 21*, 91–112.

Cummings, S.M., Cooper, R.L. and Cassie, K.M. (2009) 'Motivational interviewing to affect behavioral change in older adults.' *Research on Social Work Practice 19*, 2, 195–204.

Cutler, D., Kelly, D. and Silver, S. (2011) *Creative Homes: How the Arts Can Contribute to Quality of Life in Residential Care.* London: The Baring Foundation. Accessed on 1 March 2018 at http://baringfoundation.org.uk/wp-content/uploads/2014/09/CreativeCareHomes.pdf

Dallos, R. and Vetere, A. (2009) *Systemic Therapy and Attachment Narratives.* London: Routledge.

De Jong, P., Kelly, S., Berg, I.K. and Gonzales, L. (2012) 'Building strengths-based tools for child protection practice: a case of "parallel process".' Accessed on 8 April 2018 at www.ndti.org.uk/our-work/areas-of-work/ageing-and-older-people/circles-of-support-for-people-with-dementia

De Jong Gierveld, J. and Van Tilburg, T. (2010) 'The De Jong Gierveld short scales for emotional and social loneliness: tested on data from 7 countries in the UN generations and gender surveys.' *European Journal of Ageing 7*, 2, 121–130.

Department of Health and Social Care (updated 2018) *Using the Care Act Guidance.* London: Department of Health & Social Care.

Detering, K.M., Hancock, A.D., Reade, M.C. *et al.* (2010) 'The impact of advance care planning on end of life care in elderly patients: randomised controlled trial.' *British Medical Journal* 340: c1345.

Duschinsky, R. and Solomon, J. (2017) 'Infant disorganized attachment: clarifying levels of analysis.' *Clinical Child Psychology and Psychiatry 22*, 4, 524–538.

Equality and Human Rights Commission (2011) *Close to Home: An Inquiry into Older People and Human Rights in Home Care.* Accessed on 1 March 2018 at www.equalityhumanrights.com/sites/default/files/close_to_home.pdf

Faulkner, A. (2012) *The Right to Take Risks: Service Users' Views of Risk in Adult Social Care.* York: Joseph Rowntree Foundation. Accessed on 1 March 2018 at www.jrf.org.uk/sites/default/files/jrf/migrated/files/right-to-take-risks-faulkner.pdf

Feldman, D.B., Davidson, O.B., Ben-Naim, S. *et al.* (2016) 'Hope as a mediator of loneliness and academic self-efficacy among students with and without learning disabilities during the transition to college.' *Learning Disabilities Research & Practice 31*, 63–74.

Finlayson, S. (2015) 'Stop Worrying about Risk.' Blog: The Centre for Welfare Reform. Accessed on 1 March 2018 at www.centreforwelfarereform.org/library/by-az/stop-worrying-about-risk.html

Fivaz-Depeursinge, E., Frascarolo, F., Corboz-Warnery, A. (2010) 'Observational tool: the prenatal Lausanne Trilogue Play.' In S. Tyano, M. Keren, H. Herrman *et al.* (eds) (2010) *Parenthood and Mental Health: A Bridge between Infant and Adult Psychiatry.* Chichester: John Wiley & Sons, Ltd.

Fransham, M. and Dorling, D. (2017) 'Have mortality improvements stalled in England?' *BMJ*, 357: j1946.

Furedi, F. (2011) *Changing Societal Attitudes, and Regulatory Responses, to Risk-Taking in Adult Care.* Scoping paper. York: Joseph Rowntree Foundation.

Gawande, A. (2014) *Being Mortal.* London: Profile Books.

General Medical Council (2010) Treatment and care towards the end of www.gloucestershire.gov.uk/media/11328/care_home_whispers_project7c62.pdf

Goodman, A., Adams, A. and Swift, H.J. (2015) *Hidden Citizens: How Can We Identify the Most Lonely Older Adults?* London: Campaign to End Loneliness.

Goodrich, J. (2012) 'Supporting hospital staff to provide compassionate care: do Schwartz Center Rounds work in English hospitals?' *Journal of the Royal Society of Medicine 105*, 117–122.

Granqvist, P., Sroufe, L.A., Dozier, M., *et al.* (2017) 'Disorganized attachment in infancy: a review of the phenomenon and its implications for clinicians and policy-makers.' *Attachment & Human Development 19*, 6, 534–558.

Graybeal, C. (2001) 'Strengths-based social work assessment: transforming the dominant paradigm.' *Families in Society: The Journal of Contemporary Human Services 82*, 3, 233–242.

Gridley, K. (2017) 'Life story work in dementia care.' Presentation, Narrative in Question, Interdisciplinary Centre for Narrative Studies, University of York, 15 February.

Gridley, K., Brooks, J., Birks, Y., Baxter, K. and Parker, G. (2016) 'Improving care for people with dementia: development and initial feasibility study for evaluation of life story work in dementia care.' *Health Services and Delivery Research 4*, 23.

Hamblin, K. (2014) AKTIVE Working Paper 6: Risk, Freedom and Control in Older People's Lives: The Relevance of Telecare. CIRCLE, University of Leeds. Accessed on 1 March 2018 at www.aktive.org.uk/downloads/AKTIVE-PAPER-6.pdf

Hawkins, R.J., Prashar, A., Lusambili, A. *et al.* (2017) 'If they don't use it, they lose it': how organisational structures and practices shape residents' physical movement in care home settings.' *Ageing and Society.* https://doi.org/10.1017/S0144686X17000290

Hawkley, LC., Thisted, R.A., Masi, C.M. *et al.* (2010) 'Loneliness predicts increased blood pressure: 5-year cross-lagged analyses in middle-aged and older adults.' *Psychology and Aging 25*, 1, 132–141.

Hazan, C. and Shaver, P.R. (1990) 'Love and work: an attachment-theoretical perspective.' *Journal of Personality and Social Psychology 59*, 270–280.

Healthwatch England (2015) Safely Home: What Happens When People Leave Hospital and Care Settings? Special inquiry findings. Accessed on 1 March 2018 at www.healthwatch.co.uk/sites/healthwatch.co.uk/files/170715_healthwatch_special_inquiry_2015_1.pdf

Higginson, I.J., Gomes, B. and Calanzani, N. (2014) 'Priorities for treatment, care and information if faced with serious illness: a comparative population-based survey in seven European countries.' *Palliative Medicine 28*, 2, 101–110.

Holt-Lunstad, J., Smith, T.B. and Layton, J.B. (2010) 'Social relationships and mortality risk: a meta-analytic review.' *PLoS Med 7*, 7, e1000316.

Howe, D. (2011) *Attachment across the Lifespan.* Basingstoke: Palgrave Macmillan.

Howell, D.A., Wang, H.I., Roman, E. *et al.* (2017) 'Preferred and actual place of death in haematological malignancy.' *BMJ Supportive & Palliative Care* https://muskie.usm.maine.edu/helpkids/telefiles/may25/SB%20tools%20article.pdf

Hussein, S. (2017) '"We don't do it for the money"…The scale and reasons of poverty-pay among frontline long-term care workers in England.' *Health and Social Care in the Community 25*, 6, 1817–1826.

IDeA (2010) A Glass Half-Full: How an Asset Approach Can Improve Community Health and Well-Being. Accessed on 1 March 2018 at www.assetbasedconsulting.net/uploads/publications/A%20glass%20half%20full.pdf

Imogen Blood and Associates/Innovations in Dementia 'Evidence Review of Dementia Friendly Communities.' Unpublished report for EU Joint Action on Dementia/Department of Health.

Institute for Public Policy Research (2014) *The Generation Strain: Collective Solutions to Care in an Ageing Society.* Report. London: IPPR.

Jopling, K. (2015) *Promising Approaches to Reducing Loneliness and Isolation in Later Life.* London: Campaign to End Loneliness.

Kellett, U., Moyle, W., McAllister, M., King, C. and Gallagher, F. (2010) 'Life stories and biography: a means of connecting family and staff to people with dementia.' *Journal of Clinical Nursing 19*, 11–12, 1707–1715.

Kelly, D. and Kennedy, J. (2017) *Power to People: Proposals to Reboot Adult Care and Support in N.I.* Belfast: Department of Health. Accessed on 1 March 2018 at www.health-ni.gov.uk/publications/experts-report-adult-care-and-support

Kennedy, J. (2014) *John Kennedy's Care Home Inquiry.* York: Joseph Rowntree Foundation. Accessed on 1 March 2018 at www.jrf.org.uk/report/john-kennedys-care-home-inquiry

Kennedy, J. (2016) 'What makes a care home outstanding?' 19 September. Accessed on 1 March 2018 at www.theguardian.com/social-care-network/2016/sep/19/what-makes-care-home-outstanding

Khan, O. (2014) 'Race is no protection against loneliness.' In Campaign to End Loneliness (ed.) *Alone in the Crowd: Loneliness and Diversity.* London: Campaign to End Loneliness.

Killett, A., Burns, D., Kelly, F. *et al.* (2016) 'Digging deep: how organizational culture affects care home residents' experiences.' *Ageing and Society 36*, 160–188.

Kindell, J., Burrow, S., Wilkinson, R. and Keady, J.D. (2014) 'Life story resources in dementia care: a review.' *Quality in Ageing and Older Adults 15*, 3, 151–161.

Kissane, D.W., McKenzie, M., Bloch, I. *et al.* (2003) 'Family focused grief therapy: a randomised, controlled trial in palliative care and bereavement.' *American Journal of Psychiatry 163*, 1208–1218.

Kitwood, T. (1997) *Dementia Reconsidered: The Person Comes First.* Buckingham: Open University Press.

Klein, A. (2018) 'Husband with Alzheimer's forgot he was married to his wife of 38 years. He proposed, and they married again.' *The Washington Post* 25 January. Accessed on 1 March 2018 at www.washingtonpost.com/news/inspired-life/wp/2018/01/25/husband-with-alzheimers-forgot-he-was-married-to-his-wife-of-38-years-he-proposed-and-they-married-again/?utm_term=.b40112fe8d46

Knocker, S. (2012) Perspectives on Ageing: Lesbians, Gay Men and Bisexuals. York: Joseph Rowntree Foundation. Accessed on 1 March 2018 at www.jrf.org.uk/report/perspectives-ageing-lesbians-gay-men-and-bisexuals

Kokkonen, T.M., Cheston, R.I., Dallos, R. *et al.* (2014) 'Attachment and coping of dementia care staff: the role of staff attachment style, geriatric nursing self-efficacy, and approaches to dementia in burnout.' *Dementia 13*, 4, 544–568.

Kolb, D.A. (1976) *The Learning Style Inventory. Technical Manual.* Boston, MA: McBer.

Kolb, D. (1988) 'The Process of Experiential Learning.' In *Experience as the Source of Learning and Development.* London: Prentice Hall.

Konnikova, M. (2016) 'How people learn to become resilient.' *The New Yorker* 11 February. Accessed on 1 March 2018 at www.newyorker.com/science/maria-konnikova/the-secret-formula-for-resilience

Lawrence, V., Samsi, K., Murray, J. *et al.* (2011) 'Dying well with dementia: qualitative examination of end-of-life care.' *The British Journal of Psychiatry 199*, 417–422.

Leighton, R., Oddy, C. and Grace, J. (2016) 'Using sensory stories with individuals with dementia.' *The Journal of Dementia Care 24* (4) 28–31.

Livability (2017) *Developing a Dementia-Friendly Church: A Practical Guide.* London: Livability.

Loetz, C., Muller, J., Frick, E. *et al.* (2013) 'Attachment theory and spirituality: two threads converging in palliative care?' *Evidence-Based Complementary and Alternative Medicine 2013*, article ID 740291.

Lopez, R., Mazor, K., Mitchell, S. *et al.* (2013) 'What is family-centred care for nursing home residents with advanced dementia?' *American Journal of Alzheimer's Disease and Other Dementias 28*, 2, 763–768.

Macadam, A. and Savitch, N. (2015) 'Staying connected with Circles of Support.' *The Journal of Dementia Care 23*, 1, 32–34.

MacLeod, S., Musich, S., Hawkins, K., Alsgaard, K. and Wicker, E.R. (2016) 'The impact of resilience among older adults.' *Geriatric Nursing 37*, 266–272.

Macpherson, R., Eastley, R.J., Richards, H. *et al.* (1994) 'Psychological distress among workers caring for the elderly.' *International Journal of Geriatric Psychiatry 9*, 5, 381–386.

Manthorpe, J. and Moriarty, J. (2010) '*Nothing Ventured, Nothing Gained': Risk Guidance for People with Dementia.* London: Department of Health. Accessed on 1 March 2018 at www.gov.uk/government/uploads/system/uploads/attachment_data/file/215960/dh_121493.pdf

Manthorpe, J., Harris, J., Samsi, K. *et al.* (2017) 'Doing, being and becoming a valued care worker: user and family carer views.' *Ethics and Social Welfare 11*, 1, 79–91.

Mapes, N. (2017) 'Think outside: positive risk-taking with people living with dementia.' *Working with Older People 21*, 3, 157–166.

Maslach, C., Jackson, S.E. and Leiter, M.P. (1996) *Maslach Burnout Inventory Manual* (3rd edn). Palo Alto, CA: Consulting Psychologists Press.

McGovern, J. (2015) 'Living better with dementia: strengths based social work practice and dementia care.' *Social Work in Health Care 54*, 5, 408–421.

Mental Health Foundation (2011) *An Evidence Review of the Impact of Participatory Arts on Older People.* London: The Baring Foundation. Accessed on 19 April 2018 at www.mentalhealth.org.uk/sites/default/files/evidence-review-participatory-arts.pdf

Miesen, B.M.L. (2006) 'Attachment in Dementia: Bound from Birth?' In B.M.L. Miesen and G.M.M. Jones (eds) *Care-Giving in Dementia: Research and Applications.* Hove: Routledge.

Milberg, A., Wahlberg, R., Jakobsson, M. *et al.* (2012) 'What is a "secure base" when death is approaching? A study applying attachment theory to adult patients' and family members' experiences of palliative home care.' *Psycho-Oncology 21,* 8, 886–895.

Miller, W.R. and Rollnick, S. (2002) *Motivational Interviewing: Preparing People for Change* (2nd edn). New York: Guilford Press.

Minuchin, S. (1974) *Families and Family Therapy.* London: Tavistock.

Mitchell, S.L., Kiely, D.K. and Hamel, M.B. (2004) 'Dying with advanced dementia in the nursing home.' *Archives of Internal Medicine 164,* 321–326.

Mitchell, W. and Glendinning, C. (2007) *A Review of the Research Evidence Surrounding Risk Perceptions, Risk Management Strategies and their Consequences in Adult Social Care for Different Groups of Service Users.* Working Paper No. DHR 2180 01.07. York: York University.

Morgan, S. and Andrews, N. (2016) 'Positive risk-taking: from rhetoric to reality.' *The Journal of Mental Health Training, Education and Practice 11,* 2, 122–132.

Moriarty, J., Manthorpe, J. and Cornes, M. (2015) 'Reaching out or missing out: approaches to outreach with family carers in social care organisations.' *Health and Social Care in the Community 23* 1, 42–45.

Morrison, T. (2005) *Staff Supervision in Social Care.* Brighton: Pavilion.

Morrison, T. (2007) 'Emotional intelligence, emotion and social work: context, characteristics, complications and contribution.' *British Journal of Social Work 37,* 2, 245–263.

National Statistics (2014) *National Survey for Wales: Headline Results, April 2013–March 2014.* First release, 30 May 2014, SDR 89/2014 (R).

NHS Digital (2017) *Personal Social Services Survey of Adult Carers in England, 2016-17.* Accessed on 1 March 2018 at https://digital.nhs.uk/catalogue/PUB30045

Older People's Commissioner for Wales (2014) *A Place to Call Home?* Accessed on 1 March 2018 at www.olderpeoplewales.com/Libraries/Uploads/A_Place_to_Call_Home_-_A_Review_into_the_Quality_of_Life_and_Care_of_Older_People_living_in_Care_Homes_in_Wales.sflb.ashx

ONS (2014) Article. 'Changes in the older resident care home population between 2001 and 2011.' Accessed on 1 March 2018 at www.ons.gov.uk/peoplepopulationandcommunity/birthsdeathsandmarriages/ageing/articles/changesintheolderresidentcarehomepopulationbetween2001and2011/2014-08-01

ONS (2016a) Statistical bulletin. *Deaths Registered in England and Wales.* Accessed on 1 March 2018 at www.ons.gov.uk/peoplepopulationandcommunity/birthsdeathsandmarriages/deaths/bulletins/deathsregistrationsummarytables/2015

ONS (2016b) Statistical bulletin. *National Survey of Bereaved People (Voices): England, 2015.* Accessed on 1 March 2018 at www.ons.gov.uk/peoplepopulationandcommunity/healthandsocialcare/healthcaresystem/bulletins/nationalsurveyofbereavedpeoplevoices/england2015

ONS (2017a) Dataset. *National Life Tables: United Kingdom.* Accessed on 1 March 2018 at www.ons.gov.uk/peoplepopulationandcommunity/birthsdeathsandmarriages/lifeexpectancies/datasets/nationallifetablesunitedkingdomreferencetables

ONS (2017b) Statistical bulletin. *Families and Households: 2017.* Accessed on 1 March 2018 at www.ons.gov.uk/peoplepopulationandcommunity/birthsdeathsandmarriages/families/bulletins/familiesandhouseholds/2017#how-does-the-number-of-people-who-live-alone-vary-by-age-and-sex

Owen, T., Meyer, J., Cornell, M. *et al.* (2012) My Home Life: Promoting Quality of Life in Care Homes. York: Joseph Rowntree Foundation. Accessed on 1 March 2018 at www.myhomelife.org.uk/wp-content/uploads/2015/02/JRF-report-on-care-home-quality-of-life-full.pdf

Pattoni, L. (2012) *Strengths-Based Approaches for Working with Individuals.* Accessed on 19 April 2018 at Iriss. www.iriss.org.uk/resources/insights/strengths-based-approaches-working-individuals

Pearlin, L.I., Mullan, J.T. and Semple, S.J. (1990) 'Caregiving and the stress process: an overview of concepts and their measures.' *The Gerontologist 30,* 5, 583–594.

Peisah, C., Brodaty, H. and Quadrio, C. (2006) 'Family conflict in dementia: prodigal sons and black sheep.' *International Journal of Geriatric Psychiatry 21,* 485-492.

Perren, S., Schmid, R., Herrmann, S. *et al.* (2007) 'The impact of attachment on dementia-related problem behavior and spousal caregivers' well-being.' *Attachment & Human Development 9,* 2, 163–178.

Pike, L. and Walsh, J. (2015) *Making Safeguarding Personal 2014/15: Evaluation Report.* Local Government Association. Accessed on 1 March 2018 at www.local.gov.uk/sites/default/files/documents/L15-472%20Making%20Safeguarding%20Personal%202014-15%20evaluation%20report.pdf

Prince, M., Knapp, M., Guerchet, M. *et al.* (2014) Dementia UK: Second Edition – Overview. Alzheimer's Society. Accessed on 1 March 2018 at https://kclpure.kcl.ac.uk/portal/en/publications/dementia-uk-second-edition--overview(22d426a1-c0aa-4b3f-8fcb-1db4a3f4c4d7).html

Public Health England (2015) National End of Life Care Intelligence Network. *What We Know Now 2014.* London: Public Health England.

Pulla, V. (2013) 'What are strengths based practices all about?' Charles Sturt University, Australia. Accessed on 1 March 2018 at http://impetusglobal.com/wp-content/uploads/2013/02/VenkatPullaSBP.pdf

Residential Forum (2017) *Lionising the Rare Beasts.* Accessed on 1 March 2018 at http://residentialforum.tumblr.com/post/163941281911/lionising-the-rare-beasts

Richards, S., Donovan, S., Victor, C. and Ross, F. (2007) 'Standing secure amidst a falling world? Practitioner understanding of old age in responses to a case vignette.' *Journal of Interprofessional Care 21,* 3, 335–349.

Roberts, Y. (2012) *One Hundred Not Out: Resilience and Active Ageing.* London: The Young Foundation.

Rolinson, J.J., Hanoch, Y., Wood, S. *et al.* (2013) 'Risk taking differences across the adult lifespan: a question of age and domain.' *The Journals of Gerontology, Series B 69,* 6, 870–880.

Rolland, J. (1994) 'In sickness and in health: the impact of illness on couples' relationships.' *Journal of Marital Family Therapy 20,* 4, 327–342.

Roper-Hall, A. (2008) 'Systematic Interventions and Older People.' In R. Woods and L. Clare (eds) *Handbook of the Clinical Psychology of Ageing* (2nd edn.) Chichester: John Wiley and Sons. (Original work published 1996).

Royal College of Occupational Therapists (2013) *Living Well in Care Homes 2013.* Accessed on 1 March 2018 at www.rcot.co.uk/practice-resources/rcot-publications/downloads/living-well-care-homes

Saleeby, D. (2005) *The Strengths Perspective in Social Work Practice.* 4th edn. Boston, MA: Pearson.

Sawbridge, Y. and Hewison, A. (2011) 'Time to Care? Responding to Concerns about Poor Nursing Care.' Policy Paper. University of Birmingham Health Services Management Centre.

Scourfield, P. (2007) 'Helping older people in residential care remain full citizens.' *British Journal of Social Work 37*, 7, 1135–1152.

Sims, A. (2016) '91-year-old who inspired thousands by skipping chemotherapy to go on end of life road trip dies.' *Independent*, 5 October. Accessed on 1 March 2018 at www.independent.co.uk/news/people/91-year-old-inspired-thousands-skipping-chemotherapy-to-go-on-end-of-life-road-trip-dies-a7345951.html

Skills for Care (2015) *The State of the Adult Social Care Sector and Workforce in England.* Leeds: Skills for Care.

Skills for Care (2016) MDS-SC briefing 26. 'Registered Managers in Adult Social Care.' Accessed on 1 March 2018 at www.skillsforcare.org.uk/Documents/NMDS-SC-and-intelligence/NMDS-SC/Analysis-pages/Briefing-26-Registered-managers-in-adult-social-care.pdf

Slettebø, Å. (2008) 'Safe, but lonely: living in a nursing home.' *Vård i Norden 28* (1), 22–25.

Smith, N., Towers, A-M., Palmer, S. *et al.* (2017) 'Being occupied: supporting "meaningful activity" in care homes for older people in England.' *Ageing & Society 1–23.* https://doi.org/10.1017/S0144686X17000678

Social Care Institute for Excellence (2015) 'What Is a Strengths-Based Approach to Care?' Accessed on 1 March 2018 at www.scie.org.uk/care-act-2014/assessment-and-eligibility/strengths-based-approach/what-is-a-strengths-based-approach.asp

Social Care Institute for Excellence (2017) 'Deprivation of Liberty Safeguards (DoLS).' Accessed on 1 March 2018 at www.scie.org.uk/mca/dols/practice/care-home

Steele, H., Phibbs, E., and Woods, R. (2004) 'Coherence of mind in daughter caregivers of mothers with dementia: links with their mothers' joy and relatedness on reunion in a strange situation.' *Attachment & Human Development 6*, 4, 439–450.

Stokes, G. (2008) *And Still the Music Plays: Stories of People with Dementia.* London: Hawker Publications.

Strawbridge, W.J. and Wallhagen, M.I. (1991) 'Impact of family conflict on adult child caregivers.' *Gerontologist 31*, 770–777.

Stroebe, M. and Schut, H.A.W. (1999) 'The dual process model of coping with bereavement: rationale and description.' *Death Studies 23*, 1–28.

Stroebe, M. and Schut, H. (2010) 'The dual process model of coping with bereavement: a decade on.' *Omega – Journal of Death and Dying 61*, 4, 273–289.

Stroebe, M., Schut, H. and Boerner, K. (2010) 'Continuing bonds in adaptation to bereavement: toward theoretical integration.' *Clinical Psychology Review 30*, 2, 259–268.

Stroebe, M., Schut, H. and Stroebe, W. (2005) 'Attachment in coping with bereavement: a theoretical integration.' *Review of General Psychology 9*, 1, 48–66.

Subramaniam P. and Woods B. (2012) 'The impact of individual reminiscence therapy for people with dementia: systematic review.' *Expert Review of Neurotherapeutics 12*, 5, 545–555.

Swim England (n.d.) *The Dementia Friendly Swimming Hub.* Accessed on 18 February 2018 at www.swimming.org/dementiafriendly

The Mid Staffordshire NHS Foundation Trust (2013) *Report of The Mid Staffordshire NHS Foundation Trust Public Inquiry. Executive Summary.* London: The Stationery Office.

The National Council for Palliative Care (n.d.) 'What Does Spirtitual Support Mean to You?' Accessed on 1 March 2018 at www.ncpc.org.uk/sites/default/files/NCPC_Spiritual_support_comments.pdf

Think Local Act Personal (2016) *Developing a Wellbeing and Strengths-Based Approach to Social Work Practice: Changing Culture.* London: Think Local Act Personal.

UK Homecare Association (2012) *UKHCA Commissioning Survey 2012: Care Is Not a Commodity.* UKHCA: Sutton.

Vallelly, S., Evans, S., Fear, T. and Means, R. (2006) *Opening Doors to Independence: A Longitudinal Study Exploring the Contribution of Extra Care Housing to the Care and Support of Older People with Dementia.* London: Housing 21.

Valtorta, NK., Kanaan, M. Gilbody, S. *et al.* (2016) 'Loneliness and social isolation as risk factors for coronary heart disease and stroke: systematic review and meta-analysis of longitudinal observational studies.' *Heart.* doi: 10.1136/heartjnl-2015-308790

Wadham, O., Simpson, J., Rust, J. *et al.* (2016) 'Couples' shared experiences of dementia: a meta-synthesis of the impact upon relationships and couplehood.' *Aging & Mental Health 20,* 5, 463–473.

Warmington, J., Afridi, A. and Foreman, W. (2014) *Is Excessive Paperwork in Care Homes Undermining Care for Older People?* Report. York: Joseph Rowntree Foundation.

Weaks, D., Wilkinson, H., Houston, A. *et al.* (2012) *Perspectives on Ageing with Dementia.* York: Joseph Rowntree Foundation. Accessed on 1 March 2018 at www.jrf.org.uk/report/perspectives-ageing-dementia

Welsh Government (2015) Social Services and Well-Being (Wales) Act 2014. Part 3 Code of Practice (Assessing the Needs of Individuals). Accessed on 1 March 2018 at http://gov.wales/docs/dhss/publications/151218part3en.pdf

West Yorkshire Playhouse (2016) *Guide to Dementia Friendly Performances.* Leeds: West Yorkshire Playhouse.

Williamson, T. (2010) *My Name Is Not Dementia: People with Dementia Discuss Quality of Life Indicators.* London: Alzheimer's Society.

Wilson K., Ruch G., Lymbery M. and Cooper, A. (2011) (eds) *Social Work: An Introduction to Contemporary Practice.* Harlow: Pearson.

Woodward, J. (2015) 'Seeing beyond the immediate: listening and learning alongside older people.' *Working with Older People 19,* 3. https://doi.org/10.1108/WWOP-03-2015-0006

World Health Organization (2018) *Projections of Mortality and Causes of Death, 2015 and 2030.* World Health Organization. Accessed on 1 March 2018 at www.who.int/healthinfo/global_burden_disease/projections/en

Yu, D.S.F., Cheng, S-T. and Wang, J. (2018) 'Unravelling positive aspects of caregiving in dementia: an integrative review of research literature.' *International Journal of Nursing Studies 79,* 1–26.

Zaider, T. and Kissane, D. (2007) 'Resilient Families.' In B. Munroe and D. Oliviere (eds) (2007) *Resilience in Palliative Care: Achievement in Adversity.* Oxford: Oxford University Press.

Subject Index

64 Million Artists campaign 93–4

activities
    care home 90–6
    to help with loneliness 114–6
adult abuse 142–3
affirmations 72, 212–3
'age-related positivity effect' 122
arts-based activities 92–6
assessment process review (case study)
    188–92
attachment theory
    attunement 42
    and bereavement support 156–9
    case studies 50–4
    couple relationships 66–9
    dementia 62–6, 174
    development of strategies 40, 42–8
    Dynamic-Maturational Model 34–6
    end of life and 150–9
    and 'good life' in care home 88–90
    history of research 34
    infant development 39–41
    later strategy development 45–8
    and older people 48–54
    predictability 42
    risk-taking and 120–1
    secure base 153–5
    staff wellbeing and 179–82
    Strange Situation procedure 41
    strategies within families 58–9
    terminology used 41
    to make sense of puzzling behaviour
        36–9

Type A strategy 43–4, 46–7, 65, 67,
    111, 151–2, 157, 158, 180–1
Type B strategy 42–3, 45–6, 64, 157,
    158
Type C strategy 44–5, 47–8, 50–2, 59,
    65–6, 112, 152–3, 157, 181–2
'attuned repair' of relationships 107–8
attunement 42

behaviour, pattern and function triangle
    35–6, 200–1
bereavement
    attachment-informed approach to
        156–9
    dual process model 157–9
    grief therapy 167
    stages of grief 156–9
    supporting families 166–7
Best Friends Approach 95
burnout 173, 180–2

Care Act (2014) 17–9
Care Home Inquiry (2014) 76–7
care homes *see* 'good life in care home'
care workers' qualities 171–2
church, 'dementia-friendly' 115–6
circles of support 217–20
collaboration 19–20, 83–4, 106–7
community
    accessing mainstream activities 114–6
    'dementia-friendly' 115–6
    links with 81
    loss of 'community spirit' 101
    see also loneliness

Author Index